A FRAMEWORK
FOR THE IMAGINARY

A FRAMEWORK FOR THE IMAGINARY

CLINICAL EXPLORATIONS IN PRIMITIVE STATES OF BEING

Judith L. Mitrani, Ph.D.

with a Foreword by
Joyce McDougall, Ed. D.

JASON ARONSON INC.
Northvale, New Jersey
London

This book was set in 10 pt. New Baskerville by Alpha Graphics of Pittsfield, New Hampshire and printed and bound by Book-mart Press of North Bergen, New Jersey.

Library of Congress Cataloging-in-Publication Data

Mitrani, Judith L.
    A framework for the imaginary : clinical explorations in primitive states
of being / by Judith L. Mitrani : with a foreword by Joyce
McDougall.
      p. cm
    Includes bibliographical references and index.
    ISBN 1-56821-479-0 (alk. paper)
    1. Psychoanalysis. I. Title.
BF173.M56   1996
150.19'5—dc 20   95-35054

Manufactured in the United States of America. Jason Aronson Inc. offers books and cassettes. For information and catalog write to Jason Aronson Inc., 230 Livingston Street, Northvale, New Jersey 07647.

Dedicated to the
Treasured Memories
of
Harry David Stone
(1910–1989)
and
Frances Tustin
(1913–1994)
The Wind Beneath So Many Wings

Contents

Foreword

Those acquainted with Dr. Judith Mitrani's published articles in various international and American psychoanalytic journals will welcome this volume of her collected papers and will also have the pleasure of discovering four chapters that are published here for the first time. Those who do not yet know Dr. Mitrani's work will engage in a delightful and insightful clinical and theoretical voyage of discovery into the understanding and treatment of primitive states of mind.

Mitrani, although inspired by the work of Klein, Bion, Tustin, Winnicott, and other noted researchers of the British and American object relations schools, offers, in a pioneering spirit, extensions not only of Freud's concept of *anxiety equivalents*, but also of many other psychoanalytic conceptions in the area of primitive mental and protomental states.

Her conception of psychosomatic phenomena, particularly with regard to respiratory illness, is ground-breaking in that she conceives of certain forms of somatization as "pre-historic, self-survival tactics" against the "threat of evaporation." Drawing on Freud's etiological factors concerning the "actual neuroses" (which, as I have stated elsewhere, were the earliest papers on psychosomatic disorders), Mitrani adds those of privation, premature disillusionment, and schizoid withdrawal from the primary object as further etiological factors contributing to the development of such symptomatology.

Such original theoretical conceptions as "unmentalized experience" and "adhesive pseudo-object relations" are richly illustrated with clinical case material, and give insight into the transference–countertransference relationship that this analyst establishes with her analysands. We come to know "Robert," "Bill," "Hope," "Carla," and others in the intimate psychoanalytic experience with their analyst, in which she demonstrates that the "baby in the patient must be afforded the experience of being imaginatively conceived in the mind of the other (who is capable of being both at-one-with and distinct from the patient)."

Mitrani's reflections deal also with the survival function of various forms of pathological organization—such as severe narcissistic character pathology—and their relation to archaic experiences "of being a developing fetus, of being born—even of being an embryo in search of conception"—as potential material "for constructing an increasingly meaningful genetic link between the patient's past and his or her present phantasy life."

All those engaged in psychoanalytic work are well aware of the challenge that such analysands present, both in clinical management and in theoretical conceptualization, in view of their immense difficulty in *leaving* their survival techniques. Such readers will be moved by the sensitivity and profound empathy that Dr. Mitrani displays as she shares with us her own voyage of discovery into these little-charted regions of the mind.

Joyce McDougall
Paris, France
June 1995

Acknowledgments

There are so very many people to whom I wish to express my gratitude. First there are the supervisees, students, and especially the
patients who have stimulated my imagination, challenged me to
construct increasingly articulate models, and motivated me to seek
new metaphors and to tell better "stories."

Second, there are those who took the initiative to encourage
my creativity and independence and who often actively inspired me
to think. Among them are Prof. Charles Batten and Drs. Pierre
Ducet, Stuart Ende, William Erwin, Alain Gibeault, James Gooch,
James Grotstein, Robert Gruener, Victoria Hamilton, Donald
Marcus, Thomas Ogden, and Graeme Taylor.

Next, there are a special few who openly fostered my work.
Among them are my friends and colleagues Mr. Harold Boris, Drs.
Elizabeth Bianchedi, Joann Culbert-Koehn, Erna Osterweil, Judith
Welles and, of course, my mentor, Mrs. Frances Tustin.

A very special expression of my thanks must go to Dr. Joyce McDougall for honoring me with the foreword to this book, for her gracious and generous support, and for her appreciation for my writings. My feelings of affinity with her own work can hardly be adequately expressed.

Then there are two who have truly provided a most extraordinary framework for my growth and development over the past fifteen years: Drs. Ralph M. Obler and Yvonne Hansen.

Finally, there is but one who consistently provides me with all of the above: one who stimulates, inspires, fosters, and forms a constant framework for my imaginary and much, much more: my husband, Dr. Theodore Mitrani, to whom I am profoundly grateful. His generosity, forbearance, scholarship, intellectual integrity, and clarity of mind in editing this work are and always have been invaluable.

I also wish to thank Art Feiner, Jay Greenberg, Owen Renik, Otto Weininger, and David Tuckett for their expert editing and for granting me permission to reprint in this volume some of my papers first published in their very fine journals.

All knowledge brings us nearer to our ignorance . . .
where is the wisdom we have lost in knowledge?

T. S. Eliot, *Two Choruses from "The Rock"*

Introduction

For some years I saw a young man in analysis. Robert, as I shall refer to him here, was in such a dark and impenetrable state of distress when first we met that I feared for some time that he might not survive. Our connection was intense yet fragile, filled with moments of cruel rage, loving tenderness, and, as he once said, "everything in between." Our first major break in the treatment took place over the Christmas holiday. Before we parted, Robert presented me with a gift: a book that he had made himself. Printed on the front cover of this book was the title: *Photo Album of My Imaginary*.

Between the covers, carefully drawn in pen and ink, were simple rectangles, one to a page, with captions printed below each one. Some were dated with a year, some with a month and year, others with a precise date; still others were left untethered in time.

A preface offered a poignant explanation of thirty-one such "photographs"—perhaps not coincidentally—one for each year of Robert's painful existence.

What fascinated Robert about photography was the limits of the "frame with four sides." He wondered what there is "beyond the frame," what the photographer chooses not to let his audience see. In his book there were no pictures within the frames. In the preface he wrote that the caption and the frame were meant to "bring back not one but a multitude of images and feelings, impossible to capture in one picture alone. The frames and the captions serve as starting blocks to our imagination."

This gift was given at the end of the final hour before the holiday break. I was very moved by this gesture. Throughout the length of this separation I had many thoughts about Robert and his book. For a time the analysis became the living frame for his unimagined experiences.

It seems to me that in analysis, the four hours, like the four lines of the rectangle, provide the boundaries of the "imaginary," creating the frame for the analytic week and all that it contains. Associations, like the captions below the frames, serve to bring back not one but a multitude of images and feelings. Together within the frame, analyst and analysand strive to capture the previously unimagined-imagined; developing imaginative word-photographs within the boundaries of a common language, within the boundaries of each 45-minute hour, within the boundaries of the analytic week, within the boundaries of the analytic relationship, and within the creative overlapping of two minds.

In the end, both analyst and patient are left to wonder what lies outside the frame, outside the bounds of what each has chosen, consciously or unconsciously, to let the other "see."

This collection of essays serves as a simple framework for my "imaginary," that is, for my analytic experiences of Robert and many others over a period of fifteen years. Not unlike Robert, each of my analysands at various times communicated their raw experiences in the transference, like pieces of film requiring processing by a mind. In analysis this processing calls upon the analyst to receive and respond to vivid impressions of the patient's raw and sometimes even unmentalized experiences in the countertransference, something analogous to a photographic negative. The subsequent "developing process" is one in which the analyst feels, suffers, mentally transforms, and finally verbally constructs—for and with the analysand—various possible meanings for immediate versions of life's earliest experiences as they are glimpsed through the therapeutic lens.

Within the pages of this "album" these experiences are reproduced as clinical discursive snapshots (and the theoretical transformations of these) developed in the imaginary of one psychoanalyst. Clearly, what is printed on these pages is merely a sampling of the various representations of those experiences. There is much more still to be "seen," more that lies outside the frame of this book. Left out-of-bounds is that which the author has chosen not to let the reader "see," what each member of the analytic couple has chosen not to let the other see, and, of course, the ineffable. Any theory, like any photographic print, is only a representation of our perception of reality. It is only a feeble attempt at creating an approximation of experience. Alas, as Robert once reminded me, "There is so much more that overflows the boundaries of the frame in all directions."

Unintegration, Adhesive Identification, and the Psychic Skin:* Variations on Some Themes by Esther Bick

The failure of [the] containing function of the Skin Ego results in two forms of anxiety. An instinctual excitation that is diffuse, constant, scattered, non-localizable, non-identifiable, unquenchable, results when the psychical topography consists of a kernel without a shell in physical pain or psychical anxiety: he wraps himself in suffering. In the second case, the envelope exists, but its continuity is broken into by holes. This Skin Ego is a colander: thoughts and memories are only with difficulty retained; they leak away.

[Didier Anzieu, *The Skin Ego*]

BACKGROUND

Born in Poland in 1901, Esther Bick earned her doctorate in child development in Vienna. Seeking refuge from Nazi persecution in World War II, she immigrated to London where she pursued her

---

*An earlier version of this chapter was presented as part of a series of discussions on "Classic Papers in Psychoanalysis" spon-

analytic training at the London Institute of Psychoanalysis of the British Psycho-Analytical Society. Along with John Bowlby, Bick established the training program at the Tavistock Clinic. She founded the technique of infant observation practiced there to this day (Bick 1964), the same technique that was later adopted as an integral part of the training at the Institute of Psycho-Analysis, London, of the British Psycho-Analytical Society, and one of the cornerstones of the training program at the Psychoanalytic Center of California.

It was Bick's conviction that learning to become a good observer aids in learning to become a good psychoanalyst. She felt strongly that throughout the yearlong observation each candidate-observer comes to learn how a baby grows and becomes increasingly interested in the complexity of his development. She noted that this increasingly interested observer reinforces the mother's own interest in her baby and encourages her to value her own capacity to understand him and to tend to his needs. Similarly, Bick also believed that the analyst, observing the patient, comes to learn how he has arrived at this point in his life. It seemed to her that the analyst who could sustain an appreciative interest in the complexity of that individual's development reinforced in the analysand the healthier and more mature aspects of his personality and the inclination to value his own capacity to comprehend experience and to minister to his own needs.

Although Bick underwent her training analysis with Michael Balint, she was later analyzed by Melanie Klein and is remembered by many as a devout follower and a respected teacher of Kleinian theory and technique. Her own work, however, observing infants

---

sored by the Extension Division of the Psychoanalytic Center of California on January 28, 1994. It was subsequently presented at a scientific meeting of The Los Angeles Institute and Society for Psychoanalytic Studies on October 31, 1994, and was later published in *Melanie Klein and Object Relations* in December 1994.

and treating and supervising the treatments of autistic children and severely disturbed adults, led to the development of some new models for understanding patients in analysis. These models of understanding form what can now be considered the basis for an essential extension of classical Kleinian thinking.

In her published work Bick (1964, 1968, 1986) delineated an extremely primitive type of "narcissistic identification" which developmentally precedes that which is implied in Klein's theory of projective identification (M. Klein 1946). Bick's notion of this very early form of identification subsequently provoked many workers to revise their psychoanalytic thinking by inspiring them to begin charting yet another dimension of object relations that had previously been little explored. This is a dimension in which the centrality of the process of "getting into" is subordinated to the primacy of "getting in contact with" the object: a very archaic process that always appears to be linked to an object of psychic reality equivalent to the skin (Etchegoyen 1991).

After a review of Bick's work, I will touch upon the evolution and refinement of the concepts she introduced as they later appeared in the work of Donald Meltzer (1975) and his co-workers (Meltzer et al. 1975) and subsequently were extended by Frances Tustin (1972, 1980, 1981, 1983, 1984b, 1986, 1990) and others. As I trace these later efforts, I will also elaborate on the notion of adhesive pseudo-object relations (J. Mitrani 1994a), a term I have coined for the purpose of communicating about an archaic mode of object relations, more elemental than that which has been so well defined and documented by Melanie Klein and her exponents.

THE WORK OF ESTHER BICK

In her 1968 paper Bick wrote about certain behaviors that caught her attention time and again in those infants she—as well as her colleagues and students—observed. Such observations led Bick to hypothesize that very young babies may initially experience the absence of boundaries sufficiently capable of holding together their mental and emotional contents, not yet distinguishable or differentiated from bodily contents. In her compact communication Bick proposed the notion of a "psychic skin" that ideally serves to passively bind together the experiences or parts of the nascent self on their way toward integration into a cohesive sense of self.

She described this psychic skin as a projection of or corresponding to the bodily skin, and she proposed that it is "dependent initially on the introjection of an *external object, experienced as* capable of fulfilling this function" (Bick 1968, p. 484).

The external object Bick refers to here is a complex, undifferentiated object composed of *experiences of continuous interaction between a physically and emotionally "holding" and mentally "containing" mother, and the surface of the infant's body as a sensory organ.* This notion is one that Freud (1923) alluded to when he suggested that "the ego is first and foremost a bodily ego; it is not merely a surface entity, but is itself the projection of a surface" (p. 26).

Bick (1968) further hypothesized that "later, identification with this [psychic skin] function of the object supersedes the unintegrated state and gives rise to the [ph]antasy[1] of internal and external space" (p. 484). She forwarded the idea that this phantasy of space is the essential basis for the *normal adaptive splitting* and *projection* necessary to the processes of idealization and separation described by Klein. However, Bick warned that ". . . until the containing function has been introjected, the concept of a space within

---

1.   The word *phantasy*, spelled with a "ph," was used by Melanie Klein and elaborated by Susan Isaacs to denote an *unconscious* process or the product of one such process. Spelled this way, the word phantasy discriminates these processes and their products from those subsumed under the term *fantasy* with an "f," which refers to a *conscious* process or its product. All defenses, arising from the unconscious, are phantasies.

the self cannot arise . . . [and] construction of an [internal containing] object . . . [will be] impaired" (p. 484).

Along with her description of the primary tendency to relate to objects in a two-dimensional way preceding the development of a sense of internal space, Bick made a crucial distinction between *unintegration* as a helpless, passive state of maximal dependency and the active *defensive* maneuvers of splitting and disintegration. She explicitly associated unintegration with the earliest catastrophic anxieties, while correlating disintegration with later persecutory and depressive anxieties. Along these lines, she stated that

> the need for a containing object would seem in the infantile unintegrated state to produce a frantic search for an object—a light, a voice, a smell, or other *sensual* object—which can hold the attention and thereby be experienced, momentarily at least, as holding the parts of the personality together. [p. 484]

She continues to explain that

> the optimal object is the nipple in the mouth, together with the holding and talking and familiar smelling mother . . . experienced concretely as a skin. Disturbance in the primal skin function can lead to development of a "second skin" formation through which dependence on the object is replaced by a pseudo-independence. [p. 484]

In a further clarification of the subject, Bick (1986) additionally noted that these "secondary skin devices may arise in collaboration with peculiarities of the maternal care such as muscular or vocal methods" (p. 292). Stated another way, these psychic skin substitutes may be patterned after perceived sensual characteristics of the mother or other primary caretakers. Bick also suggested that such primeval defenses come under the heading of "second skin formations" and are originally "non-mental" phenomena

constructed to protect the very young infant against what she
described as

> the catastrophic anxiety of falling-into-space, and the dead-
> end [which] haunts every demand for change and which
> engenders a deep conservatism and a demand for sameness,
> stability and support from the outside world. [p. 299]

Although her published papers are brief and few in number, in
them Bick provides us with many excellent clinical examples to
illustrate her ideas. For example, she vividly describes one infant,
Baby Alice, who was moved to develop a premature muscular type
of second skin in compliance with the needs·of an insecure mother
who early on requires proof of her infant's vitality and who later,
out of the necessity of her situation, pushes her baby toward pseudo-
independence. She also reports her treatment of Mary, a schizo-
phrenic 3-year-old, who spoke of herself as a "sack of potatoes," in
constant peril of spilling out due to the holes that she picked in
her sack. One adult patient was observed in oscillation between an
experience of herself as a "sack of apples," in which she felt easily
bruised and threatened with catastrophe, and "the hippopotamus,"
who was aggressive, tyrannical, and stubborn. And Jill, a 5-year-old
child, conveyed the sense of how precariously she felt held together,
insisting that her clothes be firmly fastened and her shoes tightly
laced during the absence of her therapist. I will here add an example
from my own practice.

Carla

> When Carla was still a fairly young child, her mother died of
> respiratory failure in the child's lap on the way to the emer-
> gency room. The mother's death occurred only a short time
> after she, Carla, and four younger siblings had been abandoned
> by a philandering father. Carla presented herself in analysis,

and to the world, as a hard, sassy, streetwise "chick," whose toughness served as a second skin resembling the tight leather clothing she often wore. On the surface, the form of her defense might well have been traced to an idealized image of the father's erect penis and the paternal function of protection. In the second year of her analysis, however, a fragile baby part of Carla began to emerge, crying out to be born and to be allowed contact with what she seemed at times to experience as the caring presence of a mother-analyst.

In one session Carla began to cry as we had not heard her cry before, a cry that penetrated me deeply. I felt that the depth of Carla's cries corresponded to the strata from which they emanated, as if they came up from some very deeply buried experience in infancy. When I told her as much, she said, "I feel like something terrible wants out of me. I can't let myself breathe. I don't want it to come out. I'm afraid I'll never stop crying." She seemed to be communicating about that terrible feeling that she would spill out and be gone, unable to collect herself at the end of the hour as she experienced the loss of some very basic sense of security: a loss that would certainly have originated even earlier than the memorable events of either her father's abandonment or her mother's death.

Months later we were to come closer to understanding some of the most primitive origins of Carla's fear of being spilled and gone, as well as the template for the development of her leathery protection against the threat of such dissipation. Both this anxiety and the defense against it appeared to be connected to a primary experience of the mother.

In the third year of her analysis, I noticed that almost invariably when Carla returned from the weekend breaks she would at first greet my arrival at the waiting room door with a warm and enthusiastic smile. She would then scan my face quite intensely before passing through the doorway on the way to my consulting room. It often occurred to me that she was perhaps looking for an expression on my face that might reflect her own, which nearly always ranged somewhere from mild pleasure to sheer joy at the sight of me.

By the time she reached the couch, however, this enthusiasm for her analysis and for me would dissolve into a tough, leathery air of indifference, if not downright disgust, at having to submit to *my* requirement that she return for yet another hour and another week. When I turned our attention to this transformation one day, suggesting that it might somehow be connected to feelings and fantasies provoked by what she seemed to see in my face when I came to the door, she said with despair, "You always look the same."

Carla then went on to tell me that she had been happy that day when she arrived in plenty of time to use the restroom. However, when she found that it was "all locked up," she was left feeling as if she might burst. Then, as if to deny the importance of her disappointment, she added resolutely that it was "really O.K."

At that moment it seemed to me that the story of the locked restroom contained clues to the meaning of her radical transformation. She had indeed been filled to bursting with emotion, which she could barely hold inside when she arrived. But she was soon disappointed, feeling me to be emotionally shutting her out as she searched my face for signs of joy as evidence that I might be open to the overflow of her excitement and therefore able to provide her with some relief from these as well as other overwhelming feelings.

I told Carla that it seemed to me that she had been hoping that my face would reflect the enthusiasm with which she had come to see me that day, especially when she felt that it was *not* too late for her to get some relief, but that her hopes had somehow turned rapidly to disillusionment. She nodded in agreement and I continued, telling her that I thought she might be communicating to me about a little-she who was unable to bear that feeling of disillusionment, so that she had consequently resolved to toughen up for fear of bursting open.

Carla replied that she had only hoped I would be as happy to see her as she was to see me. I acknowledged this hope and added that she seemed to need to feel that the over-flowing joyous baby-she could be seen and held in my facial expression so that she would not spill away and be lost again. I added that I also thought that today this need was so intense that, when it seemed to her that I *could not* reflect and recip-rocate her joyous feeling for me, she transformed herself to match what must have felt to her like a locked-up, leathery, tough mommy-analyst, this in order to create a sense that she could catch herself by bringing us closer together with no gap in between.

Now crying, Carla told me that as I was speaking she had flashed back on the image of her mother's face, looking just as it had when Carla, as a very little girl, would watch her mother admiringly at her dressing table. She then told me, for the first time, that her mother had been disfigured in a car accident as a child. As a result, her face had always looked strange, disgusted and remote, with a leathery skin full of scar tissue resulting in a frozen, unchanging expression. Carla admitted that she could never tell if her mother really loved her. It seemed to me that the baby-Carla may never have felt held safely and responsively in her mother's gaze, as Mother's unalterable expression would have hindered her ability to reflect her daughter's joyous states of ecstasy and love.

Carla's story is an example of a rigidified and therefore patho-logical second-skin formation. In contrast to this, I would like to give one example of the temporary loss of the psychic skin and the transient development of a second skin made up of muscular and visual sensations. This example is an excerpt taken from records of my own infant observation.

Matthew

During one observation hour, 6-week-old Matthew, upon being undressed for his bath, began to show signs of distress while his clothes were removed as he lay on the changing table, his mother's attention diverted momentarily to the observer. His response to this gap in maternal attention—as well as the concomitant loss of the sensation of his mother's close and affectionate handling and the clothing that contained his body, all perhaps felt as a part of his physical as well as psychic skin—was to rigidify his muscles by arching his spine, clenching his fists and toes, and drawing these together in rhythmic movements, thus attenuating the distress, as if to hold himself together.

These actions were relinquished as soon as Matthew was once again held in his mother's arms and as she slipped him into the warm, soothing bathwater, which seemed to provide a continuous sensual experience of contact, both with the warm waters of the bath and with his mother's constant and attentive gaze and touch. Subsequently, as he was lifted from the bath and dried, Matthew again appeared to grow distressed at the loss of this comforting sensation. The signs of his distress escalated markedly as Mother's undivided attention was withdrawn while she resumed her conversation with the observer.

Becoming more and more agitated, Matthew seemed to search frantically with worried eyes until he was finally able to focus and fix his gaze on the mirror to the side of the counter on which he lay. He gradually began to quiet down again, as if he were now feeling held securely within his own image in the glass. However, when his mother abruptly turned him away from this holding mirror-image, Matthew let out a shriek, accompanied by a burst of tears, sudden urination, and a stream of wind from both mouth and bottom. It seemed as though he had felt torn away from that holding image in the mirror, and that this tearing feeling had undermined the integrity of his tenuous experience of being held together. The tear in this illusory psychic skin seemed to precipitate a spilling out from his eyes and penis and a diffusing or evaporating through both his mouth and his anus, as if these orifices had become equated with that tear.

WINNICOTT'S CONTRIBUTIONS

It may be of interest to note that although Winnicott's work has been largely overlooked in the Kleinian literature, he actually preceded Bick, addressing the subject of unintegration (1945) as well as the importance of the skin in early object relations (1960a). Winnicott pointed out that a part of the development taking place in the holding phase of infancy is the establishment of the baby's psychosomatic existence, a primary integration that he earlier referred to as the "indwelling of the psyche in the soma" (1949).

In connection with this, Winnicott noted (1960a) that in the course of normal development

> there comes into existence what might be called a limiting membrane, which to some extent (in health) is equated with the surface of the skin, and has a position between the infant's "me" and his "not-me." So the infant comes to have an inside and an outside, and a body-scheme. In this way meaning comes to the function of intake and output; moreover, it gradually becomes meaningful to postulate a personal or inner psychic reality for the infant . . . the beginning of a mind as something distinct from the psyche. Here the work on primi-

tive fantasy, with whose richness and complexity we are familiar through the teachings of Melanie Klein, becomes applicable and appropriate. [p. 45]

In his theory of mental development, Winnicott proposed that in the event of a deficiency in "good-enough mothering," the infant is likely to be subjected to sudden and/or chronic awareness of disconnection, leading to "unthinkable anxieties" associated with the *felt* state of "unintegration." The unthinkable anxieties to which Winnicott (1962) referred were enumerated by him as the fear of going to pieces, of falling forever, of having no relationship to the body, and of having no orientation in space.

Winnicott also noted that such unthinkable anxieties arise out of the primary state of unintegration, experienced in the absence of maternal ego-support. He further stated that these anxieties result from privation, characterized by a failure of holding in the stage of absolute dependence, and are thus to be differentiated from those of disintegration or fragmentation, which stem from an active production of chaos related to the more sophisticated omnipotent defenses associated with *deprivation* and activated only after some measure of ego integration has taken place.

I believe it is important to note that the capacity to experience unintegration as relaxation—what Winnicott referred to as the "capacity to be alone" (1958b)—also occurs *only* after the child has had the opportunity, through "good-enough mothering" and the "experience of being alone in the presence of the object," to build up a belief in a benign environment. Without this experience the baby may fall into a void of meaninglessness, and his otherwise normal state of unintegration may become a *feeling* of disintegration. This feeling of disintegration must be differentiated from disintegration as a defensive phantasy. Disruptions in the baby's sense of his own continuity of being may produce an "over activity of mental functioning" (Winnicott 1962, p. 61)—a precocious development of omnipotent phantasies of a defensive nature—produced "to take over and organize the caring for the psyche-soma; whereas in health it is the function of the environment to do this" (Winnicott 1962, p. 61).

This usurpation of environmental functions by the mind may lead to confusional states, second-skin adaptations, and the development of mental functioning as a thing in itself. Winnicott (1949) coined the term *pathological mind-psyche* for this phenomenon, which, he stated, is perceived as an enemy to the "true" self and must therefore be localized in the head for purposes of control.

I have introduced Winnicott's ideas here, not only because they are overdue for acknowledgment in the context of what are often thought to be original Kleinian notions, but also because they add much needed elaboration to the concept of unintegration and its anxieties, and may also serve to flesh out Bick's concept of a second skin by articulating its mental component. It is my understanding that Winnicott's pathological mind-psyche is a pseudomental apparatus that develops in the event that the environment fails to support the integration of psyche and the soma. I believe that this pathogenetic state, in which intellectual functioning is employed as a protective shell, may be one and the same as that which Meltzer observed and described as a mental apparatus that falls apart in the process of what *he* understood as unintegration.

It appears that, unlike Winnicott, Meltzer and colleagues (1975) understood unintegration to be a passive *defense* against anxiety. Meltzer (1986) used the term *dismantling* in relation to unintegration. He described dismantling as a splitting of the sensory apparatus, and consequently of the experience of the object, into its sensory components, resulting in the obliteration of common sense. He also used the term *reversal of alpha function*, assuming that the mental apparatus, and the thoughts processed and/or generated by it, is stripped of meaning that has previously been established. In viewing unintegration in this light, Meltzer—and Ogden after him—seemed to suggest that pathological psychogenic autism is related to a passive type of destructive "regression" and the collapse of previously developed mental structures.

Again, in contrast to Meltzer's use of the term, Winnicott, Bick, and Tustin used the term unintegration to designate a natural state of being in infancy, one that exists prior to the mother's application of her capacities to sort out the baby's nascent sensory experiences in her feelings, thoughts, and behaviors, thereby lending support to the baby's innate tendency toward the integration of such experiences. For these authors, unintegration is understood as a state of being that is only *experienced* by the baby as a dangerous disintegration *if and when* maternal containment becomes inaccessible and prior to the development of a stable psychic skin. Viewed in this context, unintegration may be seen as a normal primary state that is only experienced, felt, feared, and evaded when needed environmental supports are absent. Here, unintegration is conceptualized as a feeling-state, rather than a pathological development occurring at the expense of normal mental and emotional growth.

In this model it follows that a baby, chronically deficient in his experience of a suitable skin-object, out of necessity may organize his primary sensory experiences, without benefit of meaning, into an impenetrable second skin. This second skin thus provides an illusory and tentative form of integration that is false. The result is a sort of pseudo-mental-maturity, not unlike what Winnicott described as a pathological-mind-psyche, which may also be akin to what Bion referred to as a *beta-screen*.

It may be helpful at this point to look at one example of the intellect, and more specifically the use of words—either the patient's own or those of the analyst—to create a second skin as a container for unbearable experiences.

Vickie

Vickie had been raised by a severely disturbed mother who, as the patient was told, closed the door to her newborn infant's room when she heard her cries because she did not know how to mother her. In brief, Vickie seemed to re-experience in the transference a time in early infancy when, while lying in her crib, she had attempted to make meaning of her mother's failure to attend to her. I often had the impression of a baby who must have been continually obsessing about whether she had cried too loud or perhaps not cried loudly enough. Maybe the pitch of her cry was too high or maybe too low. Maybe she should continue to cry out or perhaps she should stop at once, and if so, for how long? Vickie seemed to wonder if Mother was ill or asleep, or perhaps she had finally left forever. Was Mother dead? Or was she?

I had the feeling that this patient had been unable to be a baby-at-one-with-her-mother, and so she was pushed to develop a pseudo-mind in service of avoiding a dreadful experience of perishing as well as a rather precocious concern for her caretaking object. She would often become terrified when, in this avoidant state, she could no longer feel her own body.

Initially my interventions ran the expected gamut: transference interpretations addressing the weekend breaks, the holidays and the endings of sessions, and the experiences of abandonment, along with the anxieties and defenses against these anxieties provoked by painful separations. But, although Vickie's material was quite communicative of this type of experience, it became apparent that her ruminations were not really thoughts connected to experiences of loss, but rather that these were an agglomeration of words that provided a cocoon of sensation within which she could wrap her precarious self for protection against the awareness of loss. She seemed also to use those interpretations that addressed the *content* of her associations as additional *stuff* for the construction and maintenance of that cocoon, and I was often left feeling that we were going nowhere together.

Indeed, I was puzzled by this for some time, but when I was able to understand that this was the point, that we were

to be prevented from going anywhere, and was finally able
to communicate to her my sense of her perpetual activity—
spinning me and my words as well as her own into a safe and
impenetrable cocoon within which she might be able to protect herself against some catastrophic experience of being
gone—Vickie had the following association.

   She recalled having once been told by a family member
that, on the day she was brought home from the hospital, she
was left wrapped up in a blanket in the middle of her mother's
bed, where no one was permitted to enter or pick her up in
order to offer her comfort when she cried. Vickie's naive if
well-meaning mother believed that this treatment would help
to "toughen up" her baby and would diminish her dependency
upon her caretakers.

   It might be seen that, with such patients, if we attend *only* to
the *text* of their communications, we run the risk of colluding with
their attempts to toughen up and to protect themselves against
(while failing to help them to contain) these early experiences. Such
toughening left little room for the emergence and development of
a genuine "felt-self" that, over time in Vickie's case, became more
and more compressed and out of reach of feeling.

SYMINGTON'S EMPHASIS ON THE SURVIVAL-FUNCTION OF THE "SECOND SKIN"

In a further expansion of Bick's concept of the second skin, Joan
Symington (1985) discussed the survival function of such omnipotent protections. She explicitly described one such protective
maneuver as a tightening or constricting of the smooth muscles of
certain internal organs, providing an illusory sensation of a continuous skin, without gaps through which the self risks spilling out
into space, never again to be found and held securely.

Symington's many examples from infant observations, as well as her experiences with adult patients in the analytic setting, give credibility to her conclusions that

> the primitive fear of the state of disintegration underlies the fear of being dependent; that to experience infantile feelings of helplessness brings back echoes of that very early unheld precariousness, and this in turn motivates the patient to hold himself together . . . at first a desperate survival measure . . . gradually . . . built into the character . . . the basis on which other omnipotent defense mechanisms are superimposed. [p. 486]

Symington emphasized that these catastrophic unintegration anxieties are likely to be present at times in the majority of people, and she suggested that, while holding themselves together through the use of these primitive as well as more sophisticated methods, patients are likely to appear to be in opposition to the analytic relationship. Mutism, blocking, stubbornness, immutable rage, falling asleep, intellectualizing, forced speech, superficiality, zoning-out on the analyst's voice, appropriating the analyst's interpretations, reading books about analysis, flitting from one subject to another, and other such behaviors *might* mistakenly be interpreted as a turning away from the analyst and as intentionally destructive to the analytic process. However, Symington warned that interpretation of the defense and its destructiveness, without acknowledging the patient's fear of catastrophe and his conviction that he must hold himself together, risks leaving him feeling uncontained and misunderstood, and often results in silent hurt and increased defensiveness.

I would like to further emphasize this point by saying that, in my experience, this increased defensiveness often takes the form of extreme compliance that, while simulating improvement, merely constitutes the development of a new and more subtle version of *j* the second skin, one that is patterned on the personality and theories of the analyst and is therefore acceptable to him. Once this transformation in the second skin is achieved, it is no longer accessible to interpretation, as it has become scotomatized in the mind of the analyst.

TUSTIN'S CLARIFICATION
OF ADHESIVE IDENTIFICATION

Frances Tustin (1986) pointed out in a discussion of "autistic objects" that, in the absence of a containing presence, chronically "unintegrated children" (p. 127) quell their unbearable terrors of falling or spilling away forever by creating sensations of adhering to the surfaces of hard things. These sensations afford the child an immediate if ephemeral experience of bodily continuity and safety, as the child becomes equated with the surface of the object. In the case of autism, the child is addicted to this mode of survival.

Tustin (1992) suggested the use of the term *adhesive equation* rather than Bick's *adhesive identification*, a term she thought more descriptive of certain pathological processes unique to the problem of autistic encapsulation.

In her most recent work she clarified that autistic children are chronically "stuck" to their mothers in such a way that there can be no space between them, that is, no space in which the development of a true object relationship can take place. She noted that Bick, who had an early influence upon her own professional development, was aware that autistic children, in contrast to schizophrenic-type or symbiotically psychotic children, cannot identify with an object, and came to rename this phenomenon *adhesive identity*. Tustin emphatically underscored the point that, without an awareness of space, there can be no relationship, and without relationship, the process of identification cannot be set in motion. It might be said that adhesive equation or adhesive identity serves to establish a *sensation of existence* rather than a *sense of self and object*, each with its own identity.

In a personal communication, Tustin (1992) additionally clarified that "In *adhesive equation* the 'subject' feels the *same* as the 'object' with no space between them, while in *adhesive identification* the 'subject' feels *similar to* the 'object' and there *is* space between them."

Tustin (1986) also called attention to Gaddini's (1969) term *imitative fusion* as yet another way of conceptualizing this phenomenon, reiterating that

> It is important to realize that, since the child's body seems fused with "autistic objects," these have scarcely reached the status of an "object" in the usual sense of the term . . . [and these also] need to be differentiated from Winnicott's "transitional objects" which . . . can facilitate ongoing psychological development. [p. 128]

Gaddini (1969) understood this phantasy of fusion as "an attempt to gain a vicarious identity, magically acquired through [fusional] imitation" (p. 478), an idea very much in keeping with Bick's description of the second skin as the resultant of an act of "mimicry."

Preceding Gaddini, Hélene Deutsch (1942) described the "as-if personality" as one existing in a state of "imitative identification." She noticed that these patients behaved "as-if" they themselves *were* their loved objects. Through her years of work with autistic patients, Tustin came to understand this as a "delusory state of fusion" rather than a special case of identification.

My patient Robert displayed this type of adhesive identification as well as the somatic expression of unmentalized experience typical of such patients whose secondary skin constructions create autistic enclaves.

Robert

Robert was referred for analysis after a series of hospitalizations following his mother's suicide. In one hour Robert told
me of a visual handicap from which he had suffered all of his
life, a "lazy eye" through which he saw the world in only two
dimensions, an anomaly that one physician had attributed to
his traumatic birth. Because of this lazy eye, Robert had no
depth perception. He had no sense of space or distance, and
no sense of an inside, only the sensation of a flat outside. Over
time we came to understand his lazy "I" as a somatic *presentation* of the psychologically unborn-he who could not bear
changes in light, temperature, or textures. Thus he felt he
could not be "fixed" *by* the analysis but could only be "fixed"
onto it.

This patient always seemed to feel at the end of each
hour as if I was peeling him off the "placental" walls next
to the couch in my consulting womb. Both in session and
between times on the telephone, Robert seemed to stick to
me for dear life, and he expressed his experience of the weekend breaks and holidays as an excruciating "rip-off" during
which he would intentionally engage in behavior that might
result in his being put on "hold" in the hospital.

He would often and quite poignantly describe, in great
detail and with much emotion, episodes in the hospital prior
to our work together when he was actually placed in four-point
restraints in a padded room. Frequently he longed to return
to that safe, if constricting, environment. The last time he
overdosed on a mixture of substances, he was hospitalized and
required renal dialysis. Thus, in a very dramatic way, Robert
brought home to me his felt need, not just for the womb, but
for the umbilical cord and its functions as well.

On one occasion Robert came up with what he thought
was a viable solution to "the problem of the analysis" that was

felt to force him to be an "I" in three dimensions. He articulated the fantasy of placing his camera on a tripod in my consulting room, setting it for a 30-minute exposure that, in his words, "would blur the two of us into a state of oneness" with no space between and no distinction of sex, age, or position in the relationship. The resultant photograph would serve, not as a souvenir of this perfect state, but an amulet without which he felt always at risk.

At a later point in his analysis, Robert began to bring new photographs—this time in vivid color and clearly three-dimensional—of ancient structures gently and loosely shrouded and surrounded by supportive scaffolding, all in the process of restoration.

MELTZER'S HISTORICAL AND TECHNICAL CONTRIBUTIONS

Meltzer (1975) has provided a historical context for the saga of the development of Kleinian thinking, which culminated in the conceptualization of adhesive identification, suggesting a primitive narcissistic state preceding that subsumed under the paranoid-schizoid position. This illuminating paper enriched the findings that he and his co-workers reported in the classic volume *Explorations in Autism* (Meltzer et al. 1975), especially in the area of the technique working with such elemental states in adults as well as in children. Meltzer reports:

We . . . began to notice that interpretations along the lines of projective identification didn't seem to carry any weight in certain situations. We were in trouble with certain kinds of patients and saw that something else was going on that certainly was connected with identification processes; it was certainly connected with narcissism, but it seemed to have quite a different phenomenology from what we gathered together under the rubric of projective identification . . . something that had to do with states of catastrophic anxiety in certain infants whose mothers seemed somehow unable to contain them. When these infants got anxious, their mothers got anxious too and then the infant got more anxious and a spiral of anxiety tended to develop . . . which ended with the infant going into some sort of . . . disorganized state. [p. 295]

Meltzer recalled how Bick began to observe that some adults were also subject to similar states.

Suddenly they wouldn't be able to do anything. They would have to sit down and shake. It wasn't that they were anxious in the ordinary sense . . . they just felt muddled, paralyzed and confused and couldn't do anything. They just had to sit down or lie down until it went away. The material of the analysis at these times and the dreams began to throw up an image of something . . . not held together, not contained . . . these people all had disturbances related to the skin or their experience of the skin . . . that they weren't properly held together by a good skin, but that they had other ways of holding themselves together . . . with their intelligent thinking and talking . . . with explanations . . . [or] muscularly. [p. 296]

Meltzer reported that he and his group of child therapists had observed similar phenomena in autistic children. At certain stages these children

functioned as if there were no spaces, there were only surfaces, two dimensions. Things were not solid, only surfaces that they might lean up against, or that they might feel, smell, touch . . . get a sensation from . . . they didn't seem to hold things well . . . words went right through them. Their responses [to

interpretation] seemed so delayed often that one felt that all
that had been left behind of what you had said was a kind of
musical disturbance that they eventually reacted to or reacted
against. [p. 299]

Most useful for the clinician is the distinction Meltzer explicitly
made with regard to the course of treatment with such patients.
He clarified that what was previously thought to be associated with
motivation—the problem of "negative therapeutic reaction" related
to envy, masochism, jealousy, and unconscious guilt—could be seen
as a manifestation of a *structural defect*.

[These patients] do just fall to pieces occasionally, and one
has to be very patient with particular counterference problems that have to do with being able to contain the patient
. . . the chief manifestation of this is the ability to worry about
the patient . . . these seem to be patients who need to be
worried about, although they are not the kind of patients who
clamor for it . . . one cannot expect such patients to move very
fast . . . they have to develop an internal object that can really
hold something, that doesn't have a leak in it and they are very
slow to develop this because they have a leak and they can't
hold anything very well themselves . . . one just has to wait for
something to accumulate ["like rust or corrosion"] . . . one
just can't plug up the hole. [p. 306]

It would seem that a skin object must be incorporated very early
on in mental development to allow a space within the self to develop
so that the mechanism of projective identification, as the primary
method of nonverbal communication between the mother and the
baby in search of detoxification and meaning, can function without impediment. Indeed, the work of Mauro Mancia (1981) supports the notion of a potential for this early development of a psychic skin *in utero*.

In consideration of each of the abovementioned findings, it appears that, until such time as a sense of personal existence is securely established, allowing for some awareness of a human object and the intermittent space between subject and object, there can be no true development of relationship. Only through human relationship can a sense of internal space develop. Without this sense of internal space, the phantasy of getting inside the object cannot develop and the unyielding sensation of being at-one-with, equated, and contiguous with the object, prevails, perhaps as a remnant of the earliest intrauterine experience of existence. In such a hyperbolic and therefore *pathological* state of "at-one-ment," there can be no psychological birth and consequently no *meaningful* experience of a physical life outside the womb, since the awareness of such physical separateness, when it impinges upon these as yet unformed individuals, can only be felt as catastrophic.

When considering the form and function of what Bick first termed *adhesive identification*, it becomes clear that such primitive auto-sensual survival tactics do not really coincide with normal or narcissistic object relations. However, it is important to note that neither does it imply the "normality" or even the existence of a primary "objectless state" (Mahler 1958). Instead, one might postulate a mode of *pseudo-object relationship* in which adhesive identification predominates, a state that may be seen to fill the conceptual gap between normal/narcissistic object relations and an objectless state.

This state of existence entails the obliteration of any experience of space, thus inhibiting the development of genuine human relationship and its associated identificatory processes. I will here introduce the term *adhesive pseudo-object relations* for this state. This new term may provide a helpful designation for the discussion of a mode of object relationship that is *apparent* (to the observer/analyst) rather than *actual* (in the subjective experience of the analysand); a *mode of being* in which *adhesive identification* or *adhesive equation*—rather than true identification—predominates; a state in which the superimposition of subject and object is so complete, continuous, and chronic that the concepts of "otherness" and "space" have little or no relevance. While in this mode of being, the awareness of space and otherness only serves to confront the analysand with an unbearable experience of catastrophe and a felt-threat to a fragile sense of "going-on-being."

One example of the subjective experience of space, while one is in this state of existence, is the "black hole with the nasty prick" as it was articulated by Tustin's autistic patient, John (Tustin 1981). As Grotstein (1990) so aptly put it, the experience of the black hole is an "experience of the awesome force of powerlessness, of defect, of nothingness, of 'zero-ness'—expressed, not just as a static emptiness but as an implosive, centripetal pull into the void" (p. 257). Thus space is not experienced as an area within which human relationship might be allowed to develop, but rather it is felt as the *presence of an inhumane and malevolent absence* that must be blotted out of awareness at all costs.

Ogden (1989a,b) coined the term *autistic-contiguous position* to denote a distinct psychological organization more primitive than Klein's paranoid-schizoid and depressive positions. Ogden suggested that this position is "an integral part of normal development through which a distinctive mode of experience is generated"; a position, rather than a stage, with its own form of object-relatedness, set of anxieties, and defenses against these.

Although I find Ogden's ideas valuable, my own diverge from his in several ways. While Ogden describes the nature of the infant's "autistic-contiguous" object relationships as a presymbolic dialectic between continuity and edgedness, between boundedness and at-one-ment with a subjective-object, I consider the development of an enduring mode of "adhesive pseudo-object relations" (J. Mitrani 1994a) as an asymbolic aberration of normal development, rooted in traumatic experiences of extreme privation occurring *in utero* and/or in early infancy, which have prematurely interrupted the necessary development of and trust in the "rhythm of safety" (Tustin

1986) between mother and infant, resulting in the crippling of this emerging elemental state of subjectivity and the gradual development of true objectivity.

While I believe that such an aberrant mode of pseudo-relating may, like the autistic enclave in the neurotic personality, exist on a "dual track" (Grotstein 1986) alongside normal/narcissistic object relations, I maintain that, in an enduring and rigidified form, adhesive pseudo-object-relations are nearly always *pathologically defensive* and, in turn, pathogenetic and obstructive to the ongoing development of normal object relatedness.

In other words, whereas normal presymbolic autosensuality, as described by Tustin, is the seed that, when cultivated and nurtured within the context of human relationship, germinates, sprouts, and grows into object relations proper, I believe that if experiences of a sensory nature are left unprocessed by a thinking and feeling object, symbolic meaning fails to evolve out of the rudiments of the existential experience inherent in sensory contiguity and rhythmicity, and that these untransformed and "unmentalized experiences" (J. Mitrani 1993b, 1995b) become rigidified and hypertrophied as fortified protections against the awareness of those primeval experiential states of terror related to bodily and emotional separateness.

In Chapter 8 I will attempt to operationalize and add clarity to the term *adhesive pseudo-object relations* by comparing and contrasting this with normal/narcissistic object relations.

2

On the Survival Function of Autistic Maneuvers in Adult Patients[1]

The skin is an envelope which emits and receives signals in interaction with the environment; it "vibrates" in resonance with it; it is animated and alive inside, clear and luminous. The autistic child has a notion—doubtless genetically pre-programmed—of such an envelope, but for want of concrete experiences to bring it into being, the envelope remains empty, dark, inanimate, dumb. Autistic envelopes thus provide a proof a contrario of the structure and functions of the Skin Ego.

[Didier Anzieu, *The Skin Ego*]

BACKGROUND

Francis Tustin (1972, 1981, 1986, 1990) devoted her life's work to the psychoanalytic understanding of the bewildering elemental world of the autistic child. Her realization that some of our more neurotic adult patients are haunted by the same primeval forces

---

1. A version of this chapter was presented at a scientific meeting of the Psychoanalytic Center of California on May 17, 1991, and was subsequently published in the *International Journal of Psycho-Analysis* in 1992.

that constitute an enclave of autism has been profound. The notion that autistic maneuvers serve as a protective shell against the terrifying awareness of bodily separateness and dissolution into nothingness has had a substantial impact upon the rethinking of such notable analysts as Boyer (1990), Grotstein (1983), D. Rosenfeld (1984), and H. A. Rosenfeld (1987).

In the last decade several other authors have taken up Tustin's work to expand our understanding of certain personality organizations that impede development in our adult patients and constitute an impenetrable resistance within the analytic relationship, leading to unresolvable impasse and interminable treatment.

For example, Sidney Klein (1980) described those patients who, despite the appearance of progress in the analysis, remain untouched in some essential way due to encapsulating forces that cut the patient off from the analyst as well as the rest of the personality. He posited that walled off in these cystic areas of the mind are intense and unbearable fears of "pain, and of death, disintegration or breakdown" (S. Klein 1980, p. 400) related to unmentalized separation experiences of early infancy, and he suggested that such phenomena "are strikingly similar to those observed in so-called autistic children" (p. 400).

Innes-Smith (1987) has eloquently discussed the overinvestment in sensation objects as a factor in the etiology of adult psychopathology. He emphasized the importance of attending to that preoedipal state of mind in which dyadic communication is achieved on a nonverbal level, and those moments in the analysis when such states predominate.

Ogden (1989a,b) proposed a primitive mental organization, prefacing those of the paranoid-schizoid and depressive positions, which he termed the *autistic-contiguous position*. He suggested that, like the two aforementioned positions, the latter constitutes an ongoing state of mind, a way of being and experiencing with its own set of defenses, anxieties, and a mode of object relating that persists throughout life, one which may be mobilized in the transference at times in the analytic process.

In Chile, Gomberoff and his colleagues (1990) have focused upon certain aspects of the transference/countertransference interaction wherein there develops a collusive tendency, in the analytic couple, to transform the analysis, particularly some aspects of verbal language, into an autistic object that wards off anxiety over twoness for both analyst and analysand.

In this chapter I will first highlight some of the main features of Tustin's work, particularly those pertaining to the analysis of adult patients, as a prelude to several clinical illustrations which, it is hoped, will emphasize the survival function of autistic shapes (Tustin 1984b), autistic objects (Tustin 1980), and other sensation-dominated delusions.[2] These may be understood as serving to contain *unmentalized experiences*,[3] protecting the patient from unbear-

---

2. Tustin distinguishes autistic objects from objects (inanimate or animate) in the ordinary sense, in that the former are *not related to as objects*, but rather *used for the tactile sensations that they engender* upon the surface of the skin of the subject. Autistic shapes may be differentiated from objective shapes (such as a square or a circle) in that they are idiosyncratic, endogenous swirls of sensation produced upon the surface of the skin or internally with the aid of bodily substances or objects. These distinctions, first based upon observations with autistic children, are now widely extended to include numerous other behaviors observable in adults and children with an enclave of autism, which may be conceived of as sensation-dominated delusions. The key word here is "sensation." Such sensations serve either to distract one's attention away from anxiety, providing an illusion of safety, strength, and impermeability, or they may have a numbing or tranquilizing effect upon the individual which acts to block out the terror of awareness.

3. I use the term *unmentalized experience* to denote elemental sense data, internal or external, which have failed to be transformed into symbols (mental representations, organized and integrated) or signal affects (anxiety that serves as a signal of impending danger, requiring thoughtful action), but which are instead perceived as

able feelings of the catastrophic loss of and painful longing for the primary object, which threaten the subject with overwhelming anxiety. Finally, I will suggest that further discrimination is necessary in our work to distinguish between the analysis of these autistic states of being that are related to the threat of unintegration and those still primitive yet more organized states of mind that involve anxieties of a paranoid-schizoid or depressive nature (M. Klein 1948, 1975a,b).

In some of her most recent work, Tustin (1986, 1990) demonstrates the important link between autistic pathology in children and such autistic states of mind in adult neurotic patients seen in analysis. Her capacity for observation and self-reflection has enabled her to describe, in an evocative way, some of the most elemental human fears and anxieties alive and active in each of us, as well as the specialized protective forms that our patients create for purposes of survival.

Throughout her work, Tustin describes the sensations of mutilation, of spilling and falling, of dissolving and evaporating that characterize the intolerable terror of two-ness. Tustin traces the problem of psychogenic autism to the troubled nature of the earliest relationship between mother and nursling. She points out that the mothers of many autistically disturbed children, as well as those of our more neurotic patients, seem to have unwittingly reacted

---

concrete objects in the psyche or as bodily states that are reacted to in corporeal fashion, e.g., somatic symptoms or actions. Such experiences are merely "accretions of stimuli" that can neither be used as food for thought nor stored as memories in the mind. Paraphrasing Bion (1942) Bianchedi (1991) calls these "the 'unthoughts' . . . perceptions and sensations, not yet subjected to 'alpha function'" (p. 11). I believe Freud's notion of the "anxiety equivalent" (1895b, p. 94) in the actual neurosis was the first attempt to characterize this phenomenon in psychoanalysis.

toward their babies as if they were parts of their own bodies. Thus they have somehow failed to provide a satisfying and reliable experience at the breast, which could subsequently be internalized—this perhaps due to their own feelings of inadequacy, loneliness, and depression. Instead, they have overprotected their infants out of an unconscious wish to bring them, projectively identified with their own infantile selves, back to fetal bliss within their own bodies, while at the same time filling in the black hole of their own inadequacy, emptiness, and loneliness.

This pathogenic distortion of normal primary maternal preoccupation (Winnicott 1956) leaves the baby tied to and overly reliant upon the mother's bodily presence, abandoning him to the terrors he must inevitably experience during times of felt absence, this due to the mother's own deficient capacity to contain the experience of separation. In such cases separation and closeness have been achieved concretely, not symbolically. There is no apprehension of psychic distance or symbolic closeness. Strong emotion is felt in terms of physical sensation rather than sentiment.

Too much closeness on a physical level, compensating for a frailty of emotional contact, has impeded the development in such individuals of a safe space in which psychic objects might otherwise be created. To quote one patient about her mother: "She's so demanding. I felt I had always to be beside her. Like we were Siamese twins attached at the hip. I was never allowed to turn to anyone else, and yet she seemed so cold toward me, as if she never really recognized my existence."

These mothers are felt to be both too close and too far away, failing in both their holding and containing functions, unable to make sense out of their infants' nonverbal communications. Such children are then at grave risk; their own capacity to give the rudiments of meaning to what they experience is underdeveloped, and they are pushed to action rather than psychic activity and thinking as forms of containment. As one patient who resorted to numerous affairs when her husband was out of town on business expressed it: "I only feel that I exist when I'm making love. Somehow my body seems to come together around my vagina when I feel a man inside me."

Another patient told me of feeling reconstituted temporarily through the use of cigarettes. Perhaps the cigarette in her mouth, like the nipple in the mouth of the baby-she, was felt to reassemble her dissolving sense of self. The smoke screen she created through this activity was used to hold, protect, and lend visibility and substance to a diffused self.

Tustin (1986) helps us to understand how autism acts as a protective shell made up of what she terms *sensation-dominated delusions*, which serve to block out the unbearable agony of awareness of two-ness, and the threat such awareness represents to a sense of personal continuity and integrity. She uses the term *delusion* not in the common psychiatric sense, which implies some symbolic process and thought, but in a very concrete sense on the level of what Segal (1957) called *symbolic equation*. These delusions are the thing-in-itself, not to be confused with a representation.

Tustin also demonstrates how this protective barrier acts as an impediment to the healing effects of the relationship with the therapist. Her pioneer work, within the primordial territory of autistic states of consciousness, has enabled psychoanalytic therapists to proceed where our work with such patients had previously been stopped. She has given us a key with which we may gain entry into the once-forbidden and foreboding area of our patients' earliest experiences.

She draws our attention to her observation that certain neurotic adults have much in common with autistic children in that both share a sense of tentativeness in their existence as persons. In these adults development has taken place by circumventing an area of truncated development that is callused over or encapsulated. As one patient explained: "I have this hole—an empty spot deep inside me—maybe I'm just afraid to find that nothing is there." This patient seemed to cover over the hole with a "chip on his shoulder."

Eventually we came to understand this "chip," or callused,

cynical attitude, as a "chip off the old block," which referred to his feelings about his father. "He protected me," my patient said one day. "But he just didn't seem to know what to do with me when I couldn't throw the ball right. He thought I was a sissy—I threw the ball like a girl." This man was perhaps also telling me about a growing awareness that, like his father, he could protect the soft, tender part of his experience by covering it over with a hard "daddy chip," but that he was frightened of, and did not know how to help or handle, the baby-he with the soft spot on his head, the soft skin that was easily bruised, and the tender, loving feelings he had for the mommy-me.

As this patient demonstrates, some of our analysands struggle courageously in analysis to give verbal expression to those primitive states in which development has been impaired. Their symptoms and actions are often valiant attempts to give expression to their bodily experiences and to communicate their terrors so that we may lend meaning to them through our interpretive work. Many of our patients are moved to communicate their states of terror as they are re-experienced in the transference situation, provoked by the innumerable separations engendered in the analytic frame at the end of the analytic hour, the analytic week, and around vacations.

In my own experience with patients, I have found that Tustin's model of understanding is far more applicable to adults in psychoanalytic treatment than I had first imagined possible. As exemplified in the following clinical vignettes, *autistic-like shapes, hard objects, and delusions function to contain the unmentalized experience of the catastrophic loss of and painful longing for the primary object.*

Hope

Hope, a woman in her early thirties, came to analysis after many years of therapy. Having recently lost her father after nursing him through a painful illness, she moved to this city to be closer to an aged mother who she feared was needy and infirm. Hope thought her own depression attributable to a recent abortion she had, and complained of her relationship with the father of the aborted baby, a man she described as unprepared for the responsibilities of marriage and children.

As she was predisposed to see almost all those around her as needy and dependent upon her, it seemed there was ample evidence that much of my patient's suffering was a result of excessive intolerance toward a needy-baby part of herself and the tendency to handle this painful aspect of her experience through excessive splitting and projective identification. However, the handling of this over time, as it appeared in the transference, seemed to result in only a limited measure of relief, and it soon became apparent that Hope had hidden away, in an enclave of autism, a very dependent, sick, and dying baby-part of herself, and that this encapsulation was interfering with her relationships as well as her work.

Relevant to the material I present here, I will give a bit of Hope's history. Hope's mother had been severely depressed after the death of her own mother and, just six weeks after the birth of my patient, her milk suddenly dried up. Around this time it seems that the father dropped the baby Hope while holding her in his arms, and her lip was painfully split open in the fall, the scar remaining to this day.

In this session, the first of the week in the third year of the analysis, Hope began with a long silence characteristic of her re-entry on Monday after the three-day break. During this silence, which lasted several minutes, I had the unsettling sensation of falling, as if my chair were being progressively lowered into the floor beneath me. When finally I broke the silence by asking what she had been thinking, she began by telling me that over the weekend her boyfriend had gone out with friends, and that she had awakened at 3 A.M. to find herself still alone in their bed. She said she could not fall asleep, as she was hurt and angry at the boyfriend and fearful about being alone, thinking she heard noises outside as if someone were trying to break in.

Immobilized by her fear of intruders, she told me she had lain very still looking up at the ceiling, concentrating upon one single spot. She felt physically that she was being lifted up into a soft, pink cloud as she spread her tongue between her teeth, filling her mouth from corner to corner, touching her lips with her own fleshy organ. She reported how soothing the sensation was of uniting with this soft pink cloud, and how she soon drifted off to sleep. In fact, she said she had been doing that same thing—trying to get back there—when I interrupted her silence.

She then went on to tell how on the previous morning she had made love with her boyfriend, and how delicious this had been, but that he had immediately jumped out of bed to prepare for work, leaving her feeling as if her heart had been "torn out of her chest." I told Hope that she seemed also to be telling me about how it felt to be deeply touched and fed by me throughout the last analytic week, only to feel me wrenched painfully away from her on the weekend, as if a vital part of her had been torn away, as if I had dropped her, just as she may have felt her mother's nipple torn from her mouth, leaving a terrible wound in its place.

As Hope's hand went to her mouth and she began to weep, I told her that she also seemed to be saying something about how she experienced me on Monday as transformed into a dangerous predator-intruder; how this betrayal of her trust paralyzed her capacity to allow me to help her with these feelings of being dropped and wounded. By filling the space between us with these soft sensations of her own tongue in her mouth, I believe Hope gave herself the continuous com-

fort that I failed to offer. However, this also seems to stop up
the analytic work, interfering with the kind of healing that
comes through interaction with a caring human being.

Hope went on in the session to say she had often taken
refuge in the pink cloud as a child, feeling its suffocating sweet-
ness, getting lost in the pinkness of it all, as if this pink were
the soft, wet, and full sensation of her own tongue in her
mouth. This feeling filled her mind at times when she felt unbearably disappointed and alone. Tustin reminds us that we
must be able to bear these lonely and disillusioned states for
our patients for quite some time, so that we may be better
equipped to weave, out of the threads of our own experience,
a blanket of understanding that may adequately hold and
warm them, if we are to expect them to relinquish the self-
soothing protections they have come to rely upon so heavily.

Bill

In contrast to Hope, who used soft sensation shapes to protect against unbearable feelings of falling and emptiness, Bill,
a professional man in his forties, seemed to rely more upon
the hard autistic objects that Tustin tells us about. Bill's mother
had a history of clinical depression that predated his birth. A
peculiar characteristic of this patient was manifest in his lack
of verbal expression for any feelings such as sadness, anger,
or even pleasurable excitement. These emotional states were
instead expressed in terms of substances, movements, and
physical sensations in various parts of his or others' bodies.
He spoke of his tears as moisture, without reference to feeling sad; of his nostrils twitching, without the notion of anxiety; of his feet moving, without the experience of arousal; and
I struggled to decode this idiosyncratic mode of expression
for over a year.

He seemed to feel always at risk of having his feelings spilled out through what he referred to as "the hole in his body" or "the hole in his head" that constituted the deep emotional wounds impacting both his physical and intellectual functioning. His longing for me over the weekend was not felt, but heard as a barking dog that startled him, hurtling him out of bed onto the floor, gasping for air. He threatened to kill the dog if only he could find him, and I imagined that he was communicating about feeling caged up by an uncaring owner who left him out alone to whine and howl. I took his murderous threat to be an expression of his almost suicidal despair, and his preference for death by his own hand over the feeling of spilling and falling uncontrollably when left by an uncaring mommy-analyst over the long weekend break.

He often spoke of masturbation as a means of stopping the twitching nostrils and the wiggling feet in a rhythmic way, and he referred to this as "getting rid of sex." Quickly and controllably by his own hand, he would have his "little death." Earplugs were also used to keep him from spilling, frightened, out of bed, and often in the sessions he would present an impermeable hostility toward me, or a stone wall of silence, or he would bite his fingers mercilessly in a desperate attempt to ward off contact with the more vulnerable soft center of his experience.

By the beginning of the third year of his analysis, Bill had revealed much of surprise to both of us. For example, murderous jealousy and paralyzing guilt experienced toward a child patient he had encountered in the waiting room led to the unearthing of a long-buried memory of a baby sister, Kathleen, who had died of pneumonia when Bill was 2 years old. Such memories would come in spurts, as though these moments in his history had leaked out in times of intense affect; then, just as quickly, these would be sealed off during subsequent weekend or holiday breaks in the treatment, leaving us to contend with many mysterious gaps in his experience.

Often I felt certain that these surprise revelations had leaked out, like some vital substance from deep within an inner capsule, when the emotional contact between us was such that he could be certain I would retain and contain for him, in my consciousness, this precious if painful overflow.

In the twenty-ninth month of the analysis, Bill was able to tell me more about the nature of this deeply hidden reservoir to which those painfully traumatic and unbearably pleasurable early experiences were relegated for safekeeping, albeit out of reach of his awareness and the analytic process.

One Monday Bill had returned from a trip to the mountains on horseback where he had experienced some sense of his own progress. He proudly told me that he had ridden a horse up and down miles of narrow switchback trails without fear of tumbling to his death, since he had faith that his mount had been along these same trails before, and that she seemed surefooted and confident. He felt that perhaps his lifelong fear of heights had been somehow overcome, and he was quite pleased and encouraged by this accomplishment, which he connected with the work of the analysis. This was Bill's first open and direct acknowledgement of being helped by the analysis. He spoke of how gratifying it was for him to tell his colleagues at work about his weekend, and noticed this as a deviation from the usual feeling that he had nothing to share with others of his personal life, which felt so dead and empty, especially after a weekend away.

In the Tuesday hour Bill was quite sullen and sarcastic, and spent a good portion of the session in a customary mute silence, which I felt to be impenetrable. I found myself falling into a state of despair, feeling him lost to me, unreachable and almost dead, followed by the feeling that he was punishing me for some heinous crime I had unwittingly committed. When asked about his silence, he would simply reply, "I'm empty."

On Wednesday we came to understand that he had felt lost and alone at the end of the Monday hour as I became transformed first into a deadly, depressed mother who had left him alone, spilling over with excitement, and then, on Tuesday, into a mean, withholding, and envious mother who would take from him all that of which he was so proud. It seemed his impermeable muteness was employed primarily as a primitive survival tactic to stem the flow of disillusionment into nothingness, and secondarily as a means of preserving his good objects from attack.

Having somewhat mitigated his disillusionment in the Wednesday hour, I found Bill in the waiting room on Thursday, socks and shoes off, stretched like a hammock between the two benches that he referred to as "love seats." "I wouldn't have thought I could do this," he exclaimed when I invited him in. "But it wasn't as uncomfortable as I thought," he added, referring to his new position. I said that I thought he was also telling me something of how he felt after the Wednesday hour: that the two of us were somehow linked together, connected in a comfortable if awkward way between the sessions, and that he felt it was unnecessary to hide his tender parts from me today.

Seemingly touched by my remarks, Bill then recalled how he had felt on Monday with Sarah, his supervisor, when she seemed to reach out to him in a personal way, asking how his holiday had been. He said, "I was afraid—no one wants to get into that shit—my loneliness. I guess I felt that she was like my mother. I called Mother over the weekend, finally asking her about Kathleen [the dead baby sister he had resurrected some months before in the analysis]. But she seemed too busy, superficial with me, and preoccupied with others, and I felt so disappointed. I guess I just felt that I had nothing personal to share with Sarah."

When I observed how curious it was that with Sarah he had felt empty, and that he seemed to have forgotten his experience of the weekend trip he had been so proud of, just as he had felt empty with me in the Tuesday hour, he fell suddenly silent. When he finally spoke, it was only to utter the words, "Four worn-out tires."

I had come to know such utterances as Bill's attempt to share with me various pictographs that flashed across his mind. These flashes of his experiences seemed often to startle him, and rarely could he comment on them. However, this time he seemed physically to struggle in his prone position as if to give birth to some thought, and he added, "I'm wondering if they have inner tubes or not." I replied that it appeared that it might be important to know. "Yes," he explained, "an inner tube is for protection—in case of blowout, it would be less dangerous."

I then said, "I think these four worn-out tires are the analysis, felt perhaps like the mommy-me on the weekend, when you experience me as too worn out to get excited about you and your progress, or too preoccupied with my other children to help you bear your dreadful losses, fears, and loneliness. This must feel to you like some kind of dangerous blowout—like going mad or exploding to pieces, or leaking out everywhere."

His nodding response to this urged me on to tell him that I thought of the inner tube as a way to protect himself from the feeling of losing everything. "You keep all these personal experiences sealed up in this tube for safety. But it's so tightly sealed that you become cut off from the very things you feel you need in order to have a relationship with Sarah and also with me, which is like forgetting, and this leaves you feeling empty inside."

Perhaps this patient's material speaks to the notion that the body image as a system of tubes (D. Rosenfeld 1984, Tustin 1986) is one which is even more elemental than that of the whole body being contained by a skin (Bick 1968). For Bill, the skin, or "four worn-out tires," representing the experience of the four analytic hours during the break (the "blowout"), must be fortified by the "inner" tube or the encapsulation of experience during felt absences and loss.

I believe the use made of autistic encapsulating maneuvers throughout this analysis is apparent in the material presented. In his muteness the patient was indeed sealed off from his experiences, past and present, and future contact was in jeopardy as well. Going forward in an imaginative way, rather than giving in to our despair, distinguishes the analyst from objects in the patient's past, who perhaps could not tolerate such narcissistic wounds, or the feelings of abject loneliness these patients engender in us.

Like autistic objects and shapes, psychosomatic representations seem to take the place of unconscious fantasies and are not to be confused with mentational processes. Tustin (1987) calls these *innate forms*, and sees them as innate biological predispositions with psychic overtones. In psychosomatic patients, as with autistic patients, these have remained untransformed by reciprocal interactions with the attentive thinking mother, and thus find expression in physical illness in which the symptoms may act as bodily containers or a second skin—depositories for unmentalized experiences that ensure survival but which block further development and transformation.

Carla

Like Bill, my patient Carla, who was asthmatic, seemed to rely upon a hard, impermeable object to protect her from spilling uncontrollably. However, this hard object took the form of a hard mucous plug in her bronchial tubes. Having lost her mother at a very early age shortly after she, her four sisters, and her mother were abandoned by her father, Carla presented herself mostly as a tough, sassy, streetwise kid whose toughness served as a second skin resembling the tight leather clothing she often wore, and that we eventually traced to her image of the father's erect penis and the paternal function of protection.

In the second year of her analysis, however, a fragile baby part of Carla began to emerge, crying out to be born and to be allowed contact with the caring presence of the mother-analyst. In one session Carla began to cry as we had not heard before, a cry that penetrated me to a depth as no other, and I felt this correspond to the strata from which it emanated, as from her deepest and earliest experience of infancy. When I told her as much, she said, "I feel like something terrible wants out of me. I can't let myself breathe. I don't want it to come out. I'm afraid I'll never stop crying." She seemed to be saying that she would spill out and be gone, unable to collect herself at the end of the hour as she experienced once again the father's abandonment and the loss of a sense of security.

Robert

Many patients, like Carla, lacking the mental containment necessary to catch the unbearable overflow of their painful experiences, take refuge within areas of their own body, just as they had once been protected deep inside the recesses of the body of the mother. Others substitute the delusions of being inside the body of the analyst. Such was the case for Robert, a 34-year-old man referred to in Chapter 1, who had been referred for analysis after a series of hospitalizations following his mother's suicide. His history and his lack of a sense of continuity were extreme to the degree that I felt he should be seen six times per week. Even so, he suffered extreme despair and anxiety between the analytic hours and during the Sunday break.

It was in the seventh month of treatment that Robert was reminded of the events surrounding his actual birth. The doctor was unavailable when his mother commenced labor, and thus the delivery was effected by his father, resulting in trauma for both mother and infant. The grief, rage, and terror of this event were re-experienced by my patient in the transference, provoked by my moving office.

From a quiet, dark brown paneled room that he described as "humming," and in which we spent the first few months of the treatment, he suddenly found himself in what he felt to be a "sunny environment," with light-colored walls and carpeting. The catastrophe was felt in a thoroughly sensation-dominated way, as though the sounds, sights, and textures were painful impingements uncontrollably entering his body in unmitigated form, leading to an experience of physical pain.

He often cried out from such painful assaults, and could not open his eyes for many months while on the couch in this new office. Every sound precipitated a bodily start, and he longed for the feel of the wooded wall next to the couch in my old consulting room, which he had often stroked as a soothing presence in times of extreme distress, just as he had stroked and been stroked by his mother in her bed throughout childhood and early adolescence, to soothe both of them in their seemingly shared and undifferentiated depression.

Not unlike patients described by Tustin (1986, 1990), my patient too had an unduly close relationship to his mother, which had fostered false hopes that his body could be one with an ever-present immortal being and so could never come to an end. When Robert's mother died, he was forced to become aware of his bodily separateness. She had jumped from a ten-

story window to her death, but he was left falling forever—
out of windows, out of spaces and absences.

Unable to cope with such terrors, Robert was tenaciously
insistent that I was the reincarnation of this immortal mother,
and he attempted to maneuver me in ways that would give
credence to this belief, since he felt certain that his life
depended upon physical continuity with me. The loss of my
old consulting room, as the womb-mother, re-evoked in him
the earliest experiences of being barbarically torn from the
mother's body and the later versions of this event, which were
numerous, all leading to the mother's suicide as the final straw
that toppled what he called his "house of cards."

In the following session, occurring midway between the
move to my new office and the spring break, Robert demonstrated one of the numerous ways in which he attempted to
reinstate some sense of safety by reconstituting a concrete
delusion of bodily continuity with me. In this session Robert
began by telling me about a woman who had just had a spontaneous abortion, a miscarriage, and of how sad he felt as she
appeared to him like a wounded animal. He told me how
desperately he felt the need to photograph various scenes that
came into view during his day in order to bring them to my
attention in palpable form. I told Robert about the unspeak-
able frustration of his separateness from me between the
hours, and his desire to have me know what he experienced,
but to tell me about these experiences only attested to the
harsh, cruel fact of our separateness and added to his frustration and grief.

Though somewhat grudgingly, Robert then told me
about having come upon a shop that sold large statuary, displayed in front of it in great numbers. He described the
atmosphere of the day as gray and gloomy, the same color as
the plaster from which the statues were made. He said that

although the figures were of varying styles, shapes, and sizes, some replicating ancient works of art, others more contemporary, arranged with some in the foreground and others behind, he could envision in his mind's eye the composition of a photograph in which all discrimination between background and foreground, old and new, large and small, would be lost. As there was no sun, there would be no shadow; all would appear as one. Time would be compressed, spaces would be obliterated, as would any distinction between these varied objects.

I said that he seemed also to be telling me about a state of pristine at-one-ment that could be frozen in time with the click of his camera shutter, providing the concrete proof of this blissful state of affairs. I also called his attention to the urgency of such proof positive at night and on Sundays, when the separation between us became unbearable to him. His response was to tell me that the pronoun "I" was the thing he hated most in all the world. He recalled the first time he knew the "awful truth," as he watched his own hand reach out to grasp his coat in his teens, when he was sent away from home for the first time. He felt then, for the first time, alone inside his skin. He said, "It was the first time I knew. It wasn't 'I think, therefore I am,' a sense of being, but just 'I am alone'."

As reported in Chapter 1, the solution Robert eventually proposed to "the problem of this analysis which made [him] be an 'I'" was the fantasy of placing his camera on a tripod in my consulting room, setting it for a 30-minute exposure, blurring the two of us into a state of oneness with no space between and no distinction of sex, age, or position in the relationship, the resultant photograph being a "souvenir," a concrete memory of this perfect state, as well as a guarantee of his existence, without which he seemed to feel ever at risk.

Such autistic delusions have permeated the analysis of this young man, and he often yearns for the safe, if constricting, enclosure of the hospital and the four-point restraints he had known many times prior to the beginning of treatment. Perhaps the unthinkable, uncontrollable overspill of emotions that threaten Robert with dissolution is what we call madness, and the straitjacket or four-point restraints are, like the autistic shell, a defense against this madness. However, like the locked ward of a mental hospital, such delusions disallow the establishment of caring connections with the therapist—the "gentle straitjacket" to which Tustin (1986) referred.

LITERARY AFTERTHOUGHTS

I believe that Tustin not only helps us with her insights to open ourselves up to fresh perspectives on our patients' communications, but she also encourages us to attend to the poets and artists who can further help us to develop an even greater understanding of the experience of breakdown that most of our patients fear and some may have already encountered. For example, in her novel *Celestial Navigations*, Anne Tyler (1974) describes one character who lives in a fragile yet impermeable world created as a variation on a design by his mother. Tyler describes the constant terror that threatens to overwhelm her hero should he emerge from his self-made fortress. I believe she describes Jeremy's experience of the "black hole" in a most sensitive way:

> These are some of the things that Jeremy Pauling dreaded: using the telephone, answering the doorbell, opening mail, leaving his house, making purchases. Also wearing new clothes, standing in open spaces, meeting the eyes of a stranger, eating in the presence of others, turning on electrical appliances. Some days, he awoke to find the weather sunny and his health adequate, and his work progressing beautifully;

yet there would be a nagging hole of uneasiness deep inside him, some flaw in the center of his well-being, steadily corroding around the edges and widening until he could not manage to lift his head from the pillow. Then he would have to go over every possibility. Was it something he had to do? Somewhere to go? Someone to see? Until the answer came: Oh yes! Today he had to call the Gas Company about the oven. A two-minute chore, nothing to worry about. He knew that. HE KNEW. Yet he lay on his bed feeling flattened and defeated, and it seemed to him that life was a series of hurdles that he had been tripping over for decades, with the end nowhere in sight.

On the Fourth of July, in a magazine article about famous Americans, he read that a man could develop character by doing one thing he disliked every day of his life. Did that mean that all these hurdles might have some value? Jeremy copied the quotation on an index card and tacked it to the window sill beside his bed. It was his hope that the card would remove half of every pain by pointing out its purpose, like a mother telling her child, "This is good for you. Believe me." But in fact, all it did was depress him, for it made him conscious of the number of times each day he had to steel himself for something. Why, nine-tenths of his life consisted of doing things he disliked! Even getting up in the morning! He had already overcome a dread before he was even dressed! If that quotation was right, shouldn't he have the strongest character imaginable? Yet he didn't. He had become aware lately that other people seemed to possess an inner core of hardness that they took for granted. They hardly seemed to notice it was there; they had come by it naturally. Jeremy had been born without it. [pp. 76–77]

Tyler also tells us something of the nature of Jeremy's survival tactics: what it feels like inside his protective shell—the price he pays for protection.

Jeremy Pauling saw life in a series of flashes, startling moments
so brief that they could arrest motion in midair. Like photographs, they were handed to him at unexpected times, introduced by a neutral voice: here is where you are now. Take a
look. Between flashes, he sank into darkness. He drifted into
a daze, studying what he had seen. Wondering if he HAD seen
it. Forgetting finally, what it was that he was wondering about,
and floating off into numbness again. [p. 37]

CONCLUSION

Like Jeremy Pauling, the patients discussed in this chapter frequently experience, and often attempt to describe, the numbness
resulting from the use of autistic protections. There is a certain
quality of poignancy conveyed as they complain of isolation from
their own internal experiences and objects as well as from the potential healing effects of contact with the analyst. *I believe this must be
distinguished from the triumphant pleasure of manic flight from depressive anxiety, which we often observe in these very same patients who, while
on another track, evade and avoid the shame and guilt of the depressive
position or the persecutory feelings associated with the paranoid-schizoid
position.*

Like Jeremy Pauling, Bill often experiences his life in flashes;
Carla calls this "checking out" on herself; Hope refers to these states
as "losing" herself; Robert describes this as "falling through windows." When we as analysts listen carefully to our patients, I believe
we can detect their desperate appeals for our help in finding a way
out of the autistic tomb, this numbness that incarcerates them. Just
at the analyst must discriminate between unintegration and disintegration, between paranoid-schizoid and depressive, between internal and external, between "attacks on linking" and links yet to
be formed (or that are at best tenuous in nature) between active

and passive, between words as communication and words used
defensively as action, between the varying dimensions and geo-
anatomical locations of mental experience—so must we make the
fine discriminations between these various primitive states of mind
in order to be maximally responsive to our patients in the analytic
relationship.

3

Notes on an Embryonic State of Mind*

Is there any part of the human mind which still betrays signs of an "embryological" intuition, either visual or auditory?

[W. R. Bion, *Clinical Seminars and Four Papers*]

INTRODUCTION

Over the years, a number of psychoanalysts in the United States and abroad have displayed an increasing interest in expanding the scope of our understanding of prenatal and perinatal mental states (Hansen 1994, Mancia 1981, Osterweil 1990, Paul 1983, 1989, 1990, Piontelli 1985, 1987, 1988, Share 1994). Although Wilfred Bion made reference to these states of mind in many of his last works, he sometimes called his thoughts on the subject "science fiction,"

---

*A version of this chapter was presented at a scientific meeting of the Southern California Psychoanalytic Society on September 18, 1995.

not because he intended them to be taken lightly, but because he could not represent them as "scientific statements" of observable fact. In one paper (1976) he made the following statement:

> It seems to me that from a very early stage the relation between the germplasm and its environment operates. I don't see why it should not leave some kind of trace, even after "the impressive caesura of birth." After all, if anatomists can say that they detect a vestigial tail, if surgeons likewise say they can detect tumours which derive from the branchial cleft, then why should there not be what we would call mental vestiges, or archaic elements, which are operative in a way that is alarming and disturbing because it breaks through the beautiful, calm surface we ordinarily think of as rational, sane behavior? [p. 236]

I believe that in his professional lifetime Bion did indeed observe the operation of such "mental vestiges" or "archaic elements," which had a disturbing effect upon him and his patients, defying what was ordinarily considered in those more "rational" theories of the time. Even so, Bion's exceptional capacity for "imaginative conjecture" seemed to allow him to transcend those rational theories, in spite of the lack of conventional scientific data.

Along with the aforementioned analysts working in this tradition, I have previously written on my own clinical observations of the operation of such mental vestiges and archaic elements, which constitute but one of the many facets explored in the analysis of certain patients (Mitrani 1992, 1994b, 1995a,b). I will here add some additional material from this very circumscribed aspect of my experience with one particular analysand.

Robert

Robert was referred to me for analysis after a series of hospitalizations. Each one of these hospitalizations was precipitated

by an equal number of attempts to end his life by such extreme methods as hanging and suffocation following the suicide of his mother, who ended her life and pain by jumping
from a very tall building. It was not surprising that Robert
carried with him a primordial terror of such an experience
of falling endlessly, which seemed to be inexorably linked with
a pathological identification with his depressed mother, with
whom he was unusually close. Robert's suicide attempts
appeared to be related to his periodic need to escape from
these overwhelming terrors of falling out of control.

In the first months of the analysis, I met with Robert
six times per week, a frequency that served somewhat to limit
his terrors of falling to manageable proportions. These terrors were somewhat and quite gradually attenuated by the
development of an interpretive connection. However, in the
second year of the treatment, Robert told me of a visual handicap from which he had suffered all his life—a "lazy eye"
through which he viewed the world in only two dimensions.
This anomaly had been noticed upon examination by a
physician, who questioned Robert about his birth experience. Upon hearing that Robert had been wrested from his
mother's womb by his own father's hands, the umbilical cord
wrapped precariously about his throat, during a one-month
premature and quite protracted labor under the most primitive of circumstances, the doctor informed Robert that his
visual handicap was almost certainly a consequence of this
traumatic birth.

Robert had no depth perception, no sense of space or
distance, and no sense of an inside. He appeared to have only
the sensation of a flat outside. Over time we came to understand his lazy eye as a somatic *presentation* of the psychologically unborn-he; an "I" for whom separations of any length
were sheer agony, often evoking states of unbearable terror.
He also could not bear changes in light, temperature, and

textures. He felt he could not be "fixed" *by* the analysis, but could only be "fixed" *onto* it.

This patient often expressed the feeling, at the end of each hour, that I was peeling him off the "placental" walls next to the couch in my consulting "womb." Both in session and between times on the telephone, Robert seemed to stick to me for dear life, and he experienced weekend breaks and holidays as excruciating rip-offs during which he would intentionally engage in behavior that might result in his being put on "hold" in the hospital. He would often describe, in great detail and with much emotion, hospital episodes prior to our work together, when he was actually placed in four-point restraints in a padded room, and he frequently longed to return to the safe, if constricting, environment of a locked psychiatric ward.

At the end of one week in the second year of his analysis, as the time for my vacation grew near, Robert's material spoke to a very strong feeling that I was about to abort him. This feeling seemed to be, at least in part, associated with the fact that this time, unlike previous weekend, holiday, and vacation breaks, I was going out of the area, and was therefore not on call for my patients. Robert was insistent about his inability to bear the break if he could not maintain a telephone connection with me in case of emergency.

As if to underscore this point, a few weeks before I left, Robert overdosed on a mixture of substances that resulted in his hospitalization over the weekend, during which he received a course of renal dialysis. In this very dramatic way, Robert brought home to me his felt need, not just for the womb, but for the umbilical cord and its detoxifying functions as well.

Work with Robert and other analysands has often provoked me to wonder what prompts us to use words like *attachment* at times and *connection* at other times when speaking to our patients? What prompts us to describe the feelings we have of our patients as *cling-ing* or *sticking* or *hanging on*, or even as *intrusive*? In the literature we analysts have delineated and discriminated between states of "projective identification" (Klein 1946) and "adhesive identification" (Bick 1968, 1986; Meltzer 1975; Meltzer et al. 1975). We seem to have made a distinction between patients who get under our skin or who get into our minds, and those who make contact with our minds or with whom we are able to make emotional contact.

Common sense and linguistics tell us there must be something more than just the issue of semantics to these discriminations. Per-haps they attest to the variation that exists between or within cer-tain primitive states of being; the subtle shadings and gradations that color the deeper layers of the evolutionary strata of human experience from conception to "the impressive caesura of the act of birth" (Freud 1926, p. 138).

While Robert seemed to be living a predominantly "inside" or "prenatal" experience, another patient, whom I shall call Jarrod, seemed to be re-enacting his "coming-out" experience. It often appeared to me that this patient's reports of his most perplexing relationships could best be understood as communications about once-lived and presently-alive and active states of mind related to his birth experience, his immediate perinatal existence.

Jarrod

Right from the start, Jarrod made a point of telling me he was the "elder" (by several hours) of identical twin brothers. In one session near the beginning of his analysis, he complained about his wife, whom he felt was lacking in energy, enthusi-asm, and passion. She was often felt to hold the patient back. It seemed that Jarrod's wife nearly always had to be "dragged" out of the house to go anywhere with him. He was exasper-ated that they rarely went out with other couples or away on vacation unless he initiated the trip and made all the arrange-ments for them both, including all the packing.

He was growing more and more frustrated with their restricted social life, feeling fed up that he had to practically "pull teeth" to get her to go out. When they did have plans to attend a concert, a play, or a party, she was always late and he had to wait for her, which often made him anxious and angry. I was aware that Jarrod would often come into the waiting room a quarter of an hour ahead of his scheduled time, and later during the hour he would comment on having to wait so long for me to come through the door. Eventually, Jarrod brought the following dream, the first of his analysis:

The patient was moving through a dark and narrow cavern, tethered to his brother Jacob by a long and sturdy rope. As Jarrod emerged into the light, he tugged on the rope, but Jacob was nowhere in sight. Jarrod continued to pull and pull, calling to Jacob to hurry up.

It appeared that Jarrod had both a personal and professional history of such relationships in which he nearly always felt held back by those less "forward looking" and "outgoing" than himself. He frequently felt he had to be the responsible one, to set an example for others, always feeling frustrated when this example was not followed.

He bemoaned the fact that he could not "let go" and "just relax." Instead, he felt compelled to "pull teeth," to get others—like his wife—to come along with him. He found it painful if not impossible to merely "separate" and "do his own thing." It was surprising that, prior to our discussion of the above-reported dream, Jarrod had never made any connection between his earliest experiences of being a twin and what appeared to be a consistent expression of this very primitive, core identity theme, originating at or even before birth.

It seems very likely that such primordial identity themes play a significant role in shaping the infantile transference and may profoundly influence the analysand's mode of communicating. Perhaps the earlier the experience, the greater the impact these themes have upon the patient's internal and external life.

The following material is from a case brought to me for consultation by a colleague. It may serve to exemplify these points, while also introducing the possibility of the operation of vestiges from the "earliest relation between the germplasm and its environment" that seem to leave traces, decades after the impressive caesura of birth.

Cora

Cora was in the process of undergoing intensive fertility treatments, including artificial insemination, when she began therapy twice weekly. Within a few months it became clear to the analytic couple that "more frequent treatments were needed to facilitate conception" of the baby-she to whom the patient was desperate to give life. Subsequently, the frequency of the sessions was increased to four hours per week.

During the next several months of the analysis, as analyst and patient grew more and more compatible with one another, it became apparent that the analyst was gradually able to conceive of the patient, and could now begin to formulate, and to transmit in a timely way, some rudimentary understanding of the patient's most primitive fears. However, Cora's dread of the weekend break seemed to increase in direct proportion to her experience of being understood by the analyst.

One Thursday, the last day of the analytic week, the patient came in and spoke of how she had felt relieved at the end of the Wednesday hour, although her voice was flat as she reported on the previous day's improvement. There was a long silence until Cora finally announced that she had felt "still" all morning long waiting for the time of her session. She then added that she was wondering if, in the previous hour, she had been accurate in her perception that the analyst had tears in her eyes.

Cora recalled feeling good about seeing these tears because she thought that it meant that her analyst could feel something of what she was going through. However, she was also disturbed when this good feeling was suddenly followed by the thought that these tears were merely a part of the analyst's technique.

Cora explained that she really felt she needed to know if the tears were an aspect of technique, even though she could not imagine herself leaving the analyst, even if it was. She said that it was only that she thought she should know whether her initial perception was correct or not. Cora also added that she was aware that even if the analyst did confirm the genuineness of her tears, she probably would not believe her anyway.

When the analyst did not respond to this immediately, Cora went on to say that she was also having qualms about the week's fertility work. She had undergone three inseminations that week and, although she had been more hopeful than usual, feeling that maybe this time she had conceived, she now feared that, like all the other times, the fertilized egg—the embryo—would fail to implant itself in the womb and she would begin her period, the little embryo sloughing off, draining away into nothing; "so much money and so much pain and hard work flushed down the toilet like nothing."

The analyst took all of this up as the patient's way of making herself "still," of deadening her own feelings about the weekend break as well as making the analyst's interventions inconsequential, as if she were sloughing them off or flushing them down the toilet like so much waste.

The patient responded to this line of interpretation with quite a passionate rage, telling the analyst that she couldn't really describe what she was feeling about the weekend, that she could only say that she was growing less and less certain that the analyst would be there for her on Monday. In fact, she was not even sure that *she herself* would be there by Monday.

Tearful and clearly frustrated, Cora then demanded to know the answer to her original question. The analyst queried what might lie beneath the question, which seemed to provoke more frustration in the patient, who offered that she feared that, if she said anything more about why she needed to know the answer or what she herself thought or felt about the question, she could not be sure that the analyst was really answering truthfully about the tears; that she would never know if the analyst was being real or if she was just using a technique. The analyst ended the session at this point, and the patient left in an angry huff, slamming the door of the consulting room behind her.

In her next supervisory hour the analyst reported that, after the session, she was left feeling very anxious and upset. She simply "could not get her patient out of [her] mind." She said she feared that when Cora said that she was "not even sure that she herself would be there by Monday" that the patient was in fact telling her that she was breaking off the treatment. The analyst not only feared that she had lost this patient forever, but she was left feeling abandoned and at a loss to understand what had gone wrong.

The analyst added that she had pored over these feelings of abandonment in her own analysis on Friday, finding them related to the weekend break as well as resonating with her feelings about her own analyst's upcoming vacation. However, she reported little relief from her anxiety, and said that she hoped that I could help her to understand what she might have missed with respect to Cora.

Together we were able to work out that Cora had been telling her, in the beginning of the session, that she had felt hopeful after the Wednesday hour (her third of that week), just as she had felt hopeful after the three inseminations, that they had been able to "conceive" of the patient and her difficulties. However it seemed to us that Cora was also attempting to communicate that, by Thursday morning, she had been feeling the impending weekend discontinuity in their contact; she was not just fearing separation from the analyst, but was already actually feeling herself as "still" born. Cora then seemed to take the analyst's interpretation of her omnipotent denial and denigration of the value of the analytic work as further confirmation of her own fearful sense of a "mis-conception."

I believe that Cora was attempting to communicate something about the level of her current and most troublesome state of mind. She was already feeling "sloughed off" while waiting for her Thursday hour, which stirred up feelings of a lack of contact over the weekend. She felt as if she were prematurely losing the experience of the reality of the analyst's presence, which she feared was merely a technique, like the insemination technique that had thus far failed to lead to the conception of the baby she wanted so much to give birth to.

It seemed that Cora not only feared the loss of the experience of the analyst, in whose mind she was conceived, but the loss of that she-to-be embryo that had just been conceived during the three inseminations/sessions. Since she had yet to firmly establish a consistent and enduring experience of herself in the mental womb of the mother/analyst, she had yet to securely implant an internal containing object in her mind. The analyst's apparent misconception of her dilemma threatened to "abort" the beginnings of this internalization process, and Cora felt herself slipping away even before the weekend.

Then, as Cora experienced the analyst's lack of receptivity, the patient's attempts at a successful implantation grew more and more hyperbolic. In a passionate attempt to re-establish contact with and to embed herself in the mind of her analyst, she angrily slammed herself into the analyst's mind, just as she slammed the door to the consulting room. In this way she succeeded, at least temporarily, in making a place for herself. Indeed, this analyst truly "could not get the patient out of [her] mind" all weekend long.

When Cora returned after the weekend break, she reported that she had been angry with the analyst the entire time, except for a brief period of time on Sunday, when she felt momentarily grateful, feeling the analyst had "stood her ground." I believe this was a hopeful sign that the patient had been able to maintain an affective contact with her analyst and, if for only a moment, had experienced a certain constancy in the analytic connection that was relieving to her.

Running contrary to *this* Cora's need for "conception," as well as gestation in the mind of the analyst, was its polar opposite: *another* Cora's need to avoid any such conception. This opposition to being conceived—that is, to being understood by the analyst—might have been interpreted as an expression of the patient's envy. However, I believe that on another level it may also be understood as a function of a very primitive instinct for survival, which may be illustrated in the following material from a subsequent session, some weeks prior to what was to be the first major break in the analysis.

"Another" Cora

In this session, which I report here, the patient told the analyst about a dream she found quite disturbing. She was hesitant to talk about it because she thought the analyst might think her crazy.

The patient had an undiagnosed tumor that had been left too long, causing her to lose both speech and motility. Without a voice, legs, or arms she could only lie in her bed, totally helpless and dependent,

*and the analyst, although thoughtful and caring, could do nothing
to help her.*

Although Cora had no "designated" associations to the
dream, she brought forward material related to her upcoming hiking trip and her feelings about the separation from her
analyst. She had been preparing herself for the vacation by
taking short hikes on local mountain trails, equipped with a
hunting knife with which she planned to defend herself in case
of attack. She also spoke of the conflict she was experiencing,
about whether she should attempt another course of inseminations before going on holiday. Cora said that, in a way, she
wanted to try one more round, but was afraid that this would
weaken her too much; that it would "wipe her out," and leave
her in a very "bad state" for the trip.

Here Cora seemed to be expressing her fear of attempting conception in the mind of the analyst once again before
the holiday break. She seemed to be saying that she dreaded
the feeling of being rendered a defenseless embryo, totally
dependent upon the analyst-mother-womb to give meaningful voice to her experience, and to supply the needed suste-
nance to live and to grow, as well as the essential protection
from dangerous predators.

While in this kind of regressed state, Cora feared she
would be in "no shape" to be on her own outside the womb
of the mother-analyst's mind. The fear of becoming weak-
ened—of being rendered "easy prey"—seemed to constitute
this patient's version of the fear of madness; her phantasy of
the experience of a psychotic regression. It was not surprising that Cora could not bear any awareness of dependence
on the analyst, which would leave her in this most vulnerable
embryonic state throughout the trip into "unknown territory"
without her analyst.

DISCUSSION

In this chapter I have tried to demonstrate the appearance of various archaic states of being that may be observed to struggle to the surface during the analytic process at certain times and in certain patients. It has been my experience that when these states do manage to come to the fore in analysis, the feelings and fantasies evoked in the analyst by them (if we remain receptive) are unusually disturbing and unmistakably primitive in nature. I daresay that one of the most primitive states may somehow be linked to "the relation between the germplasm and its environment," one that may be said to "betray an embryological intuition."

It always strikes me that some of these patients seem to have gone to great lengths—and have endured much suffering—in order to find some medium for communicating to the analyst (to paraphrase Winnicott) what could otherwise not be remembered, and what therefore has never been forgotten. Such re-enactments in the transference, and in other relationships outside during the course of the analysis, seem often to be motivated not only by the desire to "get rid of" or "to evacuate" these "unmentalized experiences" (Mitrani 1995b), but by some innate human striving to "be known" and "to know"—perhaps one's need to be imaginatively "conceived of" in the mind of an "other" in order that one might eventually be able to be "born" (and therefore "borne") at last in one's own mind.

The importance of detecting the appearance of these archaic experiences in our patients' communications—of being born, of being a developing fetus, and yes, even of being an embryo in search of conception—may not only lie in their value as aids in the articulation of evocative metaphor for the sake of communication, but may also include their potential as material for constructing an increasingly meaningful genetic link between the patient's past and his or her present phantasy life, a link that might otherwise remain missing.

Both the metaphoric and genetic aspects of such interpretations provide a certain grounded coherence or "continuity of being" (Winnicott 1949), and thus may act to gradually fortify our patients' capacity for containing, for keeping in mind, for subsequent thinking about, and quite possibly for modifying and mitigating the constricting impact of their most vestigial experiences.

4

On the Survival Function of
Pathological Organizations[1]

*Models are ephemeral and differ from theories in this respect; I have
no compunction in discarding a model as soon as it has served or
failed to serve my purpose. If a model proves useful on a number of
different occasions the time has come to consider its transformation
into a theory.*

[W. R. Bion, *Learning From Experience*]

INTRODUCTION

Pathological organizations have been widely theorized about and
clinically illustrated in the Kleinian literature since Joan Riviere
published her seminal paper on the negative therapeutic reaction
as early as 1936. In 1964 H. A. Rosenfeld described these character structures as organized patterns of manic defenses, which have
been relied upon to ward off anxieties of a paranoid-schizoid and
depressive nature, that is, anxieties about harm inflicted upon the

---

1. A version of this chapter was presented at a scientific meeting of the Psychoanalytic Center of California on February 21, 1995.

self and the loved object. Rosenfeld observed that defenses such as omnipotence, grandiosity, denial, splitting, and projective identification, as well as the feeling of triumph over a diminished and denigrated object and dominance over the helpless, needy, and dependent baby-self—when maintained throughout childhood development without mitigation—may become a well organized, rigid, and stable aspect of the personality.

It is largely considered that the resultant cohesive grouping of internal objects, when idealized, often substitutes for those good, internalized objects that might otherwise protect and support the nascent self while continuing to foster its growth and development. Instead, these omnipotent structures have been overly relied upon to serve this protective, supportive, reassuring, and soothing function for the immature self which has now come under its control through such devices as "terror, persecution and dread" (Meltzer 1968) or "the threat of insanity" (Money-Kyrle 1969).

H. A. Rosenfeld (1971) further developed his ideas, titrating out from the concept of narcissism, the notion of *negative narcissism* and its probable relationship to the negative therapeutic reaction. He differentiated this aggressive variety of narcissism from a libidinally driven narcissism, observing that while the latter entails an idealization of the omnipotently good aspects of the self in a state of identification with the good aspects of the object, the former concerns the idealization of the omnipotently *destructive* aspects of the self in consort with the omnipotently bad aspects of the object that are constantly on the attack against libidinal object-relationships—entrapping, enslaving, and intimidating the loving and perhaps loved baby-self, attacking the baby's experience of being loved, of his own need of as well as his own desire for dependence upon the good mothering-object.

Both Rosenfeld and Meltzer conceptualized this character structure as a delinquent gang or criminal Mafia within the mind, a covert and collusive network of renegade malignant objects in hierarchical organization that provide (for the infantile self) a reliable source of protection from madness, psychic pain, and anxiety in return for absolute obedience, loyalty, and constant acts of tribute. In short, the normally dependent baby-self is rigidly controlled within a sociopathic internal family of objects.

It might be said that in analysis we can detect the existence of these structures as it becomes apparent that the patient cannot bear or is afraid of being dependent upon, of having feelings of affection for, or gratitude toward the analyst. In fact these patients—who seem as if they are enthralled to some internal god—often experience negative therapeutic reactions just as the relationship with the analyst begins to deepen and productive work momentarily proceeds.

At times, when tangible gains are achieved by the analytic couple and the patient might otherwise feel some relief from his psychic pain and anxiety, it is as if the "gang leader," in an envious or jealous rage, rears its ugly head and brings it all down with doubts, somatic symptoms, guilt, and threats of death and destruction. During these episodes, we often hear our patients complaining that the analysis is worthless or, even worse, noxious. However, what may appear as an attempt to denigrate the analyst's work and worth may well be intended as an act of appeasement toward some inner force that cannot bear the development of this fruitful alliance between analyst and analysand, since such a new alliance threatens to provide an alternate means of living and coping with and within relationships while rendering the old regime obsolete.

O'Shaughnessy (1981), in her paper on defensive organizations, reports a lengthy case of a 22-year-old male patient, making the distinction between the "defenses" and "defensive organizations" as pervasive, pathological structures that have rigidified and stabilized over time and appear to impede the progressive development of normal object relations while serving to ward off anxieties encountered in relation to objects both internal and external to the self. The necessity for prolonged analysis within such a defensive organization, that is, in the transference, to allow for an environment in which ego development may proceed while anxiety is "in recession" (or perhaps while anxieties are contained by the analyst and/or in the analytic relationship) is highlighted in her excellent case study.

Betty Joseph (1975) has referred to these patients as "difficult to reach" since we can rarely find them outside the protective shielding of the "gang," and when we do they are quite thin-skinned and are therefore easily injured by the slightest error in tact or timing. In a paper on "Addiction to Near Death" (Joseph 1982) she highlights what she views as the patient's masochistic use and exploitation of misery and his attempts to create and to draw the analyst into a perversely exciting world that is at the same time both insular and addictive.

In a trilogy of papers on the subject Steiner (1982, 1987, 1990) characterized the narcissistic or pathological organization as a buffer against or refuge from paranoid and depressive anxieties, as a mental state lying midway between the paranoid-schizoid and depressive positions. In other words, he suggested that the "manic position" (Klein 1935) may become rigidified and inflexible, a stable structure within the ego providing a safe haven for the infantile self. However, while this structure serves effectively to guard and protect the patient against the experience of anxiety, it also obliterates his capacity for the development of healthful internal object relations.

Steiner's investigations also lead him to highlight the problem of pathological organizations as obstacles to mourning and the inability of some patients to relinquish and mourn the analyst after termination of treatment due to the inability to loosen their rigid control. Steiner concludes that as a consequence, there is a failure in the development of an experience of true separateness.

Heretofore, it would seem that the emphasis in the Kleinian literature has been on the destructive-persecutory aspects of these defensive organizations, the role these personality organizations play in the negative therapeutic reaction, and the control by tyranny and seduction that such objects or groups of objects exert upon the naive, dependent, libidinal aspects of the individual.

However, from the outset of Kleinian explorations into this area, Riviere (1936) stated that "the very great importance of analyzing aggressive tendencies has perhaps carried some analysts off their feet, and in some quarters is defeating its own ends and becoming in itself a resistance to further analytic understanding" (p. 311). She went on to warn us that "nothing will lead more surely to a negative therapeutic reaction in the patient than our failure to recognize anything but the aggression in his material" (p. 311). My own clinical experience with analysands—who might frequently seem to have come under the influence of such an adversary to the analytic process—moves me to highlight in this paper yet another aspect of these so-called pathological organizations: that is, the original *survival function* of such internal objects or organizations of objects.

Along these lines, I find it has been useful to consider a model in which these internal defensive organizations function in much the same way as does a second skin, although these structures are by far more symbolically elaborate than either the sensation-dominated structures to which Bick (1968) referred or the shell or barrier of concrete defensive maneuvers employed by autistic children (and adults with a capsule of autism) extensively explored in the work of Tustin (1972, 1981, 1986, 1990).

The following case, remarkably rich in dream material,[2] first served to sensitize me to the survival function of such pathological organizations. Perhaps by providing a clearly delineated imaginary representation of these internal defensive structures, dreams may be seen to provide a unique window onto the experience of the

---

2. The number and detail of the dreams remembered by this patient from the termination phase of her first analysis as well as from the period immediately after termination, communicated in the first few hours of her second analysis and reported in this chapter, are indeed unusual and provide a unique bit of clinical data.

analysand, yielding a view that may stand *relatively* unobstructed by theoretical attribution.

Alice

Prior to the beginning our work together, Alice had been in analysis for several years with Dr. X. She had entered that analysis, spurred on by some years of severe sleep disturbances marked by difficulties in breathing, followed by a more recent history of hellish nightmares of falling into black pools filled with formless monsters, from which she would awaken fearful and inconsolable. This first analysis was eight years in length and had, in Alice's estimation, resulted in significant improvements in her ability to overcome certain intellectual and social inhibitions that paralleled similar inhibitions in her capacity to experience and tolerate separations and losses, the awareness of which was felt to be catastrophic and life-endangering.

After somewhat over seven years, the topic of termination emerged, and there were several months during which the analytic couple dealt with the anxieties aroused by the prospect of ending the treatment, after which a date for termination was set. In the final hour of the analysis, Alice reported the following dream to Dr. X:

Alice pulled her car into the driveway of her house. She could see that someone had been there before her and had driven his vehicle into the picket fence, causing considerable damage to the front entrance and garage of the house. She examined the point where the vehicle had hit, finding flecks of silver paint from the vehicle.

Alice was angry and retreated inside, only to discover that the man who had damaged her house had gotten inside too. There was a party in progress, filled with guests invited by this intruder. He was gone; however, there were all sorts of old women inside, eating and drinking and leaving quite a mess while they chattered endlessly,

*ignoring Alice when she arrived. A waitress carrying around trays
of food offered something to each of the old women, but passed by
Alice as if she did not exist.*

*As Alice went from room to room, she realized that these old
women occupied nearly every nook and cranny of her house. At first
she felt at a loss for ways to handle the situation. When she caught
several of them using the telephones, she became angrier still because
they were tying up her business as well as her personal lines. She
then checked her answering machine, only to find that it had been
disconnected and broken into pieces.*

*Feeling at wits' end, Alice decided she must take action. She
called all the old women to order, verbally taking them in hand, as
if chairing a meeting. She recalled feeling better when it seemed that
she could handle them all without throwing them out of her house,
and she woke up feeling satisfied although she was still angry at the
man who had been at the root of all of the trouble and mess.*

The silver paint had at once reminded Alice of her pet name
for Dr. X. She recalled that she and Dr. X had understood at
the time that the dream had something to do with the patient's
experience of the end of the analysis. Alice felt that Dr. X was
leaving her with a messy situation; that she alone must deal
with these maternal-objects that seemed to interfere with her
work and her personal life, feeding on her and messing up
her mind; starving her and leaving her feeling frustrated,
confused, and helpless.

However, Alice and her analyst had subsequently agreed
that it was a hopeful sign when, in the dream, she was able to
handle all the messy mothers in spite of her anger, without
having to banish them from her house/mind. Although, at
the time, Alice was aware of the extent of the anger she was
feeling toward Dr. X for leaving her with this messy situation—
furious that things were not at all smooth, easy, and tidy at
the end of the analysis—she was also filled with feelings of

profound gratitude toward him and hope at the prospect of being able to cope on her own without him.

The termination went as planned. However, soon afterward Alice had a series of dreams that gave her over to a deep-seated fear that she had ended her analysis prematurely. The last of these dreams was as follows:

Alice was in a large room, looking out over a village square. She watched as the villagers below engaged in the mistreatment of children and small animals and she became determined to do something about the situation. With this in mind, she turned to leave the room, but was stopped by a tall man who looked like "Mr. Spock," from the Star Trek *series on television. He warned Alice against going out into the village, afraid she might be hurt or lost, and presented a very logical argument for her to remain inside and safe.*

Alice was, however, compelled to venture outside, regardless of the dangers. In the dream she reassured herself that she would be protected from harm because of her special relationship to a very elderly woman who was also in the room, a woman who appeared to be like her grandmother or mother. Alice then proceeded to go out into the square.

The scene then cut to Alice's return to her room. She approached the grandmotherly person, who was standing with her back turned to her, looking out the window. Alice rushed up to the grandmother with open arms to embrace her, expecting that she would be received with approval since she had been able to do much good outside in the village. But instead of welcoming her with the loving hug that Alice had anticipated, the old woman turned suddenly, striking Alice on the bridge of her nose with a club. Shocked and hurt by the old woman's inexplicable and violent reaction, Alice awoke, crying and bewildered, physically feeling the pain of the attack.

Alice reported that, at the time of this dream, she was approximately one month post-termination. She had been certain at the time that it related to feelings about leaving her analyst, for whom she had fantisized she was a favored patient. She thought that leaving the safety of the room to go out into the village represented the termination, and that the rescue of small children and animals was linked with her desire to apply what she had learned from her analysis to the care of both her infant-self as well as others with whom she worked.

However, it seemed that this striving was being blocked by some threatening internal figure: a rational Mr. Spock, whom Alice associated with the baby expert, Dr. Spock. She was also reminded of her schoolteacher-mother who had apparently demanded total allegiance from Alice in exchange for love and protection, and who had grown cold when Alice had dared to follow her own path in mid-adolescence. Additionally, Alice remembered tales told to her by both her mother and her older siblings about the death curse placed upon her mother and the unborn baby-Alice by her maternal grandmother, who was enraged that her only child would dare have more children than she herself had given birth to.

Alice was so disturbed by the dream that she was moved to contact Dr. X. She told him about her nightmares and her feeling of need for further analysis. After hearing her story, Dr. X consented to see the patient and, in that interview, told her he thought she required a less abrupt ending to the analysis. He recommended, and Alice agreed, that it might be helpful for them to meet once weekly for some time to discuss the problem of her recurrent symptoms.

However, it soon became apparent that the patient found this infrequent contact to be painfully tantalizing. She also feared that she was undoing all the good that had come from the previous eight years of analytic work, as she spent most of each hour attacking Dr. X for his weakness, his admitted limitations, his incompetence, his refusal to take her back into a full analysis, and for what she felt to be his collusion with her flight from the treatment.

After a year of once-weekly meetings with Dr. X, Alice went away on vacation and had the following dreams:

Alice was visiting a small suburban or rural town, selling home-made cookies she had made to raise money for a worthy cause related to the care and healing of sick children. She had sold all the cookies and was about to move on, when she was apprehended by an angry gang of community members approaching her with clubs in hand. The gang accused her of peddling "inferior cookies" and demanded that she take them back and return their money.

Alice knew that the cookies were good, and she attempted to reason with the mob, but her words fell on deaf ears, and she was finally compelled to comply with their demands. However, instead of loading the cookies into her car, she found she was loading an old woman: the founder of the "cause" for which she was attempting to raise money. This old woman, who was in reality plump and quite robust for her age, appeared in the dream as extremely frail, perhaps even near death.

Alice barely managed to drive away as the rioting mob descended upon the car. She next found herself on a highway in the middle of a desert where babies and puppies were scattered here and there. She stopped the car to rescue them, but as she opened the door to get out, the highway became an escalator.

Alice was now standing at the bottom of this escalator (which was going down). A crying baby was sitting on one of the middle steps, while its parents watched at the top of the down escalator, seemingly oblivious to the baby's distress. Alice picked up the baby and struggled toward the top to return it to its parents. As she neared the top, she saw a huge Doberman pinscher dog standing there, growling ferociously. Alice grew increasingly fearful until a young girl, about 9 years old, seemed ready to intervene on her behalf, coming between Alice and the threatening hound.

As Alice reached the top of the escalator, she tried to hand the baby over to its mother. However, just as she did, the girl smiled fiend-

ishly and stepped aside, leaving the way clear for the angry dog to attack Alice. The dog then lunged at her in slow motion, and she knew in that moment that she would be mortally bitten. At the same time, the father also lunged at her. In his hand was a hypodermic syringe, and Alice thought in the dream, "He cannot stop the dog from attacking me, but he can give me an injection of anti-venom or some anesthetic to help kill the pain."

Alice then awakened, sobbing and nearly overwhelmed with fright and desperation. She could recall feeling terribly hurt and betrayed for hours afterward. It seemed that the old woman in the first part of the dream was like the good mother or perhaps the good experience of Dr. X, which Alice thought she had safely internalized. But it now felt to her that these good experiences had been ejected by a gang of suspicious rednecks who couldn't be reasoned with as they violently demanded the removal of this "inferior cookie" from within their midst. This scene seemed to parallel Alice's fears that some force within her, over which she had no control, was inexplicably and systematically destroying the progress and sense of well-being she had gained in her analysis.

The dog in the dream had reminded Alice of a neighbor's watchdog, which had bitten her when she was 2 years old, mistaking her playfulness for a threat. This event had taken place around the same time that she had wandered off and been lost on a beach, separated from her parents for several hours. That event had always been felt as yet another piece of supporting evidence for Alice's lifelong conviction that she had been unwanted by her parents and ignored and resented by her much older siblings.

Finally, Alice remembered that, around that same age, she had been hospitalized for a tonsillectomy, this at a time when mothers were not allowed to room in with their small children. She remembered that Mother had left her alone in the hospital with a promise that Alice could have all the ice cream she wished, if she behaved herself like a big girl—a cool, soothing, and sweet consolation for being left all alone. However, Alice later felt tricked and betrayed when she found that the ice cream tasted bitter after the surgery.

Considering these associations, it appeared that through the dream Alice was communicating about an experience of a watchful and protective object inside her mind: one that seems to *misinterpret* Alice's attempts to unite the baby-her with her internal parents. It seems that when Alice attempts to reconnect her split-off baby-self with her internal family—just as she attempts the uphill struggle to integrate her analytic experience into the existing psychic structure—a "watchdog" part of her mind appears to sense a threat to that family constellation, becoming a "mad dog," attacking Alice's capacity to integrate her experiences, aspects of herself, and her objects.

The function of this watchdog seems to be *to preserve the existing structure of the family and Alice's internal world*. This world, imaginatively created, had been the bedrock of Alice's existence. But it seems to be a world in which there is no place for a baby-her, only for an older sister, an older more independent-she who seems also to be cast in a protective role.

As Riviere (1936) has noted, if "the patient acts to preserve things as they are, even sacrificing his cure, it may be due to a lack of faith that things will be better, an unconscious belief that such a change will not be for the better but for the worse" (p. 312), adversely affecting not only himself but the analyst.

The father in Alice's dream—like Dr. X to whom she had returned for help—was felt as unable to provide little more than an antidote for or an anesthetic to numb the pain of these venomous attacks launched against her by this now-pathological protector. Alice was subsequently overcome with a multitude of hypochondriacal anxieties, perhaps stemming from the fear that the good objects inside, representing those good experiences gained in her analysis, might be destroyed if she could not immediately reverse this escalation of attacks through further analytic treatment.

Alice's history might suggest that at quite a young age she had experienced a premature disconnection from the parents and their protective function, represented by the screen memory of being lost on the beach and the feelings of abandonment and dissolution in the hospital. She may well have been moved to develop her own means of protecting herself from harm: a precocious older-she, a grandmother or elder sister, or a watchdog or vigilante gang that could defend her against deadly invaders and ensure her ongoing survival.

I came to learn that this defensive constellation was partly patterned after Alice's experiences of a variety of mothering persons—mother, maternal grandmother, stepmother, and eldest sister—who had been watchful, if at times intrusive, caretakers, but who had each in her own way suddenly become abandoning, accusatory, or attacking toward Alice subsequent to any act of separation on her part. This dynamic in the transference may well have been incompletely evolved and/or insufficiently addressed during the termination phase of Alice's analysis with Dr. X.

Additionally, Alice's last therapeutic experience with Dr. X seemed to replicate her experience with her father, who was largely absent from the home, but whose warm if infrequent contacts (although felt to be tantalizing) seemed to provide moments of relief from the mother's deadly attacks, mitigating the pain and fostering Alice's hopes for escape.

Here I am reminded of a point made by Grotstein (1993), addressing yet another aspect of such defensive organizations. He suggested, along the lines of Fairbairn's thinking, that some of these patients suffer from a sort of "pathological introjective identification," in which they may have swallowed the absent, uncaring, depressed, or perhaps psychotic mother whole, and in doing so are ever in danger of being swallowed up by that mother. He pointed out that in analysis this dilemma requires the patient to become a "double agent," walking a tight rope between his or her alliance with the internal organization and the function of the analyst. Perhaps an example of this may be found in the following material.

On the eve of the first hour of Alice's second analysis, she became ill with diarrhea. Fearing she would not be well enough to leave home early the following morning, she left a message on the answering machine canceling her appointment, returned to her bed, and fell asleep. When she awoke, she recalled the following dream:

Alice was standing in the lobby of the analyst's office building, waiting behind a group of elderly women for the elevator. When the elevator opened, the old women were reluctant to get in and seemed confused about whether the elevator was going up or down. Alice urged the women to enter, afraid that they would block her way, causing her to miss the elevator and her appointment. She became frantic, believing that this was the last and only way up. She pleaded with them to get in or to move aside, but the door began to close and Alice was terrified that she had lost her chance for help. Just then, a man put his foot or hand in the way of the closing door, the old women moved into the car, and Alice was relieved, feeling reassured that she would indeed be able to make it to her appointment.

In the ensuing session Alice reported the dream, associating this last portion of it to the help she had received from Dr. X and to his support for her desire to begin a second analysis. The man's foot in the door—like the experience of her previous analysis—had cleared the way for our meeting. Here the father/analyst seems to function as a boundary, allowing for some healthy separation to exist between Alice and those obstructive maternal objects. The old women once again seemed to stand for various aspects of Alice's mother—

experienced as confused, helpless, immovable, and frustrating—as well as those analogous resistant forces within herself
that had threatened to block her initial attempts to begin a
second analysis.

To conclude my discussion of this case, I will report material
from the beginning of the third year of that analysis: material that
seemed to lend additional clarity to the notion of the survival function of Alice's defensive organization and its evolution over her life
span.

During this period, Alice spoke about a film she had seen. The
film was a *Star Trek* movie and as she reported it, the main story
line went as follows:

Some sort of alien entity called "V-ger" is suspected of causing
the annihilation of life on numerous planets. The space ship
Enterprise and its crew are ordered to seek out this entity and
to make contact with it in an attempt to diplomatically halt the
destructive activities before it reaches Earth. When contact is
finally established, it is discovered that the "alien" is in fact
"Voyager," one of earth's twentieth-century space probes.

This probe had originally been programmed to seek out
life on other planets, to collect geological samples, and to ster-
ilize these in order to preserve them for later analysis and to
protect life on Earth. The probe was also programmed to pick
up signals from Earth, indicating her readiness to receive
transmissions of information gathered throughout its journey.

However, when Voyager was later lost in space in a black
hole, cut off from contact with its creator, it had linked up with
and was rescued by a race of machines. Subsequently, its original function—the preservation of life and the epistemophilic
endeavor—was altered, perverted, fragmented, and distorted.

Voyager had become V-ger and had developed an autogenerated, hyperbolic superstructure, focused solely upon its

survival in space, while V-ger continued to seek out contact with its creator. However, when its communications were not responded to, it grew increasingly hostile, sterilizing whole cultures. In the end, it is understood that this renegade probe was suffering from loneliness, neglect, and frustration in its search for meaning and communicative contact with the "parent" who created it.

I believe this "metaphor" might provide the basis for a powerful model of understanding that may add new dimension to the way we approach such pathologically organized aspects of our patients' personalities. One might conclude that *if we are not responsive enough to our patients' probing communications, we may contribute to even further perverse and destructive maneuvers.*

Tom

To further illustrate the appearance and handling of the pathological organization in the clinical situation, I will briefly describe Tom, a patient who brought the following material to light in a dream during the middle of his fifth year of analysis. I briefly preface his material to say that Tom had entered analysis late in his fifth decade of life—after already undergoing nearly thirty years of psychotherapy, first one kind and then another—as yet unable to form any affectionate, long-lasting, and intimate bond with a woman other than his mother and sister.

Tom came in for his last hour of the week, lamenting the death of a flowering plant in his garden, and reported a dream he'd had the previous night.

Tom walked out into the garden behind his home (just as he had, in reality, upon arriving home from the session that evening). He noticed that the flowers he was attempting to nurture and grow with great pains were dying one by one. These beautiful, bushy, spreading, and maturing blooms were systematically being crushed and killed off.

In the dream he thought the culprit must be a large stray cat he had previously seen coming into his yard. The cat must be pissing and shitting on a different plant each time he leaves home, or maybe the cat just comes in and lies down upon them, crushing them to death. "And why not? He's safe when no one is there to chase him off."

After reporting the dream, Tom fell silent. All possible associations seemed to be snuffed out. When after several minutes he finally spoke again, he said he was "crushed" that I had no comment on the dream. He couldn't help but think (even though something told him it might not be true) that I was daydreaming about and looking forward to my weekend, when I could "get away from" him and his "incessant caterwauling."

I noted to myself that the word *caterwauling* was one the patient had never used before. I thought it quite apropos not just in relation to the cat in the dream, but also because it seemed descriptive of the way Tom brought his criticism of the culprit-me, which indeed felt like a harsh cry, perhaps of a growing baby-he who was "crushed" when it felt to him that he could not hold my attention going into and over the weekend.

I said to Tom that I thought he was telling me about that big bad "cat" that takes over his mind on the weekend when I'm not around, spoiling and crushing the life out of that beautifully maturing, growing, and healthy baby-him we have worked so hard to nurture and grow. To this Tom replied: "I know it's got to be that cat! I caught him once in the yard and I squirted him away with the hose, so I think that now he's getting back at me. 'I'll show you,' the cat is saying. He's letting me know that there's nothing I can do about it."

Here I understood that Tom felt that, over the weekend when the contact between us was interrupted, he and I are both helpless to stop this destroying presence within his mind, one that threatens to spitefully and jealously undo or crush all we have accomplished in the analysis. I conveyed this thought to the patient, as well as my sense that this feeling was very much alive in the session, taking over his mind right now, when he also seems to experience my silence as an interruption of the much needed contact between us.

I said I thought that perhaps the silent-me in the session—like the absent-me over the weekend—was now being experienced as the "culprit" whose crushing rejection can be excused only if Tom takes the blame upon himself for "squirting me away," that is, if he can see himself as the rejecting one.

Now, although I might have left it at that, I felt it important to add that it seemed also that he was communicating to me something about how the big-cat-he feels unwanted and excluded—squirted away from our connection—and how this big bad cat feels justified in taking revenge upon us by snuffing out his thoughts about the dream, consequently making himself more comfortable when left unattended in my silence in the hour, as well as over the weekend break. This last comment brought on a broad and contented smile from the patient, who now seemed able to resume our exploration of his dream and the loneliness and discomfort he experiences going into as well as over the weekend break.

One might consider that by addressing these specific dynamics of defense and the motive of survival underlying it in the transference—the attempt on the part of the big-bad-cat-he to comfort Tom in my absence and to protect him from unbearable feelings of being abandoned—we may be making a significant move toward mitigating the feelings of isolation experienced by this seemingly destructive part of the patient, and by so doing facilitating further integration of this outlaw-aspect of mind into the mainstream of the personality and the forefront of the patient's awareness.

In the case of Tom, a transformation might be observed in both the form and function of this internal organization as it gradually loses its hold on the patient's experience and behavior, as I will attempt to illustrate with the following material from the end of the sixth year of Tom's analysis. During this period in the treatment, Tom arrived for a Monday hour reporting the following dream:

Tom was with a group of people, among these his sister and brother-in-law. There was a baby in a stroller, which needed to be lifted over an obstacle in order to move ahead. Tom felt that "a new-he" wanted to help lift the stroller, but his brother-in-law ran ahead to do it himself. In spite of his desire to help, Tom was pushed aside by the brother-in-law, who insisted on handling the task. He was angry at his brother-in-law and yelled at him, accusing him of being unnecessarily domineering and controlling.

After reporting the dream, Tom reminded me he had recently been under some pressure, from both his sister and brother-in-law, to move to the city where they had relocated the year before. However, he expressed his reluctance to do so since he felt the need for more analysis, noting his gains at work and acknowledging his progress with regard to his relationships with women. He shyly admitted that he was growing increasingly hopeful about the future and his prospects for finding a companion in his "old age." He was also concerned that such a move would leave him once again stuck and dependent on his family for everything.

In fact, until recently, Tom had used his family as a sanctuary from the anxieties aroused by his mounting desires for an adult sexual relationship. Although his family was generally experienced as nurturing and supportive of him, Tom also felt strongly that they were unable to bear any changes in the family constellation, one in which he was cast as the "unmarried son" and "dutiful brother"—an "asexual little kid" who would never really leave home—thus providing a soothing constant core within a structure shaken by a rapidly shifting and unstable series of events, including many illnesses, marriages, divorces, births, and the deaths of his younger sister and his father, as well as numerous geographical moves occurring throughout the patient's lifetime.

After confiding this, Tom suddenly went mute. After a few moments, I commented that he seemed to have just encountered an obstacle to going forward with our discussion of his dream. When he snapped back that he had "more important things on his mind than the dream," I thought perhaps that I had been moved to behave—and was therefore now being experienced—as that overeager brother-in-law, rushing in to lift a baby-he over that obstacle. With this in mind, I decided to pull back a bit, waiting to hear what Tom might say next, trusting that this "new-he" (as he had referred to himself in the dream) would find some way to get us "over the hump."

Tom soon reported that, over the weekend, he had been plagued by the next-door neighbor, who he was certain was "erecting something dangerous inside his garage." He had heard hammering, banging, and thumping, and was afraid that this meant that the neighbor was building a "family room" in the garage, out of which "loud music" would come "booming." He complained that these sounds made him "so anxious that [he] could neither read nor think." While he spoke, I was reminded that in previous hours, "hammering," "banging," "booming," "thumping," and "loud music" had all been expressions used by the patient to denote sexual intercourse.

Tom went on describing the neighbor as a "working-class stiff" and the neighbor's wife as "crazy and unpredictable." He complained that they were "unaware of other people's sensibilities," especially his own "sensitivity to noises that make [him] unbearably anxious." He spoke of how he had grown even "more anxious when they closed the door to the garage," because he could no longer see just what the man and his wife were doing. He could still hear the children screaming and the husband and wife speaking in a "strange language" [Spanish], which added to the level of his anxiety as he could not understand and was consequently frightened by the things they were saying to one another.

Later, when the husband said "Hi" to Tom over the back fence, he felt certain that this "friendly gesture" was a sign that "some new diabolical torture" was being devised for him, and he told me that he had momentarily considered allowing his condo to revert to the bank that held the mortgage so he might be free to move to city X to live near his family. In fact, the patient had actually retreated to his mother's empty house (located in a quiet retirement village, quite a long distance from his home) for the day to get some relief from these events, which were becoming overwhelmingly terrifying for him, and which he feared would never end.

This weekend happening seemed also to have brought to life Tom's experience of his "crazy and unpredictable mother"—who had been psychotically depressed after the birth of a severely ill baby girl only one year after his birth—and the loud angry noises of his parents' conversation, or perhaps their love-making, that the baby-he could not comprehend. After many minutes, during which he was reliving this situation, Tom seemed to develop some perspective on his experience, gradually noticing his overreaction to these events.

I felt now that Tom had indeed overcome the obstacle to our going forward and would be able to hear me when I told him I thought that perhaps this new-he was helping me to understand the experience of a baby-he, alone and terrified as he heard frightening noises and perhaps imagined his father's huge erection, which would bring more noise, and the sexual intercourse between the "mother and father behind closed doors," producing screaming children, like his sick and dying baby sister, and resulting in tortuous feelings that impeded his ability to think.

As he seemed alert and receptive to more, I added that I thought the closed garage door also represented the door to my consulting room over the weekend, and that when I said "Hi" as he came in from the waiting room he had grown fearful that I was not really happy to see him, but rather that I had some new torture in store for him this week, one I had been constructing while out of his sight.

I later told him that, on another level, I thought he was calling to my attention the perspective of an "old-he"—like his brother-in-law in the dream—who insisted on helping the baby-he to get over obstacles such as his anxieties over the weekend as well as in the present—by isolating him inside the safety of his empty mother-house, where he could avoid awareness of his own as well as others' erections, perhaps representing his desire to marry and build a family of his own. I thought it clear that, in the dream, Tom's anger at the controlling and domineering brother-in-law was indicative of his annoyance with that part of himself that dominates, controls, and impedes his attempts to "do-it-himself," as well as his anger toward me when I am experienced as "doing it all."

One can see how, in this hour, the "controlling and domineering" part of this patient is on its way toward being integrated into the main stream of the personality and his awareness. As Tom becomes more understanding of this part of himself, he can begin to stand up to it. Additionally, as this aspect of his personality was attended to more fully, we could begin to see the emergence of a dependent infantile part of him from within the protective and stifling confines of the organization, and he could began to allow himself to more fully take advantage of, use, and acknowledge his connection with the analyst. As Tom began to do this, we were able to see him "hatching out of his shell in all directions," developing new interests and relationships, and feeling more and more confident in his own growing physical, mental, and emotional capabilities.

One day, near the summer break of the seventh year, a curious event took place. The following emerged during the last session of a week in which Tom had brought an abundance of material that seemed to consolidate much of the work of the term; a week in which he had been feeling quite good about himself as well as about his analysis.

When I went to get Tom from the waiting room, I found him reading a magazine, but not just *any* magazine. It was a *New Yorker*, which he had previously scorned, viewing it as too "snooty," "uppity," and overly intellectual, but most of all, as inaccessible to him. I believe this magazine was associated with an inaccessible-me and my husband—with whom I share my office suite—and our life together.

Tom had always imagined that my life with my spouse must be filled with intellectual pursuits and a joyous, active, healthy sexuality leading to the kind of creativity felt to be out of reach of the capacities of a little-he "with a hole in his head and a hole in his body." So, needless to say, finding Tom so engaged with the *New Yorker* was quite an unusual scene. Added to the uniqueness of the situation, Tom appeared to be having a difficult time tearing himself away from his reading. He literally could not put the magazine down and as he came in from the waiting room, he asked if he could take it home with him over the weekend.

The patient then went to the couch and told me that he feared that I might take his request as an attempt to avoid the feeling of being separated from me over the weekend. But I disagreed, replying that I thought that today his request had more to do with his need or perhaps his desire to feel that I could actively support his recently expanding interests, as well as his developing-if-still-fragile sense of himself as being a "whole" person, rather than a nonperson with a "hole."

Tom was both surprised and moved by my words, agreeing wholeheartedly with the idea that he needed to feel acknowledged and supported by me in a positive way as he attempts to expand his horizons. Then, as he began to tell me about some of his accomplishments at work that day, there was a gradual shift in the material and the tone in which it was presented. He reported that he had been overheard by his supervisors while shouting at someone on the phone. However, he did not merely report this conversation, but instead he enacted it, at one point getting off the couch, facing me head-on, quite red-faced, and shouting at the top of his booming baritone voice while looming large over my chair. In response to his provocative behavior, my heart began to pound as I felt a quite powerful-if-irrational fear for my life.

This was not a new experience for me with Tom. In fact, in the beginning of the analysis, there were many such intimidating displays of violent anger directly aimed at me. However, these demonstrations—in which Tom always gave me quite a scare, but never touched me or anything else in the room—had lessened over our years together, disappearing in the previous two years or so. At that time we had been able to trace these fits to what seemed to be an object with whom he was then identified, one that represented his mother in a half-crazed state, engaged in the act of terrorizing a little-him, the projection of which I was called upon to bear and to suffer when he could not do so for himself.

At the conclusion of these dramatics, Tom returned to the couch and more calmly told me he had later reassured his supervisors that the call they had overheard was "just" a personal one, unrelated to business. He felt they were relieved rather than bothered to hear he was making personal calls during business hours. But he was also worried about what they might think after overhearing his angry outburst. Perhaps they would be disappointed to know that the "old-he"— that loud, angry "madman who used to intimidate and bully everyone on the job" whenever he felt unsupported or let down, even in the smallest way—still existed in spite of how reasonable, restrained, respectful, soft-spoken, thoughtful, and tolerant he had become of late.

I told Tom that I thought the old-madman-he was making his existence known to us, afraid that if he remained mute we might think him dead and withdraw our attention from this aspect of his experience, while at the same time he seemed also to be communicating about how disappointed he feels that the madman-he *does* still exist, right alongside that more reasonable and tolerant-he. I also said I thought that, while he wanted to make certain that we could see the madman and could bear to "face" him, he was afraid that I would be discouraged by its appearance. As he wiped the tears from his cheeks, I added that while fearing I might be discouraged, he felt the need to reassure me that his rage was not aimed at me—that this was not a business call. However, at the same time, he needed me to see that it was related to the impending weekend letdown for which he holds me responsible.

To this the patient replied that he did feel that, in a way, he had flaunted his personal call and his angry interaction outside his private office in a place where others, especially supervisors, would get an earful. He thought now that it was almost as if, with all the changes occurring in his way of reacting and relating to other people, there remained a need to let people know that the "old Tom" was "still alive and kicking." He even conceded that he was, at times, worried that I would lose sight of a "him" that still needed my attention, in spite of his obvious advances and improvements.

It seems here that what some might have considered a *negative therapeutic reaction* could be understood not just as an envious attack on the creative couple or the good breast, but as an attempt to re-establish contact between the analyst and that aspect of Tom's personality that needed further attention, as well as an effort to enlist the analyst's aid in furthering and fostering contact between the various parts of the patient's mind.

DISCUSSION AND CONCLUSIONS

In her 1985 paper Symington points out that

> analysis is directed toward elucidating and deepening the relationship between two people, analyst and analysand. Hence, a great many interpretations are directed towards that behavior which is felt to be counter to deepening the analytic relationship, that is the omnipotent, narcissistic aspects of the personality. [p. 481]

However, she then underlines the importance of "including in these sorts of interpretations the primitive basis for omnipotence . . . the struggle in which the young baby engages in order to survive when on his own without his mother" (p. 481). Symington wisely cautions that the interpretation of the defense and its destructive side effects, without acknowledging the patient's fear of catastrophe and his conviction that he must defend himself, risks leaving him feeling uncontained and misunderstood, and often results in silent hurt and increased defensiveness.

I would further elaborate on this point of Symington's, adding that in my experience this increased defensiveness often takes the form of extreme compliance, which may *simulate* improvement, but which merely signals the development of a new and more subtle version of the defensive organization: one patterned on and identified with the omnipotent personality and theories of the analyst. Tragically, once this transformation is achieved, the pathological organization is no longer accessible to interpretation, as it has become ego-syntonic for and effectively camouflaged in the mind of the analyst.

Perhaps by consistently recognizing and addressing the survival function of the pathological organization, the analyst might convey an attitude of respect for (rather than one of antagonism toward) this aspect of the analysand's personality, and in doing so may be afforded greater access to it in the long run. Often dream material, which can provide a clearly delineated imaginary representation of these internal defensive structures, offers us just such access. It was my hope that the dreams reported in this chapter might provide a unique window onto the experience of some patients, perhaps yielding a view of that experience relatively unobstructed by theoretical attribution.

However, paradoxically, I do believe that our theoretical attributions are important to keep in mind. I am particularly taken by Grotstein's (1993) variation on a theme of Fairbairn's. He suggests that many of our patients suffer from a sort of "pathological introjective identification," in which they have swallowed the disappointing, frustrating, or malignant object whole, and in doing so are always on the brink of being consumed by that object.[3] Grotstein also admonishes the analyst to remain cognizant of the

---

3. I am grateful to Dr. James Grotstein for calling to my attention the fact that my view of pathological organizations may complement the "American adaptive perspective," which Ego Psychology has attempted to integrate into the mainstream of psychoanalytic theory, in spite of its incompatibility with classical drive theories. I believe the work of Peter Giovacchini is quite representative of this view. Grotstein has also reminded me of the work of Lawrence Hedges, Robert Stolorow, and other Americans who view patho-

fact that this dilemma requires the patient to become a "double agent, walking a tight rope between his or her alliance with the internal organization and the function of the analyst."

I believe that, with this in mind, we can better understand, appreciate, and attend to the ever-present terror of falling provoked in our patients by the analytic work itself, as well as the probability that this terror may prompt our patients' return to an addictive reliance upon their most omnipotent and omnipresent means of survival, especially at times when our relative impotence or absence is experienced. Perhaps the consistent and predictable reappearance of symptoms and behaviors related to the ascendance of the pathological organization poses a constant challenge to our faith in our analytic abilities and the slow but steady process that works to gradually build up a mental and emotional structure—a *benign organization*—that the patient may someday come to have faith in and rely upon.

However, in order that we might afford our patients an experience of our reliability, we analysts must have the capacity to discriminate between a "negative therapeutic reaction," which is an envious attack on the creative couple or the good breast, and one that might be understood as a consequence of the terror associated with change (Bion 1966) and a temporary "loss of faith." We must be able to discriminate between reactions that are really a desperate attempt on the part of the patient to re-establish contact between

---

logical organizations as "parent-induced," which may be "especially apposite in terms of the child abuse literature," and he puts forward the idea that pathological organizations may indeed represent "an amalgamation of parental abuse and the child's defensive response to it." Rather than validating or disputing these points of view on causality, it may be useful here to focus on the subjective experiences of patients and one system of adaptation—developed in response to such experiences—and its function with respect to the baby's sense of going-on-being.

the analyst and that malignant aspect of the patient's personality in need of further attention and one that is perhaps an attempt on the part of the patient to enlist the analyst's aid in furthering and fostering contact between the various parts of his mind.

Thus we must continually strive to develop and improve our capacity to sort out and to differentiate these varied motives and meanings, one from the other. For if we are not responsive enough to our patient's probing communications, we may contribute to the development of further perverse and destructive maneuvers.

Finally, as H. A. Rosenfeld (1971) reminded us, the goal in the treatment of these challenging patients is to find, revive, engage, and even support the loving, constructive, and creative aspects of the patient's personality. To accomplish this aim we might consider "the epistemophilic instinct, the libidinal instinct, and the death instinct are but three facets of a unitary isomorphic life instinct whose function it is to keep us alive as individuals and as a group" (Grotstein 1984, p. 322).

Recognizing and addressing what appears to be the *original survival function* of certain defensively organized structures, their more sensual forerunners (J. Mitrani 1992, 1993b, 1994a,b, 1995a), and the infantile anxieties fueling these in the present has proved useful to me on a number of different occasions, especially in helping to deconstruct some potentially explosive and destructive links in the mind of the patient, allowing for a very different relationship to evolve between the analyst and that protective organization. The establishment of this new relationship may eventually lead to a modification of the pathologically organized part of the personality, as well as to the formation of a new relationship between all of the various aspects of the patient's personality, between the various objects in his internal world.

5

To Err Is Human: One Patient's Emergence from within a Pathological Organization*

Until we affirm or deny something of the ideas we have of things, the idea itself cannot be called either true or false; for its truth or falsehood consists in the relation to reality of some judgment into which it enters.

[John Locke, *On Human Understanding*]

INTRODUCTION

Often we find that people come to analysis not so much to acquire a deeper understanding of themselves, but rather to obtain relief from "something terrible" that is felt to threaten their way of being. Sometimes they come to us with some awareness of an event or series of events that has—as one patient put it—"really upset the applecart." At other times they come "without a clue." They have only a scat-

---

*An earlier version of this chapter was presented as part of the discussion series "Classic Papers in Psychoanalysis" sponsored by the Psychoanalytic Center of California Extension Division on March 10, 1995.

tered sense that their lives are "somehow not right"—"something is out of kilter." It just doesn't "feel" good. Whatever it is that has gotten out of kilter, these people have volunteered to become our analysands so that we might be able to help them "right" things once again, so that they might be able to continue on their way.

Many Kleinian analysts (Joseph 1975, 1985, Meltzer 1968, Money-Kyrle 1969, O'Shaughnessy 1981, H. A. Rosenfeld 1964, 1971, Steiner 1982, 1987, 1990) have conceptualized the "applecart" as a mental structure: a *narcissistic or pathological organization* of manic defenses that has grown rigid and stable over time and that provides the infantile self—the tender apples—with an omnipotent, omnipresent, and therefore thoroughly reliable mode of safe passage—"bruise-free"—through life, that is, free from madness, psychic pain, and overwhelming anxiety.

The relationship between "cart" and "apples" is one in which the more easily bruised part of the self—the vulnerable baby-self—is protected from life's bruises. However, there is a heavy price to be paid for such safe passage. In return, the vulnerable self must submit to being dominated, controlled, and incarcerated within this prisonlike structure.

This protective structure is often characterized in phantasy as an extremely idealized internal family of objects, interconnecting to form some sort of invincible, if pathological, containment—perhaps a gang or the Mafia or some sort of criminal "cartel." This cartel is composed of *destructive* aspects of the self in cahoots with the omnipotently bad aspects of the object. As such, this organization is constantly on the attack against any feelings of vulnerability in relationships. It seduces, extorts, and browbeats the vulnerable, loving, and loved baby-self. It is ruthless, stopping at nothing to maintain its prominence. It even attacks the baby's experience of being loved and his need of, as well as his desire for, dependence upon the good and therefore vulnerable and receptive caretaking-objects. And when this latter source of "goodness" threatens to prevail, the cartel turns its attack upon that object-source of good-ness in an attempt to diminish and denigrate its presence.

However, sometimes the cart is overturned by an unexpected series of bumps on the road of life. When these bumps are encountered, the cart is split apart, its contents spilled out, once more made vulnerable to overwhelming early anxieties that have failed to be mitigated through the course of healthy object relations.

In Chapter 4 I wrote about some of the difficulties encountered in our work with such patients—those who have found their way to analysis in order to get us to "put the thing right"—and the importance of recognizing the survival function of these personality organizations in order to render them more accessible to the analytic process.

However, I would be remiss if I did not also point out that it would be a serious error on the part of the analyst to assume that these patients wish to "learn" ways in which they might live without their customary way of going through life. On the contrary, in the beginning of the analysis and for a very long time afterward, the analysand wishes and perhaps even expects us to repair the old structure, or at least to provide a new one—one that is equally reliable—for him to get around and about inside of. The transference relationship is often mistaken for and is consequently used by the patient *as if it were* this new improved vehicle for defense.

I have noticed that patients, such as the one I present in this chapter, often live under the misconception that to be human—or humanly vulnerable and dependent—is an *error* to be corrected. Only much later might we be able to help these patients to develop the courage to emerge from within the superhuman order provided by the pathological organization, to strike out and about on their own two feet and begin to "learn from experience" (Bion 1962). Only after many years of work might we be able to help our patients to realize that to be human is *not* an error, but rather that *to err is human*.

In this brief clinical note I will give an example of the emergence of the dependent infantile part of the patient from within the protective and stifling confines of a pathological organization, as well as the beginnings of a more creative and generative way of being.

Sandra

As patients so often do, Sandra entered analysis in her midthirties owing to a breakdown in what appeared to be her previously functional narcissistic adaptation, a breakdown precipitated by the death of her father, a major geographical move, and various personal and professional disappointments and difficulties—those bumps in the road of life to which I referred earlier.

In the first three years of the analysis, Sandra had been able to establish, in the transference situation, a secondary defensive organization that was manifested in the treatment by the patient's oscillation between a narcissistic transference in which the two of us were as one, ideal, martyred mother, and her fleeting awareness of two-ness, usually precipitated by those associations of hers and interpretations of mine that brought new ideas, fresh insight, and lively feelings to our work. Such shifts—from the reassuring feeling of at-one-ment to the awful awareness of two-ness—led to her experience of me as a cold, cruel, retaliatory, mostly paternal object that threatened her with desertion. However, regardless of which way she experienced me, it was quite difficult for the analytic work to proceed effectively.

The first phase of Sandra's treatment allowed for the reestablishment of a defensive organization in which the analysis proceeded for over three years prior to the session I shall report. This defensive structure functioned at times and in some ways like a protective hammock in which we were to rock back and forth, suspended equidistant between two dangerous poles. This session seemed to mark the beginning of a new phase in the analysis in which light was shed, for both Sandra and me, on old issues and events, first presented in the earliest hours of the treatment and periodically re-emerging in various forms.

To add clarity, I will give a bit of the context of the session. It was the last session of the week as well as the last day of the month, a month in which many important developments had taken place. Near the beginning of the month, Sandra had returned from a three-week vacation abroad—her first absence of any length from the treatment initiated on her own, undertaken by herself, and financed with her own earnings. In the past the patient had taken vacations only when I was away and then only when her mother invited her and offered to pay her way.

Upon her return Sandra presented me with a check for the previous month which, according to our original agreement, was to have included payment for all missed analytic hours. Yet this portion of the payment was conspicuously deducted from the check. It seemed to me that Sandra had, in phantasy, obliterated her feelings of loss as well as that sensitive and dependent part of herself, which relied upon and valued her analysis.

Consequently, I was made to feel—in the context in which the check was given in the session, in which there was no reference to any experience of the long break—that the patient had left me and the treatment paralyzed. I thus felt caught in a terrible bind: if I said nothing to her about her omission, I would be complying with a role she wished me to play, one in which I was the ideally good, selfless mother-part-of-the-patient, attacked, abused, and of no use to her as a strong object who could receive and contain her hurt, lost, and angry feelings. In short, I would be colluding with her phantasy that we had never been separated.

However, if I pointed out her "error," I would become, among other things, that critical, demanding, and reprimanding aspect of her self that insisted on getting something for nothing. This aspect of Sandra's infantile personality—perhaps associated with an experience of Mother as vain and selfish—usually made an appearance in a sort of silent, sullen, arms-crossed-over-chest behavior that always provoked in me a feeling that I was being required to hand over my interpretations without benefit of her cooperative participation or associations.

I thought perhaps this paralysis was being brought about to bind us together, to deny the separation that would have been so unbearably painful and terrifying to her. But it also seemed to me that once again she was employing a comfortable sling between two very different experiences of me and was thus protected from danger. When I called her attention to this dilemma in which we were both trapped by this acting-in, taking care to address this as her method of *survival*, the work seemed to take on a new and lively dimension.

Much of the material during the hours following this confrontation revolved around the unfairness of our arrangement and the discordance of our individual needs and purposes, as well as issues of separation and two-ness. Complicating this painful situation was Sandra's discovery that I had recently achieved my doctoral degree, which furthered the feelings of separation between us and brought about the beginning of the end of a tenaciously held fantasy that it was I who needed her, a fantasy that the treatment was being conducted mainly for my academic advantage rather than for her own therapeutic benefit.

In this session Sandra entered the room in a somber mood; however, what was missing was even the slightest evidence of the anxiety she had displayed throughout that entire week. She announced that she had had a dream on the previous night, which she had just recalled on the way to my office while thinking about her sunglasses. Before proceeding to tell me about the dream, she explained that she had, in reality, purchased new sunglasses to replace the old ones that she hated. The new sunglasses had recently lost a screw and the "arm" had fallen off while she was at work. While these glasses were being repaired, she was forced to return to wearing the old, uncomfortable, and scratched pair, which she now disliked more than ever, but which she was nevertheless compelled to wear.

Silently I took this situation to represent, in a nutshell, the analytic one in which Sandra had grown to hate her old defensive "lenses" by which she had distorted her view of the world; the new lenses that had been substituted for the old had, like the illusion of at-one-ment with me, recently lost a screw, so to speak, in the process of the analytic work regarding the holiday break, when she had felt my arms had fallen off, leaving her feeling unheld, unprotected, and unseen. It seemed she was saying that, as these lenses (the illusion of at-one-ment with me) were no longer serviceable, she had returned to using the old ones (representing her omnipotent denial of her dependency), which seemed now to be more ego-dystonic than ever.

Confirmation of these thoughts seemed to be forthcoming as Sandra reported that, in the dream,

She was wearing the new sunglasses. They had felt odd so she removed them only to find that the "arms" of the frame had fallen off. She wondered to herself in the dream why they should be broken so soon, and then suddenly it dawned on her that they had been broken at the time of purchase, but that she had somehow overlooked or forgotten this fact.

The patient then wept for a moment or two following the telling of the dream. When the tears subsided she was silent for a moment. Then she smiled, shrugged her shoulders, and with a timid giggle explained that she had just had a curious idea. She had flashed on the thought that the way she was in the dream was typical of the way she was in the world. She said that she thought she'd always insisted upon her old ways even though she hated them, adding that she had just realized that even some of her newer ways of experiencing the world were flawed or broken, although she often forgets this and insists that her view of things is whole and right. I was curious as to the meaning of all this, but remained silent.

Moments later the clarification was forthcoming, as Sandra described an incident at work the previous day. Thinking she had made a serious error in her work, she had become panicky, although her co-workers had remained calm, supportive, and helpful to her. She was aware that the persecution she felt was coming from within (in itself a vast improvement from her usual tendency to externalize threats and accusations). It was quite apparent from the manner in which Sandra describe the situation that what still troubled her, despite the positive outcome of the day at work, was that she had needed to be human and to allow herself to rely upon other humans for their calm acceptance and support, as well as "their clear vision."

Upon my interpretation of the above, the patient recalled the single precipitating event that had prompted her to seek analysis, the last straw as it were. Mentioned only briefly in our first interview, this event now took on a more elaborate form and a most meaningful significance some 45 months later. At that earlier time Sandra had been chastised by a co-worker for making an error that had made her employer look "bad," and she was blamed for having damaged her employer's reputation in the eyes of a certain client. The employer was then associated with Sandra's mother who was engaged in the same position in another agency.

It now appeared that the incident had provoked extreme anxiety of a depressive nature, to which the patient responded at the time with a return to the paranoid-schizoid position in which persecutory anxieties were dealt with through manic triumph over good maternal objects feared to be damaged in her internal world. She had devalued her employer just as she had earlier devalued her own mother and, later, her analyst.

When I interpreted the material in this way, Sandra responded at once by telling me that she had felt overwhelmed upon leaving my office the day before by something I had said that had brought her in touch with the painful reality that she could never really have me, that is, that she could never really possess or *be* me. In response I shared with her my observation that it appeared she had felt the same way about her calm, supportive, and helpful co-workers on the previous day when she had become aware that she could not "have," "possess," or "be" them, but that she could only feel calmed, supported, and helped *by* them, by allowing herself to be human and by relying on them.

I also pointed out that the subsequent awareness of her separate yet needy and dependent state had registered in a part of her mind as a "serious error," and that in her attempt to correct this "error" she had become confused and had subsequently panicked. I also thought, but did not say, that the reality of separateness was to her an error that was to be corrected by confusion with her objects; however, this confusion left her without the sense of someone to rely upon, resulting in her state of panic.

After a very long, silent pause in which Sandra appeared to be nearly overcome with feeling, nodding her head in agreement but unable to speak, she finally said that she was now thinking, "I'm not as my mother would like me to be." Then she added that while listening to me speak, she had felt a flood of sorrow and guilt and had thought, "I drain my mother."

At once it occurred to me that the nature of Sandra's seemingly painful attempts at presenting herself to the world as the antithesis of her own mother—described as elegant, perfectly coiffed, meticulously robed, and fashionable, in contrast to the patient's somewhat sloppy, oversized, and disheveled appearance—was a defensive negation of her intense longing to have, possess, and be her mother. Sandra's life-long conviction that her mother wished her to be "like her" (and even that she demanded this) seemed now to be a distortion of her own wish to "be" mother, which caused her to despair over draining mother of her own life.

Concurrently, Sandra's refusal to acknowledge such a wish (due in part to her lack of tolerance for depressive feelings and the experience of true guilt) had led to her use of manic means of devaluing the mother (and the analyst in the transference). While kept in such a devalued condition, Mother and I were consequently experienced as unreliable and burdensome to the patient, who subsequently felt drained of her own vitality and creative energies.

Sandra's reluctance to see the value, reliability, and separateness of her objects could now be seen clearly as a major source of her difficulties. Trapped by her tenacious need to control her objects, she could never bring herself to rely upon them. No matter what, good objects were always felt to be drained, damaged, and therefore untrustworthy, while she, in confusional identification with these objects, always felt herself to be incompetent and lacking.

At the end of this session Sandra became aware of her conflict: if she was able to feel that she "had" me when she left on Friday, there was also the fear that I would not be there for her when she returned the following week on Tuesday. If she went away without me—that is, if she became aware that I was separate and of value to her—then she would remain with the feeling of being ill-equipped to be in the world alone, and would feel drained over the weekend and in danger of dying.

She told me: "It feels as if only one of us can exist." When I heard this, what crossed my mind was Sandra's recently expressed and quickly abandoned desire to return to college full-time to obtain a degree. She had stated at the time that she felt she could not support both her education and her analysis and, although the financial reality did not seem to warrant such a conflict, she had settled for an extension course in sculpting, leaving her plans for a degree in limbo.

With this in mind I told Sandra that perhaps this fantasy, that "only one of us can exist," was behind her hesitance with regard to returning to college, as if the "new letters" after my name (my Ph.D.) were a bit of me that I had obtained at her expense (by draining her) and, in like manner, if she obtained such letters after her name, this would result in a devastating loss to me, and I would become drained and deadened.

It seemed that, at least in part as a result of these developments in the Friday hour, Sandra returned after the weekend break stating she had been feeling a good deal better and much more hopeful. She then described an event that occurred in her sculpting class on the previous evening.

Sandra had received much acknowledgment from her classmates and the instructor for a piece she had been working on. She had been assigned the task of making a mask, and felt that it was the first piece she had produced "according to [her] own instincts and needs"; one that had "come together on that night." She said she felt she had "obtained the inspiration for the piece from her father."

Sandra then explained: "I was making the nose and I thought of my father's nose, a strong, prominent, Grecian nose. He was truly with me—alive. But the nose on my mask was not his, although he was definitely my inspiration. Everyone made a big fuss over it and me, including the model, but

I also felt good about the piece from inside—proud of it—my own creation inspired by my father's presence."

Perhaps, among the many other implications of this material, this is a sign of Sandra's budding capacity for reliance upon a strong, good object, one that seems to be gaining prominence in her internal world, providing the inspiration for her growing creativity.

EPILOGUE

Indeed, Sandra continued to develop areas of creativity and her relationships broadened and deepened substantially during the remaining years of her analysis as she grew increasingly able to allow herself to rely upon, trust, and love others as well as herself. In the sixth year of the analysis she fell in love with a man and married. In light of her age, she and her husband soon began to plan a family.

Unfortunately, their efforts to conceive a child were plagued by many obstacles. The patient underwent fertility treatments, including a reparative surgery that seemed successful, only to discover that her husband had irreversible reproductive anomalies as well. At this point the couple contemplated adoption.

It soon became apparent, however, that Sandra was conflicted about this last option for "having a baby." A long and careful analysis of her phantasies about adoption led to a painful realization: she would have to face the reality that she "had not created herself." She would have to accept a baby born of the "union between others," just as she would have to accept her reliance upon the union of her father and mother. Indeed, she was to struggle with this very complex conflict—between her phantasy of self-sufficiency and the reality of her dependency upon and gratitude toward not only her "real" parents, but toward the "analytic couple" as well, for having given her life—throughout the termination phase of her analysis.

The termination of Sandra's analysis took place at the end of the seventh year of the treatment. The question of whether she would abandon that "human" baby-she—brought to life by the analytic couple—or whether she could indeed "adopt" and love this or any other baby created outside her sphere of omnipotence was to be left unanswered for me—that is, until nearly one year later, when I received word by mail: the patient and her husband were proudly announcing the arrival of their adopted son.

6

The Role of Unmentalized Experience in the Etiology and Treatment of Psychosomatic Asthma[1]

The psyche and the soma are not to be distinguished except according to the direction from which one is looking.

[D. W. Winnicott, *Through Paediatrics to Psychoanalysis*]

INTRODUCTION

The creation of modern psychosomatic medicine as an integrated discipline dealing with the psychological concomitants of physical maladies, the study of psychological reactions subsequent to organic illness, and the interaction between psyche and soma in the production of disease is historically bound to psychoanalysis. Early on in his formulation of the libido theory, Freud appeared cognizant of the profound effects of the soma upon the psyche. He proposed

---

1. A version of this chapter was the recipient of the James A. Gooch Essay Prize in December 1991 and was published in *Contemporary Psychoanalysis* in 1993.

that the life force itself was derived from bodily functions and demonstrated their significant impact upon mental life (1895b,c). Freud's contribution of the two models of the pathogenesis of bodily symptoms (those seen in conversion hysteria and the "actual" neuroses) was significant in the early development of psychosomatic theory and has remained both the basis for and the problem of psychosomatic research for over half a century.

While reflecting upon Freud's early work, one is struck by his acute awareness of the "constant conjunction" (Bion's term) between mental and physical elements involved in the etiology of disease. He reminded us that "psychoanalysts never forget that the mental is based on the organic, although their work can only carry them as far as this basis and not beyond it" (1910, p. 217). In 1922 Freud defined psychoanalysis as a method of obtaining "insight into the complications of mental life and the interrelations between the mental and the physical" (p. 250). Freud's discovery of the psychic etiology of hysteria (1895c) marked the beginnings of psychoanalysis and planted the seeds from which modern psychosomatic theory sprouted and grew.

Freud proposed (1894) that his patients had maintained psychic health until a point at which an event, idea, or sensation awakened in the ego such painful feelings that the individual was compelled to "forget" for want of alternate capabilities with respect to resolving internal contradictions. Facilitated by a constitutional "capacity for conversion" (1894, p. 50), these patients made the "leap" or transposition from the psychic to the somatic realm of experience. Freud first understood these somatic symptoms as the representation of one or more incompatible thoughts. He later proposed (1905) that this transformation of the unconscious instinctual demands of infantile sexuality and somatic neutralization of forbidden thoughts and impulses constituted a special case of neurotic, although incomplete, repression.

Freud (1905) also linked the "capacity for conversion" with the concept of "somatic compliance, offered by some normal or pathological process in, or connected with, one of the bodily organs" (p. 24), and declared that the chronic or repetitive nature of the symptom could only be attributed to a psychological component, that is, to the unconscious affixing of psychic meaning to the symptom. This "conversion model" may be contrasted with a second model for the formation of somatic symptoms, which was related to the concept of anxiety.

In this second model Freud (1895b) saw somatic symptom formation as an organic "anxiety equivalent" (p. 94). He observed that disturbances of "bodily functions—such as respiration" (p. 94)—often accompany, mask, or even substitute altogether for anxiety, and, in contrast to the anxiety of the hysteric, the analysis of such anxiety failed to uncover a repressed idea. Here, in the case of the anxiety neurosis, or "actual" neurosis, the *somatic symptom resulted from physical sensations that had been denied access to the psychic apparatus—sensory experiences that failed to be mentalized*, whereas in hysterical conversion, psychic stimulation induced by conflict was repressed—banished to expression in the physical organic symptom.

In either case, Freud (1895b) cited a psychical insufficiency, as a consequence of which abnormal somatic processes arise. He suggested that in both, "instead of a psychical working-over of the excitation, a deflection of it occurs into the somatic field" (p. 115). The distinction Freud makes here is of paramount importance in that hysterical conversion is a subtype of repression in which the organic symptom is a physical representation of a psychic transformation, while the organic symptom of anxiety neurosis is a direct expression of unmentalized somato-sensory excitation—an *unmentalized experience*. In distinguishing between hysterical conversion and the anxiety equivalent, Freud described the former bodily symptoms as representations of psychic or mental experiences that could be interpreted as stemming from unconscious conflicts between the instinctual needs and the ego's defenses, as a compromise with the characteristic of a symbol standing for an idea. However, he described the latter as the *equivalent* of a state of undifferentiated or primitive anxiety, not the representative or physical expression of a psychical activity gone awry, but an indication that a psychic activity has failed to occur.

It might be said that the conversion symptom is a replacement or substitution of a bodily symptom for a conscious action that represents an unconscious desire to act upon an idea, while the organic symptom of the anxiety neurosis indicates a lack of mentation of a sensory experience, the idea of the action never having been formed. From this one might conclude a relationship between conversion and repression while relating anxiety equivalents with the more primitive defense of projective identification (Klein 1946) in service of communication (Bion 1977a). In light of these findings, Freud (1916/1917) concluded: "The problem of the 'actual' neuroses . . . offer[s] psychoanalysis no points of attack. It can do little towards throwing light on them and must leave the task to biologico-medical research" (p. 389).

And so Freud relegated those neuroses of a somatic nature, which were lacking in psychical content, to the background of psychoanalysis. Fortunately, this was not so with his students and followers, who made contributions toward a greater understanding of psychosomatic disturbances, both through an expansion of Freud's work on hysterical conversion and by further developing his concept of the anxiety equivalent. These pioneers in psychoanalytic psychosomatics proved somewhat successful at the task of elucidating Freud's original concepts, shedding light on the etiology of various physiological disorders, including bronchial asthma.

Many seminal researchers utilized clinical observation of adult intrapsychic processes as focal points in the formulation of the earliest theoretical suppositions (Alexander and French 1948, Cannon 1932, F. Deutsch 1939, 1949, Dunbar 1943) and conceptualized psychosomatic asthma in terms of "specificity," "organ choice," and "mediation," while others (Fenichel 1931, Rank 1924) linked asthmatic syndromes to early identificatory processes and birth trauma, respectively. The latter seemed to foreshadow the more recent work of Greene (1958) and Engel (1962), focusing upon the quality of early object relations to better understand the asthmatic symptom as it relates to the conflict between independence and dependence.

Contemporary thinking on psychosomatic asthma has expanded to include studies in ecology, social epidemiology, immunology, neuroendocrinology, and genetics (as well as psychology) and indicates a multidirectional effort producing complex models of respiratory psychosomatization (Knapp 1971, Reiser 1975, Weiner 1977). Studies on hypnosis reported by Mason (1959, 1960, 1965) seem to lend credibility to the idea that the majority of cases of intractable asthma are emotionally determined or contain significant emotional factors.

Regardless of the precise combination of factors present in the etiology of asthma in any one case, numerous reports of successful psychoanalytic treatment leading to complete or partial alleviation of the process of bronchoconstriction, wheezing, edema, and hypersecretion, with no substantial change in allergic sensitivity or other structural or immunological components (Barendregt 1961, Giovacchini 1984, Grinker 1953, Groen 1964, Sperling 1978), seem to highlight the attention that must be paid to emotional factors in combating this debilitating and life-threatening disease.

A number of psychoanalytic investigators, both empirical and clinical, are convinced of the central role of psychoanalysis in the treatment of asthma. Case studies implicating psychoanalytic treatment in the cure and/or the amelioration of the disease process abound in the literature (F. Deutsch 1959, Elkan 1977, Engel 1954, 1962, Fenichel 1931, Mason 1981, Mushatt 1975, Sperling 1967, 1978, Winnicott 1941). However, almost as numerous as these case reports are the seemingly divergent theoretical approaches utilized in achieving therapeutic results; oftentimes these theories are at odds with one another in an attempt to explain the etiology and subsequent resolution of asthma by psychoanalytic means.

For example, theorists writing on the subject (Coolridge 1956, Jessner 1955, Karol 1980, Knapp et al. 1970, Mohr 1963, Sperling 1955, 1968, 1978, Wilson 1980) have pointed to primal scene trauma and subsequent sadomasochistic phantasies, unconscious maternal rejection, parental overstimulation and overprotection, familial hostility, separation anxieties, control issues, special communications between mother and child, and a plethora of other dynamic issues as salient etiological factors in symptom production. Reports that cite the common occurrence of asthma, developing for the first time or recurring after a lengthy remission, during analysis are published in great numbers. Such symptoms are described in association with regressive trends relating to and/or alternating with acting-out behavior, psychotic transferences, perversions, and other primitive pathological manifestations (Atkins 1968, Freud 1905, Marty 1968, Mason 1981, Sperling 1955, 1968, Wilson 1980, Winnicott 1941). The appearance of such symptoms is apparently so frequent that almost every analyst may have to deal with them at one time or another in his/her practice.

Because the process of respiration is so very vital to human existence, psychosomatic asthma remains, from a clinical, technical, and theoretical point of view, a problem of considerable magnitude deserving of further investigation. Presently, with the aid of some of the contributions of Melanie Klein and others of the British school of object relations (which have amplified our comprehension of many of the most primitive mental and protomental states), it may be possible to conduct such an investigation, adding yet another dimension to our understanding of those cases of bronchial asthma that appear to fall under the heading of *anxiety equivalents*.

Any new bit of theory emerging as a result of an investigation such as this is not intended as a replacement for any other theory previously espoused by psychoanalysts, although it may perhaps penetrate more deeply into the preverbal archaic layers of the mind, in hopes of casting additional light on the emotional etiology of certain instances of bronchial asthma. Toward this end

I will first present a review of some salient concepts that form the basis of my own way of thinking about the asthmatic dilemma. Following this theoretical foundation, I will present a discursive fragment of a case of one asthmatic patient in analysis, which may serve to remind the reader of similar material in his/her own clinical experience with asthmatic patients, and which will provide an introduction to the theoretical statement and the discussion that follows.

THE CONCEPT OF UNCONSCIOUS PHANTASY

Derived from the work of Melanie Klein (1952) and others of the Kleinian group in London (Heimann 1952, Isaacs 1952), the concept of unconscious phantasy has amplified Freud's earlier notion. Phantasies are processes active in the infant long before they can be represented in a symbolic or verbal manner. The earliest phantasies are presented in a "somato-sensual" mode (Isaacs 1952, p. 74) as bodily sensations and then as motor action.

The infant, in a position of maximal vulnerability and minimal motoric and verbal capability, employs phantasy as a means of defense, for inhibition and control of instinctual urges, and for expression of wishes and desires, as well as for their fulfillment. The omnipotent character of these phantasies is directly proportionate to the degree to which vulnerability is experienced by the infant. As primitive anxiety increases, so the phantasies that constitute the pre-historic self-survival tactics of infancy proliferate, employing the senses, the viscera, and the bodily organs in the service of expression.

Isaacs (1952) cited the occurrence of hysterical conversion symptoms (which have a distinct and discernible meaning) as evidence of what she thought to be the earliest preverbal phantasies. However, she did not account for the notion of the anxiety equivalent (which lacks meaning). I suggest that if there is a "phantasy without words" as evidenced by conversion, then the anxiety equivalent must be considered as evidence for the existence of "phantasy without thought." These most primitive phantasies are more accurately termed *protophantasies*, as these seem to be rooted in the protomental area of experiences (Bion 1977a)[2] which are recorded as "body memories" (Federn 1952) or "memories in feelings" (Klein 1957).

The form taken by these primitive proto-phantasies in infancy is in part determined by the mother, whose own unconscious fantasies, projected into the infant at or even before birth, combine with innate infantile "preconceptions" to provide the primordial basis of the infant's first sense of self. The mother's phantasies provide the alphabet from which the infant begins to spell out the meaning of life experience—his earliest sensory and affective states. The form or shape of the mother's phantasies (as well as any deficiency in her capacity for mental elaboration) about her own as well as her baby's emotional states is, in a sense, passed on through the placenta and in her milk. I will later attempt to demonstrate how this notion can be brought to bear on the problem of symptom choice in somato-mental illness.

PRIMITIVE ANXIETIES

Early anxieties experienced in infancy can be studied as they correspond to the level of bodily integrity and degree of differentiation between inside and outside the bodily self attained after physical birth. Klein (1946) delineated two of the three categories of primitive anxi-

---

2. What I am referring to here is an area of experience and phantasy involving the prenatal, perinatal, and immediate postnatal existence of the fetus/infant, that area which Winnicott (1949) designates as *the realm of the "psyche-soma," in which experiences are recorded somatically*, an area later elaborated upon in an "imaginative conjecture" by Bion (1976, 1979).

eties. She first proposed "persecutory anxiety," arising as a result of the deflection or projection of split-off, destructive aspects of the self into an external part-object (the breast/mother), which is subsequently experienced as persecuting, vengeful and life threatening. This, Klein proposed, is the earliest object-related anxiety involving concern for the self. Later she described the development of concern for the good object, recognized as outside the self, as wholly associated with bad aspects that have been attacked in phantasy, and which is therefore in danger of destruction. Anxiety about the fate of the object is laden with remorse and regret as well as hopes and fears about the efficacy of reparative efforts and therefore is labeled *depressive anxiety*.

A third class of primitive anxieties, predating those of the infantile paranoid-schizoid and depressive positions, was observed by Winnicott (1958a) and Bick (1968) and later elaborated by Symington (1985) and Tustin (1986). I refer to these as "*unintegration anxieties*," which I believe form a more primitive basis for omnipotence in infancy. Winnicott (1945) postulated a primary state of unintegration and a tendency toward integration existing from the beginning of postnatal life, a belief upheld by the most current infant research (Stern 1985). Before the embodiment of the psyche occurs (what Winnicott referred to as the experience of psychical personhood dwelling in a physical body, or the state of "personalization"), development of a "psychic skin" (Bick 1968) must be facilitated by both the physical and mental "holding" mother of infancy. A deficiency in either aspect of this maternal holding environment gives rise to the unthinkable dreads of falling forever, nonbeing, dissolving in liquid, or diffusion in air; of dissolution and evaporation, without the possibility of recovery.

Normal states of unintegration, ordinarily the precursors of a later capacity for relaxation, may thus become associated with anxieties of a most terrifying nature. These unintegration anxieties, experienced and recorded at first by a "body-ego," predate those anxieties associated with damage to an embodied self or an

ambivalently loved whole object (in relationship with an embodied self).

To ensure survival or, more precisely, to restore the experience of *being* in the absence of maternal holding, the infant fash-
ions a second skin (Bick 1968) from threads of sensual experience.
Sights, sounds, smells, and the feel of smooth and striate muscular
actions, woven together in primitive omnipotent protophantasies,
provide a sensation of auxiliary holding and establish omnipotence
as a trustworthy ally in defending against the forthcoming persecutory and depressive anxieties.

MATERNAL HOLDING

Maternal holding, as it is described in its entirety by Winnicott
(1941, 1945, 1958a), is the infant's bulwark against awareness of
the earliest unintegration anxieties (those of dissolution and evaporation). If holding is "good enough," this obviates a premature
mental development on the part of the infant. That is, it allows for
a gradual development of phantasy life, not primarily in the service of omnipotent defense, but predominantly for the expression
of creative and epistemophilic strivings. If the environment can be
relied upon to provide the material for a sense of skin or the boundaries of a self, then the infant will be well on its way toward the
development of an internal psychic space, that is, the processes of
normal projective and introjective identification can be established.

If the good-enough-holding of the mother can be taken for
granted, then the infant is free to experience momentary separateness from the mother, what Tustin (1981) calls "flickering states
of awareness" or what one might conceptualize as pores in the
skin. Just as actual pores in the physical skin are necessary for the
elimination of waste products and toxins as well as the absorption
of life-giving substances (both liquid and gaseous), so too these
psychic skin pores are necessary to the establishment of the natu-

ral ebb and flow of those projective and introjective processes that allow for the development of an internal world of objects (Klein 1975a).

MATERNAL CONTAINING

Owing to the work of Bion (1977a), we now understand that for the processes of projective and introjective identification to proceed in a healthful manner, without mutating into pathological autistic maneuvers or hyperbolic disintegration of the self, the holding mother must also exhibit "containing" properties. The properties necessary to adequate containment are the capacities to receive and take in projected parts and feelings of the infant: to experience the full effect of these on the psyche-soma and to bear those effects; and to think about and understand these projections, gradually returning them to the infant in due time and in decontaminated form. This assumes the presence of a mother who has her own boundaries, internal space, a capacity to bear pain, to contemplate, to think, and to reflect back. A mother who is herself separate, intact, receptive, capable of "reverie," and appropriately giving is suitable for introjection as a good containing object. The identification with and assimilation of such an object leads to the development of a capacity to make meaning (what Bion termed *alpha function*), increased mental space, and the development of a mind that can think for itself.

The metabolic processing of the infant's raw sensory experiences (*beta-elements*), first through the mother's mental function and later on via its own, results in a decrease in somatization related to intense affective states and the development of symbol formation. I will later demonstrate how projective identification and subsequent introjective identification with a containing object may help to diminish concretization of emotional experience while augmenting abstract and creative thinking, leading to the replacement of action symptoms (related to painfully unbearable emotional states) with increased tolerance of psychic pain and mental transformations.

DEFICIENCIES IN MATERNAL HOLDING AND CONTAINING

In the event of a deficiency in good-enough mothering, the infant is subjected to sudden and/or chronic awareness of disconnection—of holes, gaps, or faults through which the nascent self can slip, spill, or diffuse, "never to be found and held again" (Symington 1985, p. 481). Such disruption in the infant's "continuity of being" (Winnicott 1949) produces "over activity of mental functioning" (p. 246) and the precocious development of omnipotent phantasies (proto-phantasies) of a defensive nature, produced "to take over and organize the caring for the psyche-soma; whereas in health it is the function of the environment to do this" (p. 246). This usurpation of environmental functions by the mind can lead to confusional states, second skin development, the development of mental functioning as a thing in itself; a pathological mind-psyche that is perceived as an enemy to the self and that consequently must be localized for purposes of control.

Inadequacies of the earliest holding environment may predispose the infant to experience later deficiencies in containing, either due to a realistic inadequacy of the containing object or to the infant's inability to use a proper containing object. In other words, precocious defensive psychological development may result in continued usurpation of environmental functions by the mind and the inability to make use of the mother as a container, or it may follow that a mother deficient in holding may also lack a capacity for reverie and alpha-function (Bion 1962).

If the first phantasies are truly "bound up with sensations" (Isaacs 1952, p. 91) resulting from stimuli experienced at birth and during respiration, feeding, and elimination, it then follows that the earliest object-related phantasies involve intake and expulsion of parts of the self into and out of the self and/or object, as yet an incompletely differentiated unit. Moderate and tolerable awareness of separateness from the object, whether facilitated by the sense of "skin" (as derived from the mother's adaptation to the baby) or by the baby's adaptation to the mother (which constitutes a second skin formation), is accompanied by discrimination of inside from outside and "me" from "not-me" (Winnicott 1951), as well as primary integration of hard and soft (Tustin 1980). These developments in very early infancy usher in primitive projective and introjective activities in phantasy that require a containing object. Deficiencies in the containing object or in the capacity of the infant to use his containing object may take the following forms and precipitate the following pathological events and symptoms.

The container function (Bion 1977a) can be divided, for the purpose of discussing areas of breakdown or deficiency, into three aspects:

1. *Reverie* or the receptivity of the container to the projected distress of the baby.
2. *Alpha-function* or the metabolic or transformational capacity of the container or its ability to detoxify or render meaningful those projected aspects of the infant's experience.
3. *Maternal feedback* or the mother's active return to her infant of mitigated and modified emotional experience, alpha elements, or the nonsensual component of her loving ministrations.

First, a deficiency or breakdown in the area of reverie (perhaps due to the mother's fear of being taken over, fear of penetration, absorption, injury, closeness, or connectedness) results in unmodified fear being returned to the baby. This rejection of the baby's distress can lead to hyperbolic projective identification or massive projection of parts of the helpless infant self in a frantic search for a containing object and the subsequent failure in the development of a mind for thinking about and modifying experience. Sensory experience that is denied access to a maternal psychic apparatus fails to be transformed into food for thought. Somato-sensory experience remains at just that level, unsuitable for thinking, and fit only for evacuation.

Second, a deficiency or breakdown in the area of *alpha-function* (due to the mother's inability to tolerate the infant's and/or her own pain, the fear of death and destruction, and/or an inability to mentalize such primitive anxieties) may result in the infant's reintrojecting not only its own unmodified fears, but his mother's fears as well. Worse yet, if the required alpha-function is not only absent but is actually reversed, in the case of an object that unthinks, misunderstands, or elaborates lies and hallucinations in service of evasion (Meltzer 1978), the infant's projections may be stripped of what little meaning they may bear and be returned as nameless dreads. In both cases, psychic activity or mentation that fails to occur in the mother affects the development of mental processes in the infant.

Finally, deficient *feedback* can arise in the case of a mother who fears separation or loss of part of herself in identification with her infant and who, consequently, fails to give back what is projected. Winnicott (1948, p. 94) describes this as a failure in "mirroring" of a depressed mother. However, I here wish to add to this my own elaborations. I propose that in some cases, depression in the mother may be so black as to absorb all light projected into it, reflecting back little or nothing. The "deadness" of such a mother is then felt to absorb all aliveness in the infant, sucking in or swallowing up the infant's lively, though painful, projections, without echo, recoil, or reflection, leaving the infant with an experience of depletion and emptiness. I believe that this experience, of an *absorbent mother*, could result in a diminution of normal projective identification as a means of communication with the mother, in an attempt on the part of the infant to preserve the nascent self.

The abovestated by itself or in consort with the experience of a mother whose *feedback* has a malignant quality—reflecting back to the infant elements more terrifying and unthinkable than those originally projected—may result in the infant's inability to utilize an adequately containing mother. In this instance normal projective and introjective activities are curtailed and the development of an apparatus for mentation is truncated.

In summary, the *obdurate, absorbent,* and *unthinking* objects involved in a deficient containing experience can lead either to hyperbolic or massive projective identification and an insatiable search for maternal sanctuary or the inhibition or atrophy of projective and introjective functions. In either case a mind for thinking, or the thoughts themselves, may fail to develop. As in the case of deficient holding, where a precocious enemy-mind-psyche evolves, requiring somatic localization, so too sensory experience deficiently contained by the primary object remains unmentalized, requiring evacuation or self-containment in the somatic realm.

THE IMPORTANCE OF SYMBOL FORMATION

The development of the psychic structures, necessary for effective handling of painful experiences inherent in living, is dependent upon the capacity for symbolic functioning. The earliest proto-symbols, based on sensual and perceptual input, are like "symbolic equations" (Segal 1957), undifferentiated from the object symbolized. The transformation of these concrete symbols into psychic representations of the original object relies upon the introjection of a container that can deal with anxiety in relation to the object in order for substitutions to be effected (Bion 1962). Symbol formation is the necessary prerequisite in a progression from evacuation to mentation, from the somatic to the psychic action.

As discussed previously, deficiencies in the earliest maternal holding environment abandon the infant to experience the most severe varieties of anxiety; those of unintegration (liquefaction and evaporation, non-being, and total loss). One of the many reactions provoked by prolonged exposure to such anxieties is a precocious "over activity of mental functioning" (Winnicott 1949, p. 246) or "premature ego-development" (James 1986, Klein 1930, p. 244). Subsequent deficiencies of containment, inhibiting aggressive and epistemophilic impulses, may further jeopardize the capacity to use (in Winnicott's sense) primary objects, thereby thwarting development of a mind for thinking. I will now highlight the deleterious effects of such pseudo-maturity upon normal ego development and, consequently, upon the development of symbol formation according to Klein and will show how this relates to the development of somatic symptomatology.

In her paper "On the Importance of Symbol Formation in the Development of Ego," Klein (1930) makes Winnicott's concept of over activity of mental functioning explicit as precocious ego development, which she further elaborates as premature empathy or premature identification with the object, consisting in early genitality. She later describes this as premature onset of the depressive position with its incumbent anxieties related to remorse and desires for reparation felt toward the ambivalently loved object. Constitutional intolerance of such complex anxieties, which require prior establishment of a good internal object, make further moves toward development virtually impossible. "Ruthless love" (Winnicott 1965) is not an option since the consequences are not able to be borne by the immature ego. Thus the infant retreats to an autosensual world where phantasy is restricted to expression in visceral and muscular spheres, and symbol formation is stopped at the level of symbolic equation at best, where the symbol remains undifferentiated from what it symbolizes.

Anxiety must be tolerated long enough for substitutions, displacements, and equations to be affected. Intolerance results in a retreat to a mode of prenatal existence and absolute identification with the object. This confusion between self and object extends to confusion of ego with the object and consequently to a confusion of the symbol with the object symbolized. This is relevant to the problem of somatic symptoms in general since anxiety that cannot be worked over through contact with the mother will remain at a concrete level, perhaps finding expression solely in the somatic realm. In extreme forms this dilemma can be observed in the so-called alexithymic person who lacks words for feelings or affective states and expresses these states somatically.

THE DEATH INSTINCT

I think it important to state here that I am adopting the view of the "death instinct" as representative of a phylogenetic or "primal organismic panic" (Grotstein 1984) and its derivative destructiveness as a move toward survival (Symington 1985). Such primitive defenses against early anxieties eventually, in health, give way to thinking and constructive action that is attuned to reality through repeated reciprocal interactions with "good-enough" maternal holding and containment. Subsequently, a psychic structure equipped to perform this function develops independent of an external object.

In the event that such ego structures cease developing, primitive defenses maintain ascendancy and, in their hyperbole, prove inimicable to life itself, as demonstrated in perverse, autistic, psychotic, and phobic pathologies. It must be remembered, however, that these defenses against primitive anxiety, no matter how lethal, always represent on one level an effort at reorganization and reconstitution of the self.

Paranoid-schizoid, manic, and depressive defenses are utilized in very concrete, archaic ways through somatic channels established in (but never abandoned after) infancy. For example, in autism, symptoms are not symbols or metaphors set up for the purpose of conveying distress, but are concrete things used to plug holes and gaps in the psychic skin. In perversions, pain is often a symbolic equivalent of a holding mother that lacks psychic representation, remaining at a somato-sensual level of experience. In psychosis, delusion as a system of pseudo-thought and hallucination as a mode of perception are alternatives to a painful reality that cannot be tolerated due to a lack of alpha-function. In phobic reactions, non-human objects (animals and things) are utilized as containers for terrifying aspects of self and of personal experience in the absence of a containing internal object.

In like manner, I believe that *in psychosomatosis, hypochondriasis and somatic delusion are bodily containers for unbearable pain in the absence of a capacity for mentation.* Avoidance and evasion are of paramount importance in all of these alternatives to experiencing sensations of unintegration that have no access to mentation. In each of these alternatives anxiety remains symbolically equated with the feared object or event and never attains true symbolic meaning as a signal.

THE ORIGINAL PRIMAL SCENE

Melanie Klein (1930) posited that during the stage of oral ambivalence, when the infant's sadism is in ascendancy, the mother's body, attacked and attacking, becomes a source of anxiety. If tolerance for such anxiety is innate (or if anxiety is sufficiently contained by the good breast), the experience of such depressive anxiety leads to displacement of interest from the mother's body to the outside world through symbolic equation, and the development of symbol formation proceeds along with progressive ego development.

The successful working through of this crucial phase of development requires a mother with the capacity to survive her infant's biting attacks, to contain his anxiety without loss of control, that is, without retaliation. Sarlin (1970) referred to this situation, in which the infant at the breast engages in an overtly erotic mouth/ nipple intercourse that can provoke extreme anxiety in both mother and child, as "the original primal scene." The handling of anxieties related to the infant's oral sadism in this early period of life is crucial to the development of symbolic functioning and can, through the compulsion to repeat, provide a genetic basis for later separation anxiety, patterned on the fear of losing the nipple (Sarlin 1970), as well as the basis for later phantasies of violent and sadistic parental intercourse classically described as "primal scene trauma."

The negative outcome of this original primal scene trauma has been described as a regressive step in the direction of the primal unity, a reversal of the process of separation and individuation or a blurring of the distinction between the self and the object (Sarlin 1970). In a sense, Klein (1930) came to a complementary conclusion when she observed that anxiety over premature loss of the nipple leads to a premature identification with or empathy for the mother, which becomes a decisive factor in the inhibition of all destructive impulses, eventuating in impoverishment of phantasy life and symbol formation as a result of "taking refuge in the dark, empty mother's body" (p. 245).

IN SUMMARY

Primitive omnipotent protophantasies, presented in a somato-sensual mode, are employed to protect the individual against overwhelming awareness of the experience of unintegration that threatens the infant with non-being in the event of deficiencies in maternal holding and containing. Various scenarios depicting the outcome of cumulative or chronic deficiencies in these two areas of early environmental experience highlight the lack of development of a thinking mind that modifies experience and creates meaning. The perpetuation of evasive and evacuative maneuvers, although apparently destructive, are deployed in the service of organizing and maintaining a personal sense of existence. These principles have been demonstrated with regard to autistic, perverse, phobic, and psychotic pathologies in the literature. Perhaps the following case example will demonstrate the relevance of these observations to our understanding of psychosomatic pathology, specifically in the instance of bronchial asthma.

Carrie's History

Carrie entered analysis at the age of 33 complaining of night terrors from which she would awaken with severe broncho-constriction necessitating the use of inhalant medication. She was soon to be married for the second time. The first marriage had been characterized by an almost suffocatingly symbiotic closeness from which she had "escaped" in order to return to college after some thirteen years.

Although Carrie's fiancé had been appropriately supportive of her strivings toward independence and personal as well as academic growth outside the relationship, while demonstrating affectionate involvement and interest in their mutual life together, she appeared to alternate between an experience of abandonment on the one hand and of entrapment on the other, which led to violent outbursts and displays of tearful clinging or protective, silent withdrawal from the man she was soon to marry. They were both concerned and puzzled by her seemingly inappropriate reactions and it was finally, at his suggestion, that she decided to seek analysis.

Carrie described her mother as a highly narcissistic woman who had been physically and emotionally abused by a stern and restrictive borderline mother and left unprotected by a loving, if ineffectual, father. The experience of her mother, as it was conveyed by Carrie both in the transference and in associations to childhood events, alternated between two extremes: Mother had seemed either physically and emotionally intrusive, possessive, and insensitive to her individual needs or totally unavailable—masked, asleep, and closed off in a darkened room for most of each day. Her mother was depressed during pregnancy and after Carrie's birth. Mother's depression was not only characterological, but was further exacerbated by her husband's threat of divorce, made shortly before the discovery of the pregnancy, by a series of life-threatening illnesses during the last trimester, and by the death of her father shortly before parturition.

Carrie seemed to idealize her father even though she described him as an alcoholic with a ferocious temper and considerable problems in the area of impulse control. Although the father was experienced as the more nurturing of the parents, his support was felt to be mainly intellectual and financial in nature and he finally divorced the patient's mother when the patient reached puberty, moving across the country and remarrying shortly thereafter. Carrie's two elder siblings left home shortly before the divorce and Carrie remained alone with the mother until the time of her own marriage at age 17. At the age of 21, about the time of the first onset of asthmatic symptoms, Carrie broke off relations with her mother, due ostensibly to a quarrel over financial matters; although the mother pleaded for a reconciliation, the patient remained relentless in her silent withdrawal from the relationship.

It may be important to note that Carrie reported that her mother had often told her that her own mother would punish her disobedience by pinching her so hard that her breath would be taken away by the pain. She also suffered from year-round hay fever, which restricted her breathing, and complained that the father's (and later the patient's) smoking was choking her to death. The father, a heavy smoker, was remembered as suffering from a chronic cough throughout the patient's childhood, and he would often suffer choking attacks and general respiratory distress whenever provoked to rage by the mother, especially when a meal was delayed or poorly prepared.

Shortly after analysis began, Carrie made mention of her asthma as it appeared in the sessions, stating that she had no recollection of any event precipitating the first onset. Relevant to the discussion at hand is a particular pattern of behavior that evolved early on in the treatment and acted as an impediment to free association. I will first report the behavioral pattern as it was observed on many occasions, followed by a description of the underlying "evaporation" phantasy that was slowly revealed over a number of months of analysis. In conclusion, I will present the patient's account of the first asthmatic attack complete with precipitating events, recalled for the first time only after the evaporation phantasy had been analyzed. It is my intention to demonstrate the screen value of this memory, which appears to be representative of certain early infantile experiences at the breast, unremembered and unforgotten, and which may be consistent with the notion of the original primal scene.

Behavioral Pattern

The following pattern was almost always set in motion in response to interpretations of unconscious longing for or aggressive urges felt toward the analyst that appeared in Carrie's associations. In response to such interpretive activity, Carrie would fall into a prolonged silence followed by increasing muscular rigidity, tearful cries, increasing anxiety, decreased breathing, and finally bronchoconstriction. Relief from the latter was obtained through smoking, which, paradoxically, relieved bronchoconstriction, eased respiration, mitigated anxiety, and eventually led to a return of verbal associative activity.

Feeding Phantasy

A gradual analysis of the preceding pattern revealed the following: interpretations seemed to serve as harsh reminders to Carrie of her separate existence, thus disturbing an illusion of at-one-ment with the analyst/mother. Her awareness of separation ushered in the most intense fears of discontinuity of being. The interpretations were felt-proof of rejection and constituted an intolerable "gap" or "black hole of despair" evoking the threat of unintegration. Carrie's baby-self, unheld or dropped, began to "come apart." Her tenuous solid state of bodily integration was primarily defended through rigid silence or "stonewalling."

Any attempt at breaking the silence seemed to diminish the effectiveness of this defense and necessitated reinforcement by increasing bodily rigidity. Further interventions exacerbated the sense of discontinuity as unintegration took on the form of dissolution or liquefaction, literally dissolving Carrie to tears. Feeble attempts at collecting herself in absorbent mother/analyst/tissues failed to mitigate the anxiety inherent in this state of dissolution. In this "liquid state," fears of spilling away escalated into an ever-greater fear of evaporation.

Carrie's efforts to restore a state of at-one-ment with the analyst/mother (via mental confusion) backfired as she appeared to experience her increasing inability to "gather her thoughts together" in a coherent, organized way as a "diffusion in air." In such a dilemma, breathing came to a halt as exhaling was tantamount to losing her self, now felt to be reduced to a gaseous state of invisibility. The bronchoconstriction that followed seemed to be a last ditch effort aimed at holding a self, equated with life's breath, safely inside her lungs.

Subsequent interpretations conveying some understanding of Carrie's terror seemed to re-establish an awareness of the existence of a good external object, resulting in a plethora of conflicting feelings. The constricting, autistic-like rescue attempt would have to be abandoned in favor of connecting (verbally) with the good object/analyst. Thus the desire for fusion led to a fear of loss of the invisible self, a fear of not being found or of being misunderstood; a fear of being "inhaled" or "absorbed" by the analyst, the negative consequence of fulfillment of the wish to get inside the analyst; the fear of suffocating the good object/self, which is inhaled and trapped in the lungs equated with the "good" interpretations taken in not by a mind which could think, but by way of respiratory introjection.

These conflicts appeared to be resolved temporarily through the use of cigarettes. A "smoke screen"[3] was used to

---

3. Since the original publication of the paper on which this chapter is based, I have been reminded of Anzieu's discussion (1985) in which he writes:

The fear of losing the object fulfilling the role of auxiliary protective shield is most often encountered when the child's upbringing has been entrusted to the mother's own mother . . . and when she has taken care of him with such perfection both qualitative and quantitative, that he has not achieved the possibility or necessity of self-support. Dependence on drugs may then seem to be a solution, to create a barrier of fog or smoke between the Ego and external stimuli. Support for the protective shield may be sought from the dermis if the epidermis proves deficient: this is Bick's "muscular second skin" or Reich's "character armour" (p. 103).

This passage is particularly apposite with regard to Carrie who—due to her own mother's postpartum depression—was handled by a quite competent and devoted nanny, as well as by her older teenage sister who she was told treated her like a baby doll throughout the first year of life.

hold, protect, and lend visibility and substance to Carrie's diffused self. With the return of breathing and verbal associations, bronchoconstriction decreased, anxiety was attenuated, and Carrie relaxed, once again feeling "pulled together."

The Screen Memory

This analysis of the evaporation phantasy led to the recovery of the following memory. Carrie's first asthma attack had occurred while she was in the process of feeding her horse, described as a beautiful, young, and spirited female with which she strongly identified. This young and impulsive mare had the habit of rearing up on her hind legs, in an excited display of impatience, while her mistress prepared the evening feed. Carrie recalled how this behavior would provoke anxiety within her because she feared injury to the animal who might fall or develop "colic" or a twisted intestine that could lead to a painful death. She feared injury to herself as well, if the mare should become too excited during feeding. She further explained that this mare was like a young stallion and, in her exuberance, was capable of trampling the patient to bits if she should inadvertently be knocked to the ground. Thus it was on her way to the barn, carrying the food, that Carrie experienced an acute attack of bronchoconstriction that necessitated a trip to the emergency room of the hospital where the diagnosis of asthma was made.

Over time, the following construction developed: in Carrie's mind the horse was identified with her own passive/female baby-self who, it was feared, would get colic and die, falling to pieces if not fed/nursed on demand. At the same time, the horse was also identified with an active/masculine baby-self who became excitedly aggressive toward the breast/mother in its zesty, impatient attempt at feeding. The patient, who identified with both the guilty, anxious, worried mother who fears she has harmed the horse/baby and the fearful, attacked, and injured mother who is trampled to bits while attempting to feed the horse/baby, was overwhelmed with persecutory *and* depressive anxiety. This situation resonated with Carrie's emotional experience at a primitive level of mind. Lacking the capacity for symbolic representation, she resorted to somatic activity out of necessity.

It might be concluded that Carrie's experience at the breast of a depressed and therefore unresponsive mother led to both the fear of starvation (annihilation of the self) and the fear of the destruction of the feeding breast (destruction of the object). Intolerable states of persecutory and depressive anxiety, experienced in the absence of an adequate holding and containing object (internal or external), could not be modified or transformed but were instead evaded through specific somatic channels that were sensitized by parental fantasies centered around or about respiratory processes.

In the analytic situation, the analyst's interpretive activity, equated with feeding, evoked fears of irreparable damage to the self and the object. Tears were experienced as evidence of liquefaction, and eventually, breathing was equated with evaporation. Bronchoconstriction, aimed at reorganization of a fragmenting self, was eventually replaced by the holding and containing functions of the analyst, which allowed for greater integration, and a productive capacity for mourning began to develop.

THEORETICAL DISCUSSION

The patient's history, when taken together with the analytic observations of her behavior and the uncovered phantasies and memories (associated with the asthmatic attacks in the past as well as in the analytic present), appears to support the following hypothesis.

Carrie's history, in concert with her experience of the analyst in the transference, reveals certain deficiencies in the mother's capacity for holding and containing primitive anxieties experienced in infancy. The holding capacity of the mother was seemingly diminished by her preoccupation with her own life-threatening physical illness as well as with the threat of loss of her husband's supportive presence and the death of her father in the last trimester of pregnancy. Carrie's mother's capacity to contain her baby's anxiety was decreased by her own reactive depression, her characterological narcissism, and a deficiency of alpha-function. Thus the physical presence of the mother was overly relied upon by Carrie. It might be said that this situation contributed to a psyche-soma split and consequent precocious mental activity on the part of the patient, resulting in a premature identification with and empathy toward the breast/mother and, subsequently, the premature onset of depressive anxiety, which may have in its turn contributed to the arrested development of symbolic functioning, inhibiting the elevation of anxiety to the level of a signal. Thus anxiety remained equated with the threat of evaporation. As such, the experience in infancy of primitive anxieties of unintegration, persecution, and depression appeared to have remained unmentalized due to the lack of an adequate holding and containing object; consequently, somatization of these anxieties, which re-emerged in adulthood, provided an alternative solution to psychic pain that was felt to be unbearable.

The choice of symptom appears to have been determined, at least in part, by the fantasies and behaviors of parental figures. Gradually, as the analyst proved to be an adequate container, Carrie's most primitive anxieties were made more tolerable. Subsequently, as phantasies emerged and were elaborated through the analytic dialogue, true mental representation was attained, obviating the necessity for somatic expression and containment of anxieties in asthmatic symptoms. Concomitantly, the patient was able to relinquish her protective smoke screen during the analytic sessions.

THEORETICAL STATEMENT

In consideration of the previously reported clinical material, I propose that *some forms of bronchial asthma may be conceived of as pre-
historic, self-survival tactics, aimed against the felt-threat of evaporation,
which remains an unmentalized experience in the individual due to
impairment of "holding" and "containing" functions.* Etiologically, this
concept of bronchial asthma places its emphasis upon the individual's response to deficiencies in early maternal preoccupation and
alpha-function, which underlie the later failure of the asthmatically
predisposed individual to mentalize the threat of evaporation that
is consequently defended against in a concrete, somatic fashion.

For the purpose of clarification, the terms used above will now
be elaborated more fully. First, the term *pre-historic* was originally
used by Freud (1905, p. 52), referring to the phase of preverbal
infancy characterized by both motoric and psychic helplessness
(Freud 1926, p. 167). This period appears to correspond with Bion's
"proto-mental" level of functioning (1977a), which continues to exist
as a state of mind.

The term *self-survival tactic* is used to distinguish asthma as a
passive-reflexive expression of or reaction to organismic panic
(Grotstein 1984), and therefore as a precursor to later defensive
operations of the ego, that is, to those more highly elaborated
unconscious fantasies that require a certain level of mentation. As
such, asthma may be conceptualized as a primary realization or
protophantasy of maternal sanctuary represented in a concrete,
somato-sensual mode.

The *threat of evaporation* (Carrie's term) may be one that under-
lies the asthmatic symptom specifically and respiratory symptoms
in general. I believe this to be a specific and circumscribed variety
of the unintegration experience that implies the feeling state of
invisibility, amorphousness, and diffusion and the danger of indefi-
nite expansiveness inherent in the earliest phase of infancy prior
to the formation of a psychic skin, after which a solid core self is
said to be established. Before, during, and for some time after the

establishment of this solid state of self, an external containing object is essential. The functions of the container/mother, somewhat more complex and sophisticated than that of the skin-mother that precedes her, have been previously discussed.

This containing-mother plays a critical role in determining whether or not the experience of the threat of evaporation is mentalized, that is, whether or not sense data, internal or external, are successfully transformed into symbols as mental representations that are organized and integrated, and whether or not anxiety of a primitive nature is raised to the level of a signal affect. Left uncontained, sense data, experienced in phantastic terms as a threat of evaporation, remain at a concrete level or the level of symbolic equation (Segal 1957). As a concrete object lodged in the psyche, these data lie untransformed, finding both containment and expression in the somatic symptom. Uncontained sensory experiences are merely accretions of stimuli that can neither be used to create meaning nor can they be stored as memories in the mind. Such experiences are neither remembered nor forgotten, but are instead held in abeyance in the somatic realm.

To further utilize this patient's experience of evaporation as metaphor, we might think in terms of physical chemistry. In order for a substance to be transformed from a gaseous state to a solid state, it must first be constantly contained. Heat causes the molecules of the substance to agitate in rapid and random fashion, which increases the pressure on the walls of the container. If the container is not strong enough, if it lacks flexibility, or if it is not equipped to cool down the "contained," it will surely burst and the gaseous substance will gradually dissipate in the air outside the container, lost among other substances that constitute that air.

Similarly, if the relatively unintegrated infant-self is to develop a cohesive, solid core identity, it must be consistently contained. The heat of the affective moment or sensory experience (be it the "ecstasy of one-ness" or the "tantrum of two-ness") may result in "turbulence" of raw sensory elements in rapid motion, bombarding the psychic walls of the container, producing a state of elevated emotional pressure. If she is to maintain functioning, the container/mother must have sufficient strength of character, emotional flexibility, and the capacity for cool thinking to modify the rate of projective bombardment, facilitating the development of a self-structure that has solidity and organization.

Deficiencies in holding and containing call into play improvisational methods of attaining solid organization of a self, albeit based upon false assumptions with few links to external reality. The somatic symptoms of bronchial asthma may be viewed collectively as one method of tentatively attaining a sensation of a solid organization of a self while under the threat of evaporation that has failed to be mentalized.

In the transference situation, libidinal wishes and aggressive urges harken back to the original primal scene (the nipple and the mouth). Separations are reminiscent of early disconnection, the experience of emotional unresponsiveness, intolerable ecstasy flowing over uncontained, and weaning as the final abandonment—all leading to unbearable frustration. Such intense frustration evokes aggressive, destructive impulses toward the object of longing, which leads to extreme anxieties of a depressive nature and, regressively, to paranoid anxieties and eventually those of unintegration, which are unmentalized and consequently somatized. Thus the bronchoconstriction of asthma serves to ward off unintegration anxiety by acting to form a second skin that holds the self together; paranoid anxiety, by containing the good self protected inside; and depressive anxiety, by constricting the bad self within, thereby protecting the good external object.

CONCLUSIONS

It might be concluded that certain *unmentalized experiences* in early object relations play a pivotal role in the emotional etiology of psychosomatic asthma in some patients. The selection or choice of the asthmatic symptom as an expression of a deficient environment or a sign of developmental arrest is determined (as concerns the psychic component) by the conscious and unconscious fantasies, conflicts, wishes, and fears of the primary object(s) that impinge upon the infant (and perhaps even the foetus) in the early, formative stages of development.

The concept of a psychosomatic aspect of the personality, rather than a psychosomatic personality or a psychosomatic patient, may prove to be of some merit. Likewise it may be worthwhile to consider a deficient area of alpha-function (or a circumscribed or limited deficiency in the holding and containing function of the primary object) with respect to a particular (rather than a general) vulnerability in the infant. This "coincidence of vulnerability" in both infant and the primary caretaker may be seen to have unfortunate consequences in terms of the subsequent development of mental structure.

Until recently, traditional psychoanalytic approaches to the treatment of psychosomatic asthma have been aimed toward seeking out conflicts and phantasies within the mind that seem to exert their pathological effects upon the body. With the introduction of the notion of *unmentalized experience*, an approach is implied in which the analyst attempts to shift somato-sensory memories and protophantasies from the body into the mind, where they may be represented for the first time. The aim of psychoanalysis then is to build psychic structure, to further develop a mind-ego from an original body-ego.

The capacity of the analyst to assist the patient in transcending and transforming early environmental failures and innate deficiencies is an essential factor in facilitating the gradual relinquishment of asthma as a self-survival tactic. By presenting him or herself as a reliable, durable, and flexible (although transitional) object and as a benign, reflective, and understanding presence, the analyst serves to repair and promote growth within the internal world of the patient.

7

Examining a Fragment of a Fragment: Freud's "Dora" Case Revisited

I encourage psychoanalysts to engage in psychoanalytic games, to make as many models as they choose out of any material available to them.

[W. R. Bion, *"The Grid"*]

INTRODUCTION

In this chapter, which may be considered an appendum to Chapter 6, I will compare and contrast the theory presented in that chapter with some previous notions about the etiology and meaning of bronchial asthma using, for demonstrative purposes, a hypothetical reevaluation of material from Freud's "Fragment of a Case of Hysterical Conversion" (1905), which may be familiar to most readers as the "Dora" case.

To begin with, a careful scrutiny of Freud's ideas, as set forth so elegantly in his case report of Dora, will serve to guide us through his early view of asthma as a symptom of hysterical conversion or "the translation of a purely psychical excitation into physical terms"

(Freud 1905, p. 53). Alongside Freud's original ideas, I will present new ways of considering his data and of updating his notions, utilizing our present-day knowledge of primitive mental states to transpose libido theory into object relations theory.

More specifically, in this chapter I hope to demonstrate the importance of the influence of parental fantasies on the choice of symptom, the role of identificatory processes in "specificity" of asthmatic pathology, the earliest roots of the primal scene as a contributory factor, and the sexualization of disturbances in object relations. I will also highlight the hazards of premature ego development as it contributes to the cessation of phantasy elaboration and the truncation of symbol formation, and I will bring into focus the notion of the asthmatic symptom as a beta-screen or second skin employed as a substitute for maternal containing, and the concept of bronchoconstriction as a substitute for maternal holding.

FREUD'S DORA

In many ways Dora may be compared to Carrie, the patient presented in the previous chapter. Freud (1905) points out that Dora had a "tender attachment" (p. 18) to her father, whose "lung trouble" or "tuberculosis" (p. 19) genetically predisposed Dora to asthma, rendering her own lungs "somatically compliant" (p. 41). Perhaps this concept of a "genetic predisposition" toward respiratory illness might today be expanded to include, in addition to those innate factors transmitted through the genes, notions involving complex identificatory processes, both intrapsychic and interpersonal, that utilize phantasy as a means of sensitizing specific organs and making them ripe for somatization.

Although Freud might have seen my patient Carrie, who—like Dora—was doubly endowed by both parents with such a predisposing genetic weakness on a purely biological level, I think it could also be argued that Carrie's tender attachment to both her mother and father (exemplified by her apparent introjective identification with the mother choked by the father's smoke, and father choked by his own rage at the mother) may well have contributed greatly to the designation of her lungs as a likely arena for somatic acting-out of phantasies concerning analogous objects in her internal world.

Freud portrays Dora's mother as a woman obsessed with mindless activities, having "no understanding of her children's more active interests" (p. 20) and no insight into her own illness. He tells us that Dora's mother's house was too sterile "to use or to enjoy" (p. 20), while my patient Carrie complained that her mother's house was too disorderly to use or to enjoy.

In the experience of both Carrie and Dora, the mother's house can be seen to stand for their respective minds, which were unsuited to contain and therefore to understand the active, aggressive, and epistemophilic strivings of these intellectually precocious youths. Here Freud appears to associate this failure on the part of Dora's mother with Dora's withdrawal from and subsequent critical devaluation of her.

Although Freud acknowledges the "substitution of the sexual object of the moment [the penis] for the original object [the nipple] or the finger in masturbation which serves the same function of oral gratification" (p. 52), he fails to appreciate the pivotal role of the breast/mother of infancy in the etiology of Dora's hysterical conversion symptom. Almost as if in an afterthought, Freud recognized that "Dora's homosexual (gynecophilic) love for Frau K was the strongest current in her mental life" (p. 120 n). Later on he adds that "[Dora's] remorseless craving for revenge . . . against Frau K was suited, as nothing else was, to conceal the current of feeling that ran contrary to it—the magnanimity with which she forgave the treachery of a friend she loved . . ." (p. 120 n).

Here Freud fails to link this insight with the fact of Dora's withdrawal from and criticism of her mother, which is clearly an effort on Dora's part to conceal her forgiveness of her mother, and an attempt to massively deny the wrongs (traumas) experienced at the breast of an often mindless mother who could not contain her own or her child's states of ecstasy and tantrum in the nursing situation.

Just what *was* Freud so preoccupied with and what *did* he posit as etiologically significant in the development of Dora's asthma? He tells us that the first onset of "purely nervous asthma" (p. 21) occurred at the age of 8 after a mountain-climbing expedition on which Dora presumably overexerted herself. The father was away from home during a period of improved health, and Freud tells us that on the night before his departure, Dora had overheard his heavy, labored breathing during intercourse with her mother. Therefore, Freud inferred that Dora's asthma was a "detached fragment of the act of copulation" (p. 80) between the parental couple; a symbolic equivalent of or perhaps an acting out of her identification with the copulating parents or "sympathetic excitement" (p. 80) as an expression of the wish to bring back the lost father.

Freud then correlates the cessation of Dora's masturbatory activities with the onset of her nervous asthma and her "inclination toward anxiety" (p. 80). The equation he fails to observe is that of Father's overexertion with Mother in the sexual act—Dora's overexertion with her finger in the masturbatory act—Dora's earlier thumbsucking—Dora's overexertion (mouth and nipple) in the act of nursing, the "original primal scene" (Sarlin 1970).

While Freud cites a triad of psychological determinants in the etiology of hysterical conversion (namely, psychical trauma, a conflict of affects, and finally a disturbance in the sphere of sexuality), he falls short of penetrating the deepest layer of meaning in each of these areas. He apparently maintains that the earliest sexual excitement—provoked by witnessing the primal scene at age 8, compounded by the kiss from Herr K at age 14, and the seduction at the lake at age 17 by Herr K—constitutes a cumulative trauma contributing to the formation of Dora's conversion symptoms.

The "conflict" referred to by Freud appears to be that which exists between the instincts and the outside world, while the disturbance in sexuality was identified as Dora's phobic reactions to young men in states of sexual excitement, the cessation of her masturbatory activities, and the repression of her sexual drive.

Following Freud's own suggestion when he states: "Even in cases in which the first symptoms had not already set in in childhood, I have been driven to trace back the patients' life history to their earliest years" (p. 27), I propose that the psychical traumas that laid the foundation for Dora's asthma are to be found in the original primal scene (Sarlin 1970); that the conflict of affects was one between love and hatred felt toward the mother of infancy; and that the sexual disturbance is really a profound disturbance in the sphere of object relations that has been sexualized.

To support this view of Dora's case, I will recall Freud's own brilliant investigative data as follows. Freud questioned his patient about the source of her sexual knowledge, and at first found out that ". . . she had forgotten the source of all her information on the subject" (p. 31). However, later references reveal that both her nanny and Frau K were sources of knowledge on sexual matters.

I would here posit that such knowledge of intercourse (the excitation that traumatized Dora) stemmed initially from her own experience as an active participant in the original primal scene, where she learned from her mother of the relationship of the nipple and the mouth. This knowledge was later displaced by her knowledge of the penis and the vagina, signifying the original relationship. This "true amnesia" or "gap in the memory into which not only old recollections but even quite recent ones have fallen" (p. 17) could be the consequence of experiences that remained unmentalized, and the gap into which such experiences fell could be seen as analogous to the hole or wound left by a premature loss of the nipple.

It might be even further hypothesized that this primary trauma was reinforced by the father's absence at the onset of the first asthma attack, as well as by the "disillusionment she had been caused by [Frau K's] betrayal" (p. 63), with both the father and Frau K representing Dora's mother (the original object).

Freud (1905) recognizes fellatio as "a new version of . . . a prehistoric impression of sucking at the mother's breast" (p. 52), and he later acknowledges the nursing situation as a prototype of the expression of sexual satisfaction in adulthood. But what difficulties arise when this situation at the breast is wrought with dissatisfaction and frustration?

The solution to this question may be found in Klein's expansions of Freud's theories regarding the infant's libidinal, aggressive, and epistemophilic instincts and their earliest vicissitudes with relation to the primary object—the breast. Invoking Klein's conceptualizations in the case of Dora will aid us in unraveling the complex meanings inherent in her asthmatic symptom.

First, we are told that Dora fears father's overexertion in the sexual act with the mother, leading to his respiratory distress. Her own asthmatic symptom signifies her identification with him (the father/penis). We are also informed that Dora equates the penis with the mother's nipple. From these facts we can infer the existence of an internal object that represents the nipple/mother, overexerted and in danger of destruction by the greedy, sadistic, frustrated, sucking mouth. The anxiety here is depressive in nature.

We are also notified of Dora's fear of injury to herself by thumbsucking, masturbation, the erect member of Herr K, and the sexually excited young men in affectionate conversation, all of which may signify her profound fear of the excited nipple. From this we can infer the existence of an internal object—representing the infant/Dora/mouth—in danger of illness/damage by the overexcited and exciting nipple/mother. The anxiety here is paranoid/ schizoid in nature.

Freud (1905) concludes that the asthmatic symptom "formed the boundary between two phases of [Dora's] sexual life, of which the first was masculine in character, and the second feminine" (p. 82). By transforming the concepts of masculine and feminine into those of "active" and "passive" (Freud (1905), it might be understood that Dora's asthma formed the skin or boundary between those active and passive internal objects, representing the nursing couple in the original primal scene, that were felt to threaten and destroy one another. The development of this somatic boundary may be viewed as a compensatory move toward replacing a deficient alpha-membrane (Bion 1962).

Further on in his discussion of Dora's case, Freud takes up his notion of the oedipal situation, suggesting that the conflict that plagued Dora consisted in the opposition of her sexual impulses toward her father (and Herr K) and her fear of loss of mother's (and Frau K's) love. He implies that one way in which Dora might have attempted to resolve this conflict was through an overt expression of her gynecophilic love for Frau K. He also suggested that Dora's neurotic or hysterical symptoms were an alternative to such perverse solutions to this oedipal conflict, which he "assumed to be more intense from the very first in the case of those children whose constitution marks them down for neurosis, who develop prematurely and have a craving for love" (p. 56).

This last statement foreshadows Melanie Klein's own (1945b), emphasizing "the far-reaching and lasting influence of every facet of the relation to the mother upon the relation to the father" (p. 389). She observed that early deprivation at the breast leads to the early onset of the Oedipus situation as the infant turns away from the frustrating breast toward the penis. The subsequent early identification with the mother results in archaic superego formation and the substitution of genital gratification for oral and anal pleasures. If this progress is set in motion prematurely (that is, prior to the ego's readiness to tolerate depressive anxiety), premature empathy for the mother will result in a truncation of phantasy life and severe inhibition of the development of symbol formation (M. Klein 1930).

While Freud highlights the little girl's fear of loss of the mother's love in retaliation for incestuous wishes toward the father, Klein (1928) denotes her "fear of having her body attacked and her loved inner objects destroyed" (p. 390) as the central anxiety, and posits this as "the underlying psychic cause of conversion hysteria" (p. 211).

Reaching beyond Freud's understanding of Dora's asthma (the somatic representative of the exciting act of copulation between the parents) to Klein's understanding of such symptoms (depressive concern for objects represented by the affected organ, or perhaps the omnipotent control of objects, represented by the air taken in and the restriction of exhalation) brings us a bit further toward possibly discovering the earliest roots of the emotional etiology of Dora's asthmatic conversion.

Bick (1968) and Bion (1962), however, provide the tools with which we might probe even deeper toward discovering these roots. One might see Dora's asthma as representing a phantasy of holding onto the father/mother/nipple for fear of being dropped and falling infinitely (the disillusionment as a deficiency in holding), or one might view Dora's asthma as a beta-screen existing where a deficiency in alpha-function (the "betrayal" as failure in containment) results in an inability to convert sense impressions—of the emotional experience of being dropped—into food for thought.

To postulate the role of unmentalized experience in the etiology and treatment of Dora's symptoms is consistent with Freud's statement that "the aim of [psychoanalytic] treatment is to remove all possible symptoms and to replace them by conscious thoughts" (1905, p. 18), perhaps his way of suggesting that we set our therapeutic sites on the mentalization of what has been somatized.

CONCLUSIONS

Indeed, it might be concluded that certain unmentalized experiences in early object relations play a pivotal role in the emotional etiology of psychosomatic asthma in some patients. It is also concluded that the selection or choice of the asthmatic symptom—an expression of a deficient environment or a sign of developmental arrest—is determined (as concerns the psychic component) by the unconscious fantasies, conflicts, wishes, and fears of the primary object(s) that impinge upon the infant (and perhaps even the fetus) in the early, formative stages of development.

Additionally, it may be of some merit to conceive of a psychosomatic aspect of the personality rather than a psychosomatic personality or a psychosomatic patient. Likewise it may be worthwhile to consider a deficient area of alpha-function, or a circumscribed or limited deficiency in the holding and containing function of the primary object with respect to a particular (rather than a general) vulnerability (intolerance) in the infant. This occurrence could be termed a *coincidence of vulnerability* in both infant and caretaker, which carries with it some unfortunate consequences for the development of mental structure.

The capacity of the analyst to assist the patient in transcending and transforming such early environmental failures, as well as innate deficiencies, is an essential factor in facilitating the gradual relinquishment of asthma as a self-survival tactic. By presenting himself or herself as a reliable, durable, and flexible—although transitional—object (holding), and as a benign, reflective, and understanding presence (containing), the analyst serves to repair and promote growth within the internal world of the patient.

8

On Adhesive Pseudo-Object Relations: A Theory[1]

Staring into nothingness since time began, there and yet not there she stood. In a world of dreams, shadows, and fantasy, nothing more complex than color and indiscernible sound. With the look of an angel no doubt, but also without the ability to love or feel anything more complex than the sensation of cat's fur against her face.

[Donna Williams, *Nobody Nowhere*]

INTRODUCTION

The concept of "adhesive identification" was first described by Bick (1968, 1986), further developed by Meltzer (1975, Meltzer et al. 1975) and later extended by Tustin (1972, 1980, 1981, 1984b, 1986), as a consequence of refinements in the psychoanalytic method of infant observation and child analysis, particularly the work with autistic children. In her seminal paper, Bick (1968) alluded to a more primitive type of "narcissistic identification" developmentally preceding what is implied in Klein's theory of projective identifica-

---

1. A version of this chapter was previously published in *Contemporary Psychoanalysis* in 1994.

tion. Bick's model for this very early form of "identification" has provoked some workers to revise their psychoanalytic thinking, inspiring them to begin charting yet another dimension of object relations that had previously been little explored; a process "in which the idea of 'getting into' is replaced by that of 'getting in contact with'. This process is very archaic and always appears linked to an object of psychic reality equivalent to the *skin*" (Etchegoyen 1991, p. 574).

In this chapter I will review the work of Bick and others on adhesive identification, exploring the concept of the "psychic skin" and its function with respect to the development of normal/narcissistic object relations. The evolution and refinement of this concept, primarily owing to Frances Tustin's work with autistic children, will then be traced as I attempt to elaborate on the notion of an archaic mode of pseudo-object-relating prehistoric to what has been so well defined and documented by Melanie Klein and her exponents. To accomplish my task, I will compare and contrast normal/narcissistic object relations with what I will herein refer to as *adhesive pseudo-object relations*.

THE FINDINGS OF ESTHER BICK AND BEYOND

Bick (1968) noticed certain behaviors in the infants she observed, leading her to believe that very young babies may experience the absence of boundaries sufficiently capable of holding together mental contents not yet distinguishable or differentiated from bodily contents. Bick (1968) proposed the notion of a "psychic skin"—perhaps similar to the concept of the "ego boundary" (Federn 1952) in the primitive "body ego" (Freud 1923)—which ideally serves to passively bind together the experiences/parts of the nascent self on the way toward integration. She described this psychic skin as a projection of or corresponding to the bodily skin and posited that it is "dependent initially on the introjection of an *external object*, experienced as capable of fulfilling this function" (Bick 1968, p. 484).

I have previously suggested that the "external object" referred to above is a complex, undifferentiated object composed of experiences of continuous interaction between a physically and emotionally "holding" and mentally "containing" mother and the surface of the infant's body as a sensory or sensual organ.

Bick (1968) further hypothesized that "later, identification with this [psychic skin] function of the object supersedes the unintegrated state and gives rise to the [ph]antasy of internal and external space" (p. 484). She posited this phantasy of space as the essential basis for normal adaptive splitting that allows for the idealization of self and object described by Klein (1946).

Along with her understanding of the tendency to relate to objects in a two-dimensional way due to a deficiency of an experience of internal space, Bick (1968) made the crucial distinction between *unintegration* as a helpless, passive state of maximal dependency and the active, defensive maneuvers of splitting or disintegration in the interest of survival and growth: the former associated with annihilation anxiety, the latter related to persecutory and depressive anxieties.

> The need for a containing object would seem in the infantile unintegrated state, to produce a frantic search for an object— a light, a voice, a smell, or other *sensual* object—which can hold the attention and thereby be experienced, momentarily at least, as holding the parts of the personality together. The optimal object is the nipple in the mouth, together with the holding and talking and familiar smelling mother . . . experienced concretely as a skin. . . . Disturbance in the primal skin function can lead to development of a "second skin" formation through which dependence on the object is replaced by a pseudo-independence. [Bick 1968, p. 484]

Bick (1986) later clarified that these "secondary skin devices may arise in collaboration with peculiarities of the maternal care such as muscular or vocal methods" (p. 292). It would also seem that she might concur with Greenacre's (1971) notion of the existence of "early ontogenetically appearing organismal defenses" that later undergo transformation into mental mechanisms of defense in the mature ego, thus suggesting that such primeval defenses as may be subsumed under the category "second skin formation" (for example, adhesive identification) are originally sensual, "nonmental" phenomena constructed to protect the very young infant against

> The catastrophic anxiety of falling-into-space, and the dead-end [which] haunts every demand for change and engenders a deep conservatism and a demand for sameness, stability and support from the outside world. [Bick 1986, p. 299]

Winnicott (1960a) also wrote about the importance of the skin in early object relations. He pointed out that a part of the development taking place in the "holding phase" of infancy (considered to be a phase of "absolute dependence"[2]) is the establishment of the baby's "psychosomatic existence," a primary integration he referred to as the "indwelling of the psyche in the soma." In connection with this, he notes that

> As a further development there comes into existence what might be called a limiting membrane, which to some extent (in health) is equated with the surface of the skin, and has a

---

2. Winnicott (1962) defined absolute dependence as "a stage before the infant has separated out the mother from the self . . . at this stage . . . it is necessary not to think of the baby as a person who gets hungry, and whose instinctual drives may be met or frustrated, but as an immature being who is all the time on the brink of unthinkable anxieties" (p. 57).

position between the infant's "me" and his "not-me." So the infant comes to have an inside and an outside, and a body-scheme. In this way meaning comes to the function of intake and output; moreover, it gradually becomes meaningful to postulate a personal or inner psychic reality for the infant . . . the beginning of a mind as something distinct from the psyche.[3] [p. 45]

Here the work on primitive fantasy, with whose richness and complexity we are familiar through the teachings of Melanie Klein, becomes applicable and appropriate. [p. 45 n]

In his theory of mental development, Winnicott proposed that, in the event of a deficiency in "good-enough mothering" or the earliest "holding environment," the infant is likely to be subjected to sudden and/or chronic awareness of disconnection, the "unthinkable anxieties" (or what Bion referred to as "nameless dreads") that may be associated with a *felt* state of "unintegration." The unthinkable anxieties to which Winnicott (1962, p. 57) referred were enumerated by him as the fears of "(1) going to pieces, (2) falling forever, (3) having no relationship to the body, (4) having no orientation" (p. 58). To those cited by Winnicott, one might add the fear of dissolution or liquefaction (Tustin 1980, 1986), the ter-

---

3. In 1949 Winnicott defined his use of the word "psyche" as "the imaginative elaboration of somatic parts, feelings, and functions, that is, of physical aliveness" (p. 244). Winnicott further clarified that this imaginative elaboration depends upon a fully functional brain, but that it is not localized in the brain. In health, the psyche undergoes a primary integration with the soma and, if the environment is "good enough" and if psychosomatic continuity is undisturbed, a "mind" will develop, not reactively, in order to compensate for or to adapt to a deficient environment, but creatively, as a means of meeting the environment half-way.

ror of suddenly spilling out into space (Symington 1985), and the threat of evaporation (J. Mitrani 1992, 1993b), that is, *the threat of being gone.*

Winnicott also observed that such unthinkable anxieties arise out of the primal state of "unintegration [experienced] in the absence of maternal ego-support" (Winnicott 1962, p. 61). He further stated that these are anxieties that result from privation, "a failure of holding in the stage of absolute dependence" (Winnicott 1962, p. 61), and are thus to be differentiated from disintegration or fragmentation—an active production of chaos—a sophisticated, omnipotent defense that may be associated with deprivation occurring *only* after some measure of ego integration has taken place in the individual.

It is here important to note that the capacity to experience unintegration as relaxation—that is, the "capacity to be alone" (Winnicott 1958b, p. 30) *without anxiety*—can occur *only* after the individual has had the opportunity, through "good-enough mothering" (and the "experience of being alone in the presence of the object") to build up a belief in a benign environment. Without this experience the baby falls into a void of meaninglessness and his otherwise normal state of unintegration *becomes* a "feeling of disintegration" (Winnicott 1949, p. 99), which must be differentiated from disintegration as a defensive phantasy. Such disruptions in the baby's sense of his own "continuity of being" may produce an "over activity of mental functioning" (p. 246), that is, a precocious development of omnipotent phantasies of a defensive nature, produced "to take over and organize the caring for the psyche-soma; whereas in health it is the function of the environment to do this" (p. 246).

This usurpation of environmental functions by the "mind" may lead to confusional states, "second skin" adaptation, and the development of mental functioning as a "thing in itself," what Winnicott termed a "pathological mind-psyche" that is perceived as an enemy to the "true" self and that consequently must be localized for purposes of control. Winnicott's ideas add much needed elaboration to the notion of unintegration and its anxieties, fleshing out Bick's concept of the second skin by articulating its "mental" component.

It is my understanding that Winnicott's pathological mind-psyche is a pseudo-mental apparatus that develops in the event that the environment fails to support the integration of psyche and soma, out of which a "mind" (in Bion's sense of the word) might healthfully develop. I believe that this pathogenetic entity (where intellectual functioning is employed as a "protective shell" in Tustin's sense of the term) may be what Meltzer observed when he spoke of a "mental" apparatus that falls apart in the process of what he understood as unintegration (which he seems to consider a passive defense against anxiety).

In many of his writings (Meltzer 1975, 1978, 1986, Meltzer et al. 1975), Meltzer used the term *dismantling* (in relation to unintegration), which he described as a splitting of the sensory apparatus (and consequently of the experience of the object) into its sensory components, obliterating "common sense." He also used the term *reversal of alpha-function*, assuming that the mental apparatus and the thoughts processed and/or generated by it are stripped of meaning that has previously been established. In viewing unintegration in this light, Meltzer and Ogden (1989a,b) after him seem to suggest that pathological (psychogenic) autism is related to a passive type of destructive "regression" and the collapse of previously developed mental structures.

In contrast to what seems to me to be Meltzer's use of the term, I believe that Winnicott, Bick, and Tustin used the term *unintegration* to designate a natural state of "being" in infancy, existing prior to the mother's application of her capacities for alpha-function to the baby's nascent sensory experiences (beta-elements) that lend support to the baby's innate tendency toward integration of such experiences. Unintegration seems also to be understood, by these last-mentioned authors, as a state of being that *may* be experienced by the baby as a dangerous disintegration *if and when* containment in the mother's mind is inaccessible, prior to the development of a stable "psychic skin" (i.e., the baby's experience of the mother's capacity for "reverie" and his identification of this maternal function with his own physical/psychical skin). Unintegration, taken in this context, may be thought of as a normal primary state that is experienced, felt, feared, and avoided only when average expectable environmental supports are absent, a feeling-state rather than a pathological development that occurs in place of normal mental and emotional growth.

I would suggest that the baby, chronically deficient of a suitable "skin-object," organizes his primary sensory experience (beta-elements) into a beta-screen (Bion 1963) that serves as an impenetrable second skin and provides an illusory and tentative form of integration that is false, a sort of pseudo-mental-maturity not unlike what Winnicott describes as a pathological-mind-psyche.

In a further expansion of Bick's concept of the second skin, Joan Symington (1985) discussed the survival function of this omnipotent protection. One such protective maneuver was described as a tightening or constricting of the smooth muscles of certain internal organs, providing an illusory sensation of a continuous skin, without gaps through which the self "risks spilling out into space . . . never being found and held again" (p. 481). Symington's many examples from infant observations, as well as her experiences of adult patients in the analytic setting, gave credibility to her conclusions that:

> The primitive fear of the state of disintegration underlies the fear of being dependent; that to experience infantile feelings of helplessness brings back echoes of that very early unheld precariousness, and this in turn motivates the patient to hold himself together . . . at first a desperate survival measure . . . gradually . . . built into the character . . . the basis on which other omnipotent defense mechanisms are superimposed. [p. 486]

TUSTIN'S CONCEPT OF ADHESIVE EQUATION

Tustin (1986) pointed out in a discussion of "autistic objects"[4] that, in the absence of a containing presence, pathologically "unintegrated children" (p. 127) quell their unbearable terrors of falling or spilling away forever by creating sensations of adhering to the surfaces of hard "things." These sensations afford the child an immediate, if ephemeral, experience of bodily continuity and safety as the child becomes *equated* with the surface of the object. In the case of autism the child is addicted to this mode of survival. Tustin thus suggested the use of the term *adhesive equation* (p. 127) rather than *adhesive identification*, a term she thought more apposite to understanding certain pathological processes unique to the problem of autistic encapsulation.

Tustin (1992) additionally clarified that autistic children are chronically "stuck" to their mothers in such a way that there can be no space between them, that is, no space in which a true (object) relationship can develop. She noted that "Bick was aware that autistic children [in contrast to "schizophrenic-type" or "symbiotically psychotic children"] cannot identify, so she came to call it *adhesive identity*" (Tustin 1992). Tustin emphatically underscores the point that without an awareness of space, there can be no relationship and without relationship, the process of identification cannot be set in motion. It might be said that adhesive equation serves to establish a *sensation of existence* rather than a *sense of self and object*. Tustin (1986) also called attention to Gaddini's (1969) term *imitative fusion* as yet another way of conceptualizing this phenomenon.

----

4. Tustin (1980) distinguishes autistic objects from objects (animate or inanimate) in the ordinary sense in that the former are not related to as objects, but rather are used for the tactile sensations they engender upon the surface of the skin of the subject. Such sensations serve to distract one from unbearable experiences while providing an illusion of safety, strength, and impermeability.

Gaddini (1969) understood the phantasy of fusion as "an attempt to gain a vicarious identity, magically acquired through [fusional] imitation" (p. 478), an idea very much in keeping with Bick's (1986) description of the second skin as an act of "mimicry." Even earlier than Gaddini, H. Deutsch (1942) described the "as-if personality" as one existing in a state of "imitative identification." She noticed that these patients behaved "as if" they themselves *were* their loved objects. Through her years of work with autistic patients, Tustin (1992) came to understand this as a "delusory state of fusion" rather than a special case of identification.

In France, Anzieu (1989, 1990) and his co-workers delineated an entire category of second skin phenomena. This group of clinicians, independent of the Kleinian school, has used the term *psychic envelopes* to talk about the encapsulating protections that may be constructed out of auditory, gustatory, kinesthetic, visual, and olfactory sensations as well as affects.

Ogden (1989a,b) coined the term *autistic–contiguous position* to denote a distinct psychological organization more primitive than Klein's paranoid-schizoid and depressive positions. Ogden (1989a) suggested that this position is "an integral part of normal development through which a distinctive mode of experience is generated," a position, rather than a stage, with its own form of object-relatedness, set of anxieties, and defenses.

While Ogden's ideas are both interesting and valuable, the focus of this chapter diverges from his in several ways. While Ogden describes the nature of the infant's autistic–contiguous object relationships as a presymbolic dialectic between continuity and edgedness—between boundedness and at-one-ment with a subjective-object—*I am here considering the development of an enduring mode of "adhesive pseudo-object relations" as an asymbolic aberration of normal development, rooted in traumatic experiences of extreme privation occurring in utero and/or in early infancy, which have prematurely interrupted the necessary development of and trust in the "rhythm of safety" between mother and infant, resulting in the crippling of this emerging elemental state of subjectivity and the gradual development of true objectivity.*

While I believe that such an aberrant mode of pseudo-relating may (like the autistic enclave in the neurotic personality) exist on a "dual track" (Grotstein 1986) alongside normal/narcissistic object relations, I maintain that (in an enduring and rigidified form) adhesive pseudo-object relations are nearly always *pathologically defensive* and, in turn, pathogenetic and consequently obstructive to the ongoing development of normal object relatedness. In other words, whereas normal presymbolic "auto-sensuality" (Tustin 1986) is the seed that, when cultivated and nurtured within the context of human relationship, germinates, sprouts, and grows into object relations proper, I believe that if experiences of a sensory nature are left unprocessed by a thinking and feeling object, symbolic meaning fails to evolve out of the rudiments of the existential experience inherent in sensory contiguity and rhythmicity and these untransformed and "unmentalized experiences" (J. Mitrani 1992, 1993b, 1995b) become rigidified and hypertrophied as fortified protections against awareness of those primeval experiential states of terror related to bodily/emotional separateness.

MELTZER'S HISTORICAL AND TECHNICAL CONTRIBUTIONS

In a paper that I have quoted from extensively in Chapter 1, Meltzer (1975) provided an interesting account of observations that led up to the development of the concept of adhesive identification, the hallmark of a primitive narcissistic mental state preceding the paranoid-schizoid position of Melanie Klein. That paper enlarged the findings reported by him and his co-workers (Meltzer et al. 1975) and led to alterations in their technique of working with such elemental states in adults as well as in children. Meltzer described how he and Bick began to notice that interpreting projective identification in the customary way seemed off the mark in certain cases. They felt that something else had to be going on, something that was connected with identificatory processes and the problem of narcissism, but that seemed to have a different phenomenology from that gathered under the rubric of projective identification. They were able to trace the problem to certain states of infantile catastrophic anxiety and the failure of maternal containment. "When these infants got anxious, their mothers got anxious too and then the infant got more anxious and a spiral of anxiety tended to develop . . . which ended with the infant going into some sort of . . . disorganized state" (Meltzer 1975a, p. 295).

Meltzer recalled that Bick began to observe that some adults were also subject to these states of disorganization. While in the grip of these states they were paralyzed, unable to do anything but sit and shake. This was not anxiety in the ordinary sense, but rather a confusion that had to be waited out until it went away. The material of the analysis of such patients evoked an image of something not held together, as if their skins were full of holes or missing altogether. Alternate means of holding things together—such as intelligent thinking, talking, explanations, or repetitive movements—were often employed in these patients' attempts to pull themselves together.

These phenomena were similar to those they had observed in autistic children who often functioned as if there were no spaces, as if things were not solid but were merely two-dimensional surfaces they might lean against or get some comforting sensation from. Since words went right through them, their responses to interpretations were delayed, often suggesting that little had been held inside except a sense of disturbance that they eventually reacted to or against.

As a result of these observations, what had been previously thought to be associated with "motivation"—the problem of "negative therapeutic reaction" related to envy, masochism, jealousy and unconscious guilt—could be considered as a manifestation of a *structural defect*. Meltzer warned that such patients must be expected to fall to pieces occasionally, and when they do, we must be on the lookout for particular countertransference problems that test our ability to contain the patient, and that we must have the capacity to worry about these patients who seem to need to be worried about, although they do not ask us to. He admonishes us not to expect such patients to improve rapidly. They need a great deal of time in order to develop an internal object that can hold something because they have a leak and can't hold anything very well themselves. This leak in the mind of the patient cannot simply be plugged up with interpretations. Consequently, the analyst has to wait for something to accumulate in the patient's mind, and, like rust or corrosion accumulating in a pipe, this process takes many years.

It would also seem that in health a skin-object is incorporated very early in the developmental process to allow a space within the self to develop so that the mechanism of projective identification as the primary method of nonverbal communication between the mother and the baby in search of detoxification and meaning (Bion 1962) can function without impediment. Indeed, the work of Mauro Mancia (1981) seems to support the notion of a potential for this early development of a psychic skin *in utero*.

PRENATAL DEVELOPMENT OF THE PSYCHIC SKIN

In his paper on the mental life of the fetus, Mancia (1981) integrated empirical data from embryological and perinatal research regarding the motor functions, the sensory abilities, and the appearance of REM or active sleep in the fetus (which can be observed between 28 and 30 weeks of gestation) with the work of Bick (1968) and Bion (1962) in the formulation of his hypothesis stating that

> Active sleep constitutes a "biological framework" within which the sensory experiences coming through the maternal container are transformed by the fetus into "internal representations." Such an operation would constitute the beginning of

a protomental activity in evolution which would build itself around a nucleus of an instinctual nature transmitted genetically from the parents. [Mancia 1981, p. 355]

Mancia drew an analogy between this "prenatal psychic nucleus," which is based upon unconscious fantasy elements transmitted by the extrauterine objects through the intrauterine container (the original "holding environment"), and Bion's (1962) "preconceptions." He also discussed the role of REM sleep in the prenatal development of "the psychological function of the [psychic] 'skin' which . . . may be able to contain the self of the child and to protect it from disintegrating under the pressure of impulses which come into play at the moment of birth" (Mancia 1981, p. 355). Mancia (1981) suggested that this prenatal foundation of the psychic skin favors the inception of the "container-contained" relationship, indispensable for the development of an apparatus for "feeling" and "thinking" (Bion 1962).

Mancia's interesting conjectures, based upon nonpsychoanalytic data, broadened this perspective and deepened our understanding of the profound impact of the earliest experiences upon the psychological development of the individual. Most significant were his reports of findings, in observation of both the fetus and some prematurely born infants, that the disruption of the maternal environment (whether physical or emotional) results in a reduction of active (REM) sleep and an increase in motor activity. Mancia noted this as an indication of the evacuation of beta-elements rather than their transformation into alpha-elements that would coincide theoretically with REM sleep.

ADHESIVE PSEUDO-OBJECT RELATIONS

In consideration of each of the abovementioned findings, it appears that until such time as a sense of personal existence is securely established, allowing for some awareness of a human object and the intermittent space between subject and object, there can be no true development of relationship. Only through human relationship can a sense of internal space develop. Without this sense of internal space, the phantasy of getting inside the object cannot develop and the sensation of being at-one-with, equated, and contiguous with the object prevails, perhaps as a remnant of the earliest intrauterine experience of existence. In such a hyperbolic and therefore *pathological* state of at-one-ment, there can be no "psychological birth" and therefore no *meaningful* experience of a physical life outside the womb, since the awareness of such physical separateness, when it impinges upon these as yet unformed individuals, can only be "felt" as catastrophic.

When considering the form and function of what Bick first termed *adhesive identification* (and later referred to as *adhesive identity*) in its hyperbolic and pathological form—*adhesive equation*, as Tustin termed it—it becomes clear that such primitive auto-sensual survival tactics do not coincide with normal/narcissistic object relations. However, it is important to note that neither does it imply the "normality" of a primary "objectless state" related to what Freud (1914) termed "primary narcissism," nor what Mahler (1958) once considered as a "normal phase" or "stage of primary autism" in the infant. Instead, one might postulate a mode of pseudo-object relationship in which adhesive equation predominates, a state that may be seen to fill the gap between these two extremes.

Since this state of existence requires the obliteration of any experience of space, consequently inhibiting human relationship and its associated identificatory processes, I introduce the term *adhesive pseudo-object relations* for this state. This term may provide a helpful shorthand for the purpose of discussing a mode of "object relationship" that is *apparent* (to the observer) rather than *actual* (in the subjective experience of the analysand), one in which adhesive equation rather than true identification predominates, in which the superimposition of subject and object is so complete, continuous, and chronic that the concepts of "otherness" and "space" have little or no relevance. Instead, the awareness of space and otherness *present*[5] the subject with an unbearable experience of utter catastrophe and a threat to a sense of "going-on-being."

One example of the subjective experience of space while one is in this state of existence is the "black hole with the nasty prick" described by one of Tustin's autistic patients (1981). As Grotstein (1990) so aptly put it, the experience of the black hole is an "experience of the awesome force of powerlessness, of defect, of nothingness, of 'zeroness'—expressed not just as a static emptiness but as an implosive, centripetal pull into the void" (p. 257). Thus "space" is not an area within which human relationship might be allowed to develop, but rather it is the *presence of an inhumane and malevolent absence* that must be blotted out of awareness at all costs.

I will here attempt to operationalize and add clarity to this new term by comparing and contrasting "normal/narcissistic object relations," as elaborated in the work of Melanie Klein (1946) and others in the British tradition, with *adhesive pseudo-object relations*, drawing upon the observations of Meltzer and co-workers (1975) and Tustin (1981, 1986, 1990) based upon their work with autistic children.

---

5. In a 1993 paper I have suggested that the earliest experiences are not initially *represented* or conceptualized in the mental realm but are concretely *recorded* ("presented" rather than "represented") as "body memories" later to be *presented* for expression through the visceral organs and muscular system of the neonate, which are eventually re-presented from the somatic to the psychic or mental realm with the aid of a containing object. Until these elemental experiences are "mentalized," such body memories, when reactivated, are felt as the original event and thus pose a subjectively experienced threat to "going-on-being."

Differentiating between Normal/Narcissistic and Adhesive Pseudo-Object Relations

First, in normal/narcissistic object relations, objects are perceived either in terms of "parts" (that is, as synonymous with a part of the mother's body or with some singular aspect of maternal functioning) or as a whole. Such objects are also (even if only grudgingly) recognized as animate, as possessing life, and therefore as able to move about as a result of their own or another's act of volition. These objects, in normal/narcissistic object relations, are *actual* objects; they are *not only objects apparent to the observer, but are actually experienced as human beings with separate existences by the subject*. In contrast to this, in an adhesive state of pseudo-relating, objects are not experienced as humanly animate, lively entities existing in a space of their own, but as inanimate "things" to be absorbed, exploited, manipulated, or avoided by the subject in his or her desperate attempt to gain a sensation of existence, safety, and impermeability. Objects in this sense of the word are *apparent only to an observer*.

Second, in a normal/narcissistic state some degree of awareness of separateness and/or differentiation of the subject from the object exists and is tolerated to a greater or lesser extent; while in adhesive states normal "flickering states of awareness" (Tustin 1981) are unable to be tolerated, and consequently self and object remain largely undifferentiated—they are one and the same—and the resulting pseudo-relationship with the object is mainly experienced by the subject on a sensuous level. In such a state objects are not related to per se but are instead "utilized" for the tactile sensations (and perhaps also the visual, auditory, and olfactory sensations "amodally"[6] transmitted) they engender upon the surface of the skin

---

6. According to present-day research in infant development, newborns are thought to have an innate capacity to take informa-

and/or the mucous membranes of the subject. These sensations serve either to distract the subject's attention from anxiety, providing an illusion of safety, strength, and impermeabiliity, or they may have a numbing or tranquilizing effect that serves to block out some terrifying and unbearable awareness.

Third, while normal/narcissistic object relations prevail, anxieties defended against by the subject are either paranoid-schizoid, manic,[7] or depressive in nature, as defined by Melanie Klein (1946). Those "anxieties" evaded through auto-sensual/adhesive maneuvers may more accurately be conceptualized as states of raw and unmitigated panic, equated with the fear of falling forever, of discontinuity of being, of nothingness, dissolution, and evaporation—of being a "no-body" nowhere (Williams 1992), as described in the work of Winnicott (1962) and Tustin (1986). While in the former, the individual employs complex and defensive phantasies of splitting, projective identification, and manic denial to defend against the pain and despair of envy and the awareness of helpless dependence upon the object; in the latter, the individual employs adhesive equation and the blocking out of painful and life-threatening awareness through auto-sensuous actions that protect him/her from the sensations of falling, spilling, dissolving, evaporating, and diffusing in air without hope of recovery.

---

tion received in one sensory modality and to translate it into any other sensory modality. The resultant perception exists in some "supra-modal" form (for example, wherein the breast that is seen, the breast that is smelled, the breast that is tasted, and the breast that is touched are linked together) and is encoded in what Stern (1985) refers to as an *amodal representation* that can be recognized in any of its sensory modalities.

7. In her paper "Mourning and Its Relation to Manic-Depressive States," Klein (1940) briefly mentions a third position: the manic position, lying midway between the paranoid-schizoid and depressive positions, a concept later developed by Steiner (1987) and others.

Fourth, in normal/narcissistic object relations, the ego oscillates either between a state of *nondefensive regression to unintegration* on the one hand and a state of *increasing integration* on the other[8] (Winnicott 1949, 1960) or between a state of *integration* and a state of *defensive disintegration*. However, in adhesive pseudo-object-relations the ego exists/operates predominantly in a passive *primary* state of unintegration (Bick 1968, Winnicott 1960).

Fifth, "thinking," which corresponds to normal/narcissistic states, is either abstract or concrete and may be either realistic or omnipotent in nature. However, in adhesive states there is little *actual* mentation. What *appears* to the observer as thinking remains on the level of a reflexo-physiological reaction; what Tustin (1990) referred to as "innate forms" prevail in the absence of symbolization, phantasy, and imagination, since the experience of "transitional space" is inexistent.

Sixth, while the normal/narcissistic individual reacts to separation and loss with either neediness or a tight-fisted control of need through the use of tyranny and seduction, the adhesive individual reacts with either total obliviousness or complete collapse. The awareness of dependency in the former is either experienced as the need for and the act of reliance on an object that is separate from the subject or it is defended against through pseudo-independence. In the latter, however, dependency assumes the form of a thin and tenacious clinging to the surface of an as-yet (and perhaps never-to-be) undifferentiated object felt to be part of and contiguous with the subject. This is an *appendancy* rather than a dependency (T. Mitrani 1992).

Finally, when defenses against separation and loss break down in the normal/narcissistic relationship, there is an experience of a

---

8. Perhaps this oscillatory process corresponds to Bion's (1965) notion of the oscillation between the paranoid-schizoid and depressive positions (PS ↔ D). This may also resonate with Piaget's cognitive assimilation/accommodation processes.

threat to the subject's sense of omnipotence, culminating in feelings of rejection. However, when omnipotence fails in the adhesive state, this failure is felt as a totally catastrophic collapse or as a dreadful sensation of being ripped off and thrown away (J. Mitrani 1993a). In a sense it is an experience of total and irreversible dejection; it is not an experience of the loss of the object, but the presence of "the abject" (Kristeva 1982). She suggests that the abject— a *jettisoned object*—retains only one quality of the object it once was, that of being opposed to or separate from the subject. In other words, whereas the object, in its opposition to the subject, stimulates the desire for meaning, which paradoxically creates a link between subject and object, the *abject*, having been radically excluded and its existence denied, can only draw the subject toward "the place where meaning collapses" (pp. 1–2).

In the next chapter I will strive to convey my understanding of the nature of adhesive pseudo-object relations by introducing the character Jean-Baptiste Grenouille of Patrick Süskind's remarkable novel *Perfume*. I believe that Süskind, more than any other author of our time, has captured the essence of the experience of infantile trauma and its mental and emotional aftermath, the experience of abjection and the development of an aberrant form of object relations.

9

On Adhesive Pseudo-Object Relations: An Illustration[1]

Whoever fights monsters should see to it that in the process he does not become a monster. And when you look into the abyss, the abyss also looks into you.

[Friedrich Wilhelm Nietzsche, *Beyond Good and Evil*]

INTRODUCTION

Not unlike other discoveries rooted in the observation of infants and children, the seminal work of Esther Bick (1968, 1986) on adhesive identification and her explication of the concept of the psychic skin along with its functions have impacted our psychoanalytic understanding of the development of normal/narcissistic object relations and has led to some important technical considerations in the treatment of adult patients. The evolution and refinement of Bick's ideas, especially as they have been developed in the

1. A version of this chapter was previously published in *Contemporary Psychoanalysis* in 1995.

work of Donald Meltzer (1975), Meltzer and colleagues (1975), and Frances Tustin (1969–1992), has led to the notion, discussed in Chapter 10, that there may be a mode of pseudo-object-relating, one markedly characterized by adhesive identity or adhesive equation rather than projective identification; one that may be considered as both pre-historic and pathogenetic to the normal/narcissistic object relations already well defined and documented by Melanie Klein and her exponents. I have termed this phenomenon *adhesive pseudo-object relations* (J. Mitrani 1994a).

Having already compared and contrasted normal/narcissistic object relations with adhesive pseudo-object-relations in the preceding chapter, I will now illustrate this primitive way of being, not with clinical data, but with a literary work. The practice of using literary characters to illustrate and exemplify theoretical constructs has important and obvious limitations, though it follows a rich tradition. Freud's (1906) first published analysis of a work of literature examined the protagonist Norbert Hanold in Jensen's *Gradiva*. In that paper Freud made an analogy between the burial and excavation of Pompeii and the repression and analysis of Hanold's emotional experience. In the process of developing a suitable case for his argument that dreams are mental events embued with meaning, he used the relationship between Norbert Hanold and Zoe Bertgang to illustrate a subtle point about the importance of "taking" the transference. Yet another memorable use of the imaginary patient is to be found in Klein's seminal paper, "On Identification" (1955), in which she used the character Fabian Especel in Julian Green's *If I Were You* to highlight the ins and outs of projective identification with all its associated features of envy and its destructive side effects.

It goes without saying, that the existence of these and other noteworthy contributions may not ipso facto justify the substitution of fictional characters for flesh-and-blood analysands. However, there are times when one finds that confidentiality cannot be maintained if a lengthy and detailed case history is used to illustrate a given theory, and there are often theoretical discussions, such as the one I am about to embark upon, that seem to beg for illustrations of such extended length and detail.

Indeed, I was faced with just such a dilemma when, in the early stages of formulating my ideas about adhesive pseudo-object relations, two analysands who were then at the root of my thinking on the matter each made reference to the same novel, a novel I had neither read nor heard about. Some months later I was compelled to read the novel to investigate the coincidence of the dynamics and the associative material of these two individuals. As I read it, I found Patrick Süskind's *Perfume: The Story of a Murderer* (1986)[2] to be a gripping horror tale of a fictional eighteenth-century French serial killer as well as a grotesque version of the two cases of trauma and consequence I had known in the privacy of my consulting room, but refrained from publishing except in the most abbreviated anecdotal forms.

Perhaps one may find my use of this fictive subject warranted, not only in the interest of maintaining the privacy of the patients he represents, but also because the magnification of the artist's imagination may serve to draw one's attention to those subtle conditions that might otherwise escape notice. Along the lines of the latter, I am here reminded of what Freud (1933) said in defense of the study of primitive states of mind and despite his pessimism with regard to the prospect of a "cure" for them through the use of his method of therapy. He suggested that "listening" to our severely narcissistic patients may afford us access to the innermost strata of the internal world. He seemed to be saying that narcissistic patients, more so than others less ill, provide us with a direct line of communication (due either to the extremes of regression or developmental arrest) with the primeval objects that form the foundations of many psychopathologies.

---

2. Originally published in German by Diogenes Verlag as *Das Parfum*.

If extraordinary pathology can draw our attention to normal neurotic conditions, perhaps extraordinary *fantasy* may provoke insight into those more ordinary pathological states. It might also be that certain artists, having "turned away from external reality . . . know more about internal, psychical reality and can reveal a number of things to us that would otherwise be inaccessible to us" (Freud 1933, pp. 58–59).

No doubt Süskind's story might be treated as allegory, as it seems to express by means of fictional figures and actions some basic truths or generalizations about human existence. Or it might be read as a parable, highlighting certain attitudes or principles relevant to our clinical work. However, I shall leave these areas to be addressed possibly in the future. As concerns the present work, although I am aware of its limitations, I am convinced that a compelling representation of the characteristic features of adhesive pseudo-object relations may be discovered in Süskind's protagonist, Jean-Baptiste Grenouille, whom I will evaluate, almost as if he were a patient, beginning with a summary of his history, that is, a summary of the novel.

PERFUME: THE STORY OF A MURDERER

The German author Patrick Süskind takes us back to eighteenth-century France, where we are introduced to "one of the most gifted and abominable personages in an era which knew no lack of gifted and abominable personages" (p. 3). Jean-Baptiste Grenouille was born in Paris in 1738 on a hot summer's day. The heat served to intensify the putrid odors of death and decay, life and lust, and the fish stall in which his mother stood as she began her labor of birth. Just as she had with the four "stillborn and almost born" who preceded him, Grenouille's mother squatted down under the gutting table and cut the cord with a butcher knife, expecting the "newborn thing" to be shoveled away with the offal and fish heads.

However, Grenouille's cry did not go unnoticed, as had those of his more unfortunate siblings, and he was rescued by the police and given to a wet nurse. His mother confessed to her crimes and was arrested, tried, and beheaded for multiple infanticide.

After only a few days, having exhausted several wet nurses who complained of his greediness at the breast, the police "got rid of Grenouille at the Cloister of Saint-Merri," where he was christened Jean-Baptiste and given to the wet nurse Jeanne Bussie. Alas, within a few weeks Jeanne brought the infant to Father Terrier, complaining that he was possessed by the devil. The evidence for her indictment was not based solely upon the fact of Grenouille's greed, but more owing to a peculiar trait—or lack thereof—since it seemed to her that Grenouille possessed no scent of his own. Unconvinced of the verity of Jeanne's complaint, but left with no alternative, Father Terrier received the baby indulging in the fantasy of being himself the father of the child. However, he soon found himself the target of Grenouille's olfactory attention.

> Like the cups of a small meat-eating plant Grenouille's [nostrils] seemed to create an eerie suction . . . as if the child saw him with his nostrils . . . using its nose to devour something whole . . . he could not hold that something back or hide it . . . the child with no smell was smelling him shamelessly . . . he felt naked and ugly, as if someone were gaping at him while revealing nothing of himself . . . his most tender emotions, his filthiest thoughts lay exposed to that greedy little nose . . . were he not a man by nature prudent, God-fearing and given to reason, in the rush of nausea he would have hurled [Grenouille] like a spider from him. [pp. 19–20]

Grenouille was then taken by Father Terrier to Madame Gaillard, a professional foster mother who boarded children for her living and who "had lost for good all sense of smell and every sense of human warmth and human coldness—indeed every human passion"

(p. 22) when her father had struck her across the forehead with a poker.

Just as he had survived his own birth in a garbage can, while in the custody of Gaillard Grenouille survived measles, dysentery, chicken pox, cholera, a 20-foot fall into a well, and scalding with boiling water, which had been poured over his chest. He had forgone love in favor of survival, and survive he did. He had made his decision "vegetatively, as a bean when once tossed aside must decide if it ought to germinate or had better let things be" (p. 25).

Süskind likens Grenouille's technique of survival to that of the tick,

> for which life has nothing better to offer than perpetual hibernation . . . which by rolling its blue-grey body up into a ball offers the least possible surface to the world; which by making its skin smooth [and] dense, emits nothing . . . makes itself extra small and inconspicuous [so] that no one will see it and step on it. The lonely tick, which, wrapped up in itself, huddles in its tree, blind, deaf and dumb and simply sniffs . . . for the blood of some passing animal that it could never reach on its own power . . . the tick, stubborn, sullen and loathsome, huddles there and lives and waits . . . for that most improbable of chances . . . and only then does it abandon caution and drop and scratch and bore and bite into that alien flesh . . . The young Grenouille was such a tick . . . encapsulated in himself [he] waited for better times. [p. 25]

Gaillard seemed oblivious to the fact that Grenouille gave nothing, not even his scent. But the other children in her care feared him and attempted many times to do away with him until they finally gave up, resorting to avoidance.

Grenouille grew, an ugly child, not standing up until the age of 3. He did not speak until age 4 when he suddenly cried out the word "fishes." He used nouns only for concrete[3] objects that could "subdue him with a sudden attack of odor" (p. 28). It was as if he saw, heard, or felt nothing—he only smelled. He seemed to bury himself in smells—conjuring up a blissful olfactory experience each time he uttered a word. This was how he learned to speak. Abstracts remained a mystery to him. Only things that smelled had meaning. Language seemed to lack the refinement for communicating the richness of Grenouille's olfactory world. He could even create new smells in his mind by combining those already known and these could be smelled by him through sheer force of imagination. In this way he effectively shut out the world, and some thus thought him feebleminded.

Eventually even Gaillard grew to fear and dislike Grenouille; she interpreted his uncanny aptitude for detecting and identifying smells as an ability to see through things, even into the future. Cut off from the cloister's support at age 8, Grenouille was turned over by Gaillard to the tanner Grimal, who exploited stray children, giving them tasks that few could survive. At peace with the legality of the situation, Gaillard abandoned the lad to an uncertain fate. In a twist of irony, we learn of Mme. Galliard's fate—some half century later—impoverished, mute, unable to protest being abandoned to the horror of a death shared with total strangers in the Hotel Dieu, an ending she had striven her entire life to escape.

From his first whiff of Grimal, Grenouille sensed that his life now depended upon his ability to perform the tasks assigned him in the tannery. Scraping meat from the hides, burying and unburying them and hauling water for endless hours, Grenouille contracted anthrax one year into his indenture and barely escaped death. Now bearing the scars of his illness, Grenouille was even

---

3. It may be of interest to note that the word *concrete* is used in perfumery to denote a waxy essence of flowers prepared by extraction and evaporation.

more ugly than before. He had become however far more valuable to Grimal, as he was now immune to the deadly disease that constituted the primary occupational hazard of the tanner.

His increased value to Grimal earned Grenouille more adequate treatment and a modicum of free time. Thus "the days of his hibernation were over. Grenouille the tick stir[red] again" (p. 38) and he discovered the world of scent inside the city. Standing on the banks of the river at the Place de Gréve, where his mother had been beheaded, Grenouille caught the odors of the countryside and sometimes of the sea. "He preferred to leave the smell of the sea blended together, preserving it in his memory, relishing it whole" (p. 41). He longed someday to arrive to the sea, to merge with its smell.

On one of his outings Grenouille went to Faubourg Saint-Germain, where the wealthy resided. There he smelled his first perfume. Breaking it down into its component parts, which he committed to memory, Grenouille greedily sought to possess all the smells. Without differentiating them into good and bad, "he devoured everything, sucking it up into him" (p. 43).

In the fall of his fifteenth year, Grenouille smelled something new. He followed this new scent to discover its source, which he felt must be something extraordinary. "He had to have it, not simply in order to possess it, but for his heart to be at peace" (p. 45). The source was a girl. He had never smelled anything so beautiful— more beautiful than all the perfumes of his imagination. Obsessed with the need to preserve "the least trace of her scent" (p. 50), he strangled the girl where she sat pitting plums. Then, laying her on the ground, he seemed to gather up all the fragrance of her being, as he thrust his face into her skin, over her skin, soaking up her essence and sealing it away in his "innermost compartments." Never before had this frog-of-a-creature known such bliss! He now knew the reason for his being: he was to be a creator of scents, the greatest perfumer of them all. That night, and for the weeks that followed, Grenouille dissected, sorted, and arranged the scent-memories, cataloguing them and creating an "inner fortress of magnificent odors" (p. 52).

Meanwhile, in the perfumery of Guiseppe Baldini, the master himself struggled to duplicate "Amor and Psyche," the famous perfume of a competitor, to use in the impregnation of some Spanish hides for one Count Verhamont. When Grenouille entered his shop to deliver the goatskins on behalf of Grimal, he expressed his desire for a job as an apprentice. At first Baldini laughed, but when he discovered what a fine nose Grenouille had, he set him about the task of re-creating the scent he himself had failed to capture. Once done, Grenouille offered the astonished Baldini an even better scent, "a scent so heavenly fine, that tears welled into Baldini's eyes" (p. 101).

The next day Baldini bargained with Grimal for custody of the apprentice Grenouille, and purchased him for a handsome price. Finally, Grenouille could put to use all his years of cataloguing scents in his mind. As Grenouille rolled himself up "ticklike" in his new bed in the corner of Baldini's laboratory, "sinking deeper and deeper into himself" (p. 104), Grimal left him behind, falling in his drunken stupor into the river where he floated off drowned.

With all the resources of Baldini's establishment at his disposal, as well as the new skills he had acquired under Baldini's tutelage, Grenouille was free to mix and mate all the various ingredients in the laboratory to create new perfumes for the aggrandizement of his new master's reputation. He hoped, with the aid of an alembic, to distill the odors of everything in his environment, to "rob" all things of their characteristic essence. Failing this, however, he fell mortally ill. His fever could not be contained nor could it be relieved through the pores in his skin. He developed blisters that burst open, leaving him covered with hundreds of ulcerous wounds, as if he were "some martyr stoned from the inside out" (p. 121).

Baldini nursed Grenouille back to health, not out of care or human sympathy, but out of greed for the perfume formulas yet to be recorded. Grenouille recovered, fueled by the desire to learn further methods for capturing the scents he had failed to secure through the process of distillation. He eventually satisfied his master's lust for fame in exchange for journeyman's papers. A free man at last at age 18, Grenouille headed toward Orleans. As he reached the city limits of Paris, Baldini's house of perfume, which straddled the Seine at the Pont-au-Change, collapsed into the river, killing the 'great' and greedy Baldini and submerging Grenouille's secret formulas in the process.

Surrounded by the simplicity of the countryside Grenouille felt nearly "delivered" from his constant state of olfactory vigilance. He discovered that here he "did not have to prepare himself to catch the scent of something new, unexpected, hostile—or to lose a pleasant smell—with every breath." He felt "a newfound respiratory freedom" (p. 141) in his withdrawal from the "compacted human effluvium [that] had oppressed him" (p. 139) within the city limits. He no longer wanted to go somewhere, but instead trusted his nose to lead him away from humans, to the complete solitude of the peak of the 6,000-foot-high volcano Plomb du Cantal and the bliss of "olfactory peace."

At long last he could believe he was "the only human being in the world" (p. 146). For comfort and shelter he found a small tunnel in the rocks, which were also his source of water. He licked at the rocks for moisture and found nourishment in the snakes and dry grasses which were plentiful on the mountain. As he breathed the moist, cool, salty air he was "overcome by a sense of something like sacred awe . . . never in his life had he felt so secure, certainly not in his mother's belly" (p. 148). Inside this, "his empire" (p. 152), Grenouille lived in a state of dark and silent immobility, while within his "innermost universal theater" (p. 151) he created an array of odors of omnipotent triumph over all those smells of the horrific injustices he had suffered from before birth. When he emerged from his tunnel to feed and water his "earthly" counterpart, Grenouille felt "as if he were a hunted creature, a little soft-fleshed animal, and the hawks were already circling in the sky overhead"

(p. 159) until he returned to his sanctuary where "the dark doors opened within him and he entered" (p. 160).

After seven years an "inner catastrophe" catapulted him back into the external world. It was a dream! He was surrounded in a foglike odor—his own odor—but he could not smell it, and he awoke with a scream. Leaving his cave and the threat of being suffocated by himself, he attempted to experience his own odor. However, not even in the clothing he had worn in the darkness for seven years could he locate his own scent. Discovering that the tunnel still smelled as if no living being had ever entered it, he left the mountain forever.

Grenouille soon concocted an explanation (which he thought more believable than the truth) for his shredded skin and clothing, long beard, and talonlike nails, to allay the fears and suspicions of the humans he would meet as he re-entered civilization. In Montpellier he was discovered by the Marquis de La Taillade-Espinasse, who was involved in a research project regarding the relationship between man's proximity to the earth and the "life force." His thesis was that man grew up and away from the earth to escape the *fluidium letale* (a lethal gas, emitted from the earth, that corrupts and undermines life itself). The marquis exploited Grenouille, in his deteriorated condition, to prove his point. He considered Grenouille, with his deformities of body and mind, as "more disposed toward death than life" (p. 173).

The marquis's demonstration was enthusiastically received, and he promised to further prove himself by "rehabilitating" Grenouille in a week's time, through his "vital diet" and "ventilation therapy." Indeed, the marquis made good his promise and the frog-of-a-man was transformed into a "mannerly gentleman." Feigning a relapse that threatened to ruin his benefactor, Grenouille insisted on designing a perfume of his own, which he promised would render him permanently immune to such an unfortunate and embarrassing regression. Suitably impressed with his ward's demonstration and entreaty, the marquis arranged for Grenouille to take over the laboratory of the local perfumer, Runel. There he created a perfume that smelled like a "*human being who gives off a scent*" (p. 182). Although it was frightening at first, Grenouille soon felt pride in his newfound ability to exert an effect on people with his scent.

After the newness of being a "human among humans" wore off, however, Grenouille began to glory in the notion that he had fooled them all. As his sense of superiority increased, he began to feel he could now create a superhuman scent, an enchanting and angelic scent that could compel people to love and revere him completely. "He would be the omnipotent God of scent, just as he had been in his fantasies, but this time in the real world and over real people" (p. 189). When Grenouille left Montpellier, the marquis went on to great fame, eventually meeting his fate in a mountain-climbing expedition to the Pic Du Canigou, where he was fabled to have ascended to a state of eternal life.

Meanwhile, Grenouille, wrapped securely in his polished persona, made his way to Grasse, the center for the production of perfume. Touring the town, he stopped in front of a home where he was captured by a familiar scent. It was reminiscent of the scent of the red-haired girl he had murdered in Paris. He imagined that this girl's celestial fragrance was only just emerging, as she was only just emerging from childhood. He reasoned that ripening would take at least two years, time for him to acquire the skills he needed to "possess the scent of this girl behind the wall; to peel it from her skin and to make her scent his own" (p. 208).

Toward this end Grenouille signed on as a journeyman, working in a small perfumery for the widow Arnulfi. There he practiced the craft of maceration: placing flowers in a caldron of hot oil that "appropriated" the scent of the flowers emersed in it before cooling and solidifying into a fragrant pomade to be stored in jars. He also learned to make *essence absolue* from the pomade by separating out the fragrant oil entrapped in the solid. He found some flowers too delicate to undergo maceration and so these were laid out and covered or wrapped with a cool, oil-soaked cloth until they exhaled their bouquet, which could then be pressed from the cloth as *enfleurage*.

In addition to his duties, Grenouille spent time in Arnulfi's laboratory developing a variety of scents for himself. He made one for inconspicuousness, one for occasions when he required more attention, one that aroused sympathy of others, and another that repelled people with such subtlety that they were unaware of the source of the repellent, but simply walked away from him.

Under the protection of these "magic scents," which helped to conceal his true nature, Grenouille continued to sharpen his skills, extracting scent from inert objects, aided by the absorptive qualities of oil. The essence of brass doorknob and the pomade resulting from the maceration of stone were felt by him to be "wonderful little trifles that of course no one but he could admire or would ever take note of. He was enchanted by their meaningless perfection" (p. 224). Moving on to living subjects, he boiled insects in oil and draped farm animals in "greasy bandages," but these did not give up their scent without complaint. He determined that a quick and unexpected death prior to harvesting was the only solution to the problems he encountered with living things. Having perfected a mixture of tallow, lard, suet, and oil to capture human redolence, Grenouille could now hope to preserve for himself "the odor of *certain* human beings, that is, those rare humans who inspire love" (p. 228).

From January through September 1775 Grenouille tested his method on twenty-four of the most beautiful young virgins of Grasse without ever coming under suspicion. These young women were all found naked and shorn of their tresses, having been murdered by a blow to the back of the head. People were horrified and fearful. But no sooner did the town's bishop publicly curse the murderer, then the murders ceased and the horrors were soon forgotten by all the townspeople with the exception of a widower named Antoine Richis, the town's second counsel, its wealthiest citizen, and the father of the girl Laure.

Like *Aurora's* father, Richis guarded his "sleeping beauty" with the full extent of his resources. He felt certain that "the murderer was not a destructive personality, but rather a careful collector [of beauty]" (p. 246). He imagined the murderer constructing a mosaic of beauty out of the hair and clothing of the twenty-four girls with his Laure at its center, and felt a sense of superiority in having been able to enter into and to analyze the mind of the murderer. Finding sanctuary for his daughter in the monastery of Saint-Honorat, Richis went on to Vence to arrange for her marriage in ten days. Once deflowered, Laure would surely lose her value for the murderer and Antoine would emerge as victor when what Grenouille "most desired was snatched away from under his nose" (p. 253).

Almost as soon as Laure left Grasse, Grenouille smelled her absence and was paralyzed with fright. After packing up his gear, Grenouille followed Laure's scent to the town where Richis rested for the night on his way to deliver his daughter to her betrothed. When all were asleep, Grenouille made his way into Laure's chamber. One quick blow to the back of her head and he could go about his cold-oil *enfleurage*. Before dawn, his work was complete and Laure was now a "disembodied scent" (p. 269) that he carried away, tucked under his arm, leaving only a lifeless shell for Richis to find upon awakening.

Pursued by the relentless and grief-stricken father, Grenouille was discovered, identified, and arrested. Ample evidence found in his quarters, along with his own confession, facilitated his swift conviction. The sentence was one befitting the crime: twenty-five killings for which Grenouille would be paraded through the town, beyond the city gates, there to be bound to a wooden cross, henceforth to receive twelve blows with an iron rod, crushing his body, afterward to be hanged until dead. He would then be buried by night in an unmarked grave among the remains of animals.

On the day of his execution, Grenouille was led into the public square between the scaffold and the grandstands. However, what the people perceived was not the murderer-Grenouille but "innocence personified" (p. 287). All ten thousand men, women, and children fell hopelessly in love with him and were suddenly

> touched [to] their erotic core . . . the result was that the scheduled execution of one of the most abominable criminals of the age degenerated into the largest orgy the world had seen since the second century before Christ. [p. 290]

Grenouille had

> created an aura more radiant and more effective than any human being had ever possessed before him. And he owed it to no one—not to father, nor to mother, and least of all to a gracious God—but to *himself* alone . . . he *was* Grenouille the Great! Now it had become manifest . . . just as in his narcissistic fantasies . . . but now in reality . . . he experienced the greatest triumph of his life. [p. 292]

But Grenouille was also terrified. He could not enjoy any of it because, although he finally had the love he had so longed for, he could not love back. Grenouille could feel only hatred and contempt. He could experience gratification only in being hated. But there was no such gratification, for even as he hated and wished to destroy them all, they could do nothing but worship him

> for they perceived only his counterfeit aura, his fragrant disguise, his stolen perfume . . . for once in his life he wanted to empty himself . . . to be like other people and empty himself of what was inside him—what they did with their love and their stupid adoration, he would do with his hate . . . [but] beneath his mask there was no face, but only his total odorlessness. [p. 293]

Once more, as in the cave, the fog of his odorlessness rose up to suffocate him and he was filled with a boundless fear and terror, but this time it was not a dream from which his screams could awaken him. He was finally embraced by none other than Antoine Richis, who begged forgiveness and adopted him as his son. But as soon as the perfume lost its magical fragrance, Grenouille stole away under the cover of darkness and his own odorlessness. He wanted only to return to Paris to die.

As Grenouille entered the gates of the city he came upon a band of twenty or thirty desperadoes huddled around a fire near the cemetery. He unstoppered the bottle of "his" perfume and doused himself with it. At first the group regarded him with awe, which soon turned to rapture and a frenzy of desire in which Grenouille was completely and finally devoured by the crowd. When it was over "they were proud. For the first time they had done something out of love" (p. 310).

DISCUSSION OF THE STORY

Süskind seems to possess not only an empathically keen and vivid awareness of (and capacity to be in contact with) some very elemental emotional states, but he also has a rare talent for articulating these in the story of Grenouille. I believe his story can be interpreted as a representation of some significant aspects of mental and emotional life-gone-wrong in the face of extreme environmental tragedy, the likes of which we may never have to bear witness to in our practices as psychoanalysts. However, by creating such an extreme tragedy, I believe the author draws our attention, perhaps inadvertently, to those more subtle and commonly encountered versions that might otherwise escape our mindful observation.

In Süskind's story, odor might be understood as a powerful signifier of the infant-Grenouille's earliest perceptual experiences. The rhinencephalon is the most primitive aspect of the human brain, and it may be that, by describing the era about which he writes in olfactory terms, Süskind is drawing our attention to a dimension of human experience and existence that is archaic, sensuous, invisible, amorphous, and almost totally neglected in the psychoanalytic literature.[4] In the following discussion of the story, I will suggest ways in which Grenouille's early pre- and postnatal experiences

---

4. Since the original publication of the paper on which this chapter is based, I have refound Anzieu's discussion (1989) of what he termed the "olfactory envelope." He describes his patient, "Gethsemane," and his relationship with his mother—who had suffered greatly from a protracted birthing process and who could not nurse him—and his godmother, who had rescued him from "death's door"—"his skin torn and bleeding in several places" due to "a desperate forceps maneuver"—by keeping him beside her in her bed. About the godmother, Anzieu explains that, as "a countrywoman by origin, she rarely washed herself, except her face and hands. She used to let her dirty underwear pile up in the bathroom for several weeks before washing it, and [his] patient would go in there secretly to breathe in its strong smell, an act which gave him the narcissistically reassuring feeling of being preserved from all harm, even from death. The underlying phantasy revealed itself to be that of a fusional contact with the godmother's foul-smelling and protective skin. At the same time [Anzieu] learned that Gethsemane's mother regarded it as a matter of pride to be extremely clean at all times and used quantities of eau-de-Cologne. Thus—though [Anzieu] kept this observation to [himself]—the two contradictory odors with which [Gethsemane] invaded [Anzieu's] consulting room represented an attempt in phantasy to unite upon his own body his godmother's skin and his mother's" (p. 180). Grenouille, lacking an internally autogenerated odor, seems to exemplify Anzieu's "kernel without a shell" type of individual who "wraps himself in suffering," while the doubly odoriferous Gethsemane illustrates the skin ego "broken into by holes" or "colander" type of patient who "can neither hold back nor work through his aggression" (p. 102).

rendered him extraordinarily vulnerable to subsequent environmental failures, yet provided him with the template for his peculiar method of survival. I will also demonstrate how those cumulative traumas (Khan 1964), experienced both before and after birth, contributed to the formation and transformation of Grenouille's "second skin"; finally, I will highlight the various features of adhesive pseudo-object relations (e.g., the sensation-dominated use of objects, the terror of and protections against the awareness of the "black hole," and the experience of collapse) as they appear in the character of Grenouille.

Pre- and Postnatal History and the Maternal Mental State

From the very beginning of Süskind's story we are told that Grenouille was an unwanted baby, discarded by his mother even before his birth as "dead meat," an object of contempt, an inconvenience to be expelled and forgotten in favor of "the real babies she might one day have." Although Grenouille was conceived by his mother, he was never *conceived of* by her. Mother's crimes of infanticide were intended to be concealed by the bloody remains of once-living things and the "perfume" of the death and decay of the marketplace where she toiled alone, uncontained and unsupported by a husbandly presence.

Grenouille's first perceptual contact after his physical birth was not with a mindful and caring mother's arms and bosom, but with the *smell* of death and decay into which he had been premeditatedly dropped by her. Thus we may see how his identity theme was established from the very start of his existence, both within and immediately beyond the womb. In his mother's phantasies Grenouille was born to be "inconspicuous" in a world of conspicuous odors. He was as his mother imagined him: odorless. He was born to be evil—"the presence of the absence" incarnate! Having no meaningful presence of his own, he was equated in her mind with what was bloody and smelly and intended to "cover up" her crime. Indeed, he grew up to commit crimes that served to dwarf her own by comparison.

It might be said that Grenouille suffered the "privation" referred to by Winnicott (1965).[5] His conception was totally without illusion,[6] as was he. There was neither a "holding" (Winnicott 1960) nor a "containing" (Bion 1962) object for him to rely upon, no sensory/affective "floor" (Grotstein 1986) to support him through the vicissitudes of infancy. Instead, he was subjected to a barbarically premature and abrupt experience of amputation from his mother: he was literally cut off from and by her with a butcher knife. This nearly unimaginable "traumatic weaning" seemed to lead to an accentuation of the sensual object of his environment, the hyperactivation of and overreliance on the sensory modality of olfaction and olfactory sensations that were then substituted for the

---

5. Winnicott (1965) traced the etiology of "extreme mental illness" to the failure of the environment to facilitate the baby's maturational processes at the stage of "double dependency," that is, at a mentally unsophisticated stage during which "essential provisions" are completely outside the perception and comprehension of the infant. Thus Winnicott differentiated *privation* from the more commonly used term *deprivation*, the failure occurring "on top of success, failure of the environment that was perceived by the child as such at the time that the failure occurred" (p. 226).

6. In a discussion of the "value of illusion," Winnicott (1951) explained that "the mother, at the beginning, by an almost one-hundred percent adaptation, affords the infant the opportunity for the *illusion* that her breast is part of the infant . . . under [his or her] magical control" (p. 238) and also "that there is an external reality that corresponds to the infant's own capacity to create . . . psychologically, the infant takes from a breast that is part of the infant, and the mother gives milk to an infant that is part of herself . . . the idea of interchange is based on an illusion" (p. 239). It seems that without illusion there can be no development of relationship in the true sense of the word.

nipple in the mouth as an organizing factor in Grenouille's life. As if to compensate for the "absent object" (O'Shaughnessy 1964), Grenouille created a world of scent in which he virtually swaddled himself, perhaps as a protection against the premature awareness of the overwhelming terror and unbearable psychic pain associated with his abandonment. I believe that in this way Grenouille was able to survive the repeated rejections and severe and multiple traumas and abuses suffered at the hands of his surrogate caretakers. I will review and discuss these various rejections and their consequences chronologically.

The Trauma of Environmental Failure

Following a string of earlier wet nurses, each so transient that they remained nameless in the story, Jeanne Bussie rejected Grenouille with extreme hatred, revulsion, and suspicion, misinterpreting his zest for living as an uncontrollable and boundless "greed." Rather than merely seeking the satisfaction of his greed, it seems more likely that Grenouille was attempting to establish some basic experience of continuity through a nipple–mouth connection to gain a sense of "skin" that might be relied upon to hold him together in this very early, unintegrated state. Perhaps the love-starved baby-Grenouille also appeared voracious in these preliminary attempts to "take in" some sense of himself, reflected in the eyes of an (m)other who might have the capacity to imagine him (Winnicott 1956). But Jeanne Bussie *could not* imagine this baby. She seemed to lack the capacity for receptivity that would allow her to accommodate and assimilate a new experience. Perhaps her "pre-conceptions" were saturated (Bion 1962) with the residue of previous experiences with other babies, for it seemed as though she had no space left in her mind for this one. She had expected that this baby, like so many others, would smell of "butter, milk and caramel" (i.e., that he would be sweet and easy and good), but when the baby-Grenouille failed to provide the realization for her expectation, Jeanne could not reckon with her own disillusionment, let alone his. In a state of fear and desperation, Jeanne foisted Grenouille upon an unwilling father (Terrier).

Father Terrier was unprepared for the task of parenting, of detoxifying the experience of either Jeanne or Grenouille. He failed to make meaning out of the (surrogate) mother's anxieties regarding Grenouille's "peculiarities." Instead, he met Jeanne's fears with denial, derision, and negation. Alone with this very needy baby, Father Terrier lacked the capacity to tolerate Grenouille's frantic effort to establish sensorial contact with the presence-of-the-object and his endeavor to communicate about and obtain transformation of those painful and terrifying infantile experiences of his previous attempts at attachment, the feeling of being left naked and ugly in the eyes of his primary objects.

Bion (1963) reminded us that, in the beginning, "the infant depends on mother to act as its alpha-function" (p. 27), and I believe that he vividly conveyed to us the baby's earliest sensorial experience of the (m)otherly presence in the following passage:

> The infant, filled with painful lumps of faeces, guilt, fears of impending death, chunks of greed, meanness, and urine, evacuates these bad objects into *the breast that is not there*. As it does so, the good object turns the *no-breast* (*mouth*) into a breast, the faeces and urine into milk, the fear of impending death and anxiety into vitality and confidence, the greed and meanness into feelings of love and generosity and *the infant sucks its bad property, now translated into goodness, back again.* [p. 31]

Grenouille found no such succor in the arms of Father Terrier, who appeared unable to separate out the painful experiences of the baby-Grenouille from the remnants of his own infancy with which they may have resonated. His impulse to "hurl" this baby from him seemed to represent a massive rejection of Grenouille's experience of abjection.

Next, in the custody of Madame Gaillard, Grenouille suffered from reprivation of all human emotion. Although given physical care, it was stripped of all human passion and thoughtful contemplation; thus he fell prey to physical illness until he was finally able to commit himself to bodily survival while eschewing any hope of passionate human emotional contact. He became a "tick," shelling himself off from human relatedness in favor of invulnerability in what appeared to be a state of perpetual "affective" hibernation. He emitted nothing and was impenetrable (a state, it seemed, in which normal introjective or projective processes failed to take hold and develop).

It may be significant to note that, in spite of it all, Grenouille awaited the opportunity to "bore" into a warm-blooded entity, someone upon whom he might append himself, who could perhaps tolerate his most primitive fears of dying, of "falling to pieces or liquefying" (Bick 1986, p. 296). It appeared that a glimmer of hope—a trace of the epistemophilic instinct (Klein 1932)—had remained alive at the core of Grenouille's being, inside his self-made "shell" of invulnerability.

Eventually, Grenouille was doomed to rejection once again when his uncanny ability (his exquisite olfactory sensitivity) to identify and detect odors from great distances was misinterpreted by a superstitious and fearful Gaillard as an evil omniscience. With regard to this, it might be noted that Gaillard herself had dedicated much of her life to avoiding the death she omnisciently foresaw for herself, a death as a helpless "dependent," abandoned, unloved and uncared for, in the Hotel Dieu, a paupers' hospice. She not only foresaw her own death, but took the steps she thought necessary to ensure herself against such a death. In this context her misinterpretation of Grenouille's olfactory sensitivity seems likely to have emanated from the projection of her own omnipotent ideation, further motivated by the need to obliterate the threat inherent in experiencing the helpless-and-dependent-baby-he who was physically dying, unloved and uncared for, in her own foster home, an experience that surely touched upon and exacerbated her own worst fears.

In the hands of Grimal, the tanner who cruelly exploited children, little Grenouille once again suffered a psychosomatic explosion from which he was able to emerge, all the more immunized against death. Here we find that he has developed a new physical manifestation of his second skin: the scars covering his body, permanently left in the wake of his struggle with anthrax. Afterward, Grenouille engaged in a limited sensual (olfactory) exchange with his environment, and one day, while standing in the place of his mother's execution, he experienced (in olfactory terms) the longing to merge with the idealized womb-mother, represented by the sea in Süskind's story (again, described in olfactory terms).

Grenouille's first encounter with perfume (which seems to represent the essence of goodness in this tale) occurred during these same days. This goodness was soon to be equated with the smell of a virginal girl, pure and innocent, who had "known" no one. There is a strong implication here that "perfume" is equated with the idealized-maternal-object/innocent-baby-Grenouille in an undifferentiated and unintruded-upon state. Grenouille soon discovers that only through death can he preserve this scent for himself. His experiences have taught him that objects must be frozen, deadened, or somehow immobilized to keep them from exerting their own will and eventually and inevitably abandoning the baby-he. Perhaps his attempts to freeze his objects in time corresponds with the timelessness of Grenouille's two-dimensional existence and stunted development. However, in this first attempt to preserve that sense of at-one-ment with the "good mother," he learns that he can *take on* the "essence" of the object only through skin-to-skin contact, but that he cannot hope to *take it in* and make it his own. Perhaps for the first time Grenouille experienced the bliss of at-one-ment and discovered a new *raison d'être*: to create beautiful scents (i.e., the essence of the idealized birth-mother).

Formation and Transformations of Grenouille's Second Skin

Grenouille grew up an ugly child, or perhaps he experienced himself the way others/mother had experienced him. Not unlike some autistic children, he did not stand until the age of 3; he did not utter a word until age 4, and when he did begin to speak his utterances were restricted to nouns ("things"), while pronouns, indicating acting and receiving agents, were absent in his speech. He used words only for their sensuous affect upon him. It might be understood that these words created auto-sensuous "shapes"[7] (Tustin 1984b) upon Grenouille's lips and tongue, providing him with sensations that served to calm and "subdue him."

For Grenouille, only the sensuous mattered. It may be that these essential smells were the sensuous derivatives of the "activation contours"[8] of his affective experiences (Stern 1985), "more rich in meaning than language." Although Grenouille appeared to be feebleminded from the vertex of the outside observer—presumably an objective vertex—in Grenouille's experience (which was thor-

---

7. Autistic shapes (Tustin 1984b) are distinguished from objective shapes (such as a square or circle) in that they are idiosyncratic, endogenous swirls of sensation produced upon the surface of the skin or internally with the aid of bodily substances or objects that have a numbing or tranquilizing effect that blocks out painful and terrifying awareness.

8. An *activation contour* (Stern 1985) is an engramatic pattern that is registered at the somatic or physiological level—the level of brain, not the level of mind. According to Stern, each activation contour is composed of a set of *vitality affects*, formations of feelings or somatosensory experiences, i.e., waves or rushes of feeling, perhaps laid down as a pattern of neural firing in a particular area of the nervous system. Unlike *categorical affects* (e.g., sadness, happiness, anger), they have no symbolic content. Abstract dance and music are examples par excellence of the expressiveness of vitality affects, which do not resort to plot or categorical affect signals.

oughly walled off from detection) his mind was one of "riches and imagination" that although idiosyncratic, unshared, and defensively motivated, were rich nonetheless. Although this might be put forward as evidence that indeed Grenouille had "secretly" developed some mental life—an intellect and an "internal world of objects" in the Kleinian sense—I would suggest that what *appears* to be a true mentality is *actually* what is described by Winnicott as a pathological-mind-psyche, developed to take over the function of the missing environmental mother.

Twice, both in the service of Grimal the tanner and later in the service of Baldini the perfumer, Grenouille experienced a psychosomatic explosion that was associated in the story with extremes of physical abuse and psychological disillusionment. Each time, Grenouille managed his own reconstitution through the development of an ever tougher second skin (concretely represented by the scars and ugliness that shielded and protected him from painful and even deadly contact).

The experience of being stoned from the inside out seems to be Süskind's way of describing what was perhaps Grenouille's subjective experience of the event of his disillusionment (a psychic implosion). Perhaps it might be understood that these experiences of trauma and disillusionment, which remained untransformed by tender and caring interactions with a maternal object, remained at a concrete level in the psyche, and finally found both containment and expression in the somatic symptom (J. Mitrani 1987, 1993b). As Bion (1962) suggested, uncontained sensory experiences remain as concrete accretions of stimuli that are neither used to create meaning nor stored as memories in the mind. Such experiences are neither remembered nor forgotten but are instead held in abeyance in the somatic realm. It could also be said that these unmetabolized sensations (beta-elements) are organized in somatic disease, and may then constitute a beta-screen that functions as a second skin, providing the essential protective boundary for the self—even a false self or as-if personality—within which one might survive and function.

And so, even as he was exploited, Grenouille was able to regain something resembling a life. He seems, at last, to have attained some reprieve from the bondage that had been substituted for the missing experience of bonding (Grotstein 1989). Finally he retreated into complete isolation atop the dead volcano in a never-before-inhabited cavern offering him a womb-like environment and the prospect of olfactory peace.

Within his cave inside the remains of this once-active volcano, it might be said that Grenouille recouped the primal experience, that prebirth experience of "being the only human being in the world" of the maternal body. Symbols of fetal existence abound here—from the "virgin" tunnel in which he curled up to the umbilical snakes that nourished him and the uterine wall (the rocks) that he licked in quite a sensual manner to obtain the life-sustaining moisture. Within "his empire" Grenouille engaged in a sort of "olfactory myercism," regurgitating the smells of his past "within his innermost universal theater," ostensibly as an essential means of protecting himself from the terrifying awareness of his otherwise "soft-fleshed" vulnerability.

Gaddini's (1969) concept of the "psycho-oral" may allow some understanding to emerge from this description of Grenouille's accentuated sense of smell. Gaddini (1959) explored the phenomenon of myercism in very young infants who had undergone serious oral frustrations soon after birth, which, he observed, when coupled with a traumatic weaning, led to difficulties in introjective identification. Later, developing the concept of the psycho-oral, Gaddini (1969) proposed that "all sense organs may unconsciously be perceived as mouth-like" (p. 478n), an idea in keeping with Stern's later conceptualization of "amodal perception."[9] Gaddini

---

9. According to Stern (1985), newborns have an innate capacity to take information received in one sensory modality and translate it into any other sensory modality. The resultant perception

suggested there may be an excessive intensification of other modalities of sensory stimulation that compensate for and are due to insufficient oral stimulation.

Finally, a dream penetrated Grenouille's mindlessness, creating a fog that threatened to suffocate him. Perhaps this fog, like the fog described by Meltzer (1975) as the muddled-up feeling of "disintegration" or the experience of falling apart, was felt to pose a threat to Grenouille's continuity-of-being.

> He was deathly afraid, his whole body shook with a raw fear of death . . . he sat there shivering and trying to gather his confused, terrified thoughts, he knew one thing for sure: he would change his life, if only because he did not want to dream such a frightening dream a second time. He would not survive it a second time. [Süskind 1986, p. 164]

He escaped this state, seeking human contact once again. Then he met the marquis, whose interest in him arose from an expectation that, through the rehabilitation of this loathsome creature, he might yet prove his theory, a theory of the existence of the earth's deadly pull, in opposition to the life force itself. Although the marquis thought he had rehabilitated Grenouille through his treatment, he had instead helped to create an imitation of a man, a man wearing a perfume that allowed him to smell "as-if" he were a human who gives off a scent.

At this point in the saga Grenouille's protection seemed to evolve from offal to awful. Here his omnipotence took a new direction. No longer content with his pretense of being a human

---

exists in some supramodal form (e.g., wherein the breast that is seen, the breast that is smelled, the breast that is tasted, and the breast that is touched are linked together) and is encoded in what Stern refers to as an *amodal representation* that can be recognized in any of its sensory modalities.

among humans—a pretense that had gained him acceptance—
Grenouille was overtaken by a new obsession: to create and possess a superhuman scent so that he might inspire love. He went
about his task, collecting each of the components of this super smell
from the remains of the virginal beauties he murdered. In the story,
Süskind used the character Antoine Richis to provide the necessary insight for an understanding of Grenouille's motivation. Richis
believed that the murderer's aim was not to destroy but to collect,
not an attack on beauty, but an effort to preserve beauty for himself. Like
those autistic children who conceptualize growth as occurring in
"bits" acquired from the object and stuck onto the self (Tustin 1981),
Grenouille seemed to conceive of the development of a lovable-he
through acquisition and adhesion. Indeed, after he was captured
and convicted for his murderous crimes, Grenouille appeared as if
reborn: "innocence personified" in his self-made "skin" of scent.

But his triumph was empty! As always, he could find no reci-
procity for his emotional states. Just as his overflowing love and his
craving for attachment had been met in the past with hatred, so
now his overwhelming hatred begot only love. He could find no
resonance in others for what he had walled off within himself. Once
again Grenouille was overcome by the "fog of his odorlessness,"
which might be understood as an awareness of an experience of
no-body-ness and the feeling of disintegration. Grenouille was filled
with a boundless (uncontained) terror that constituted the final and
devastating realization of the concordance between his internal and
external realities. Although Grenouille was finally embraced by
Antoine Richis, it soon became apparent that it was not he who was
"adopted," but the reflection of Richis' own omnipotent projections,
evoked by the effects upon him of Grenouille's odoriferous second
skin.

In the final chapter Grenouille grew increasingly maddened
by an uncaring world. He appeared overcome by a despair evoked
by the painful realization that he might never be seen and loved

for himself, that he might never *become* himself. Once again he sought an experience of being "one" with the body of the mother. Toward this end he provoked the band of desperadoes to cannibalism and was finally "taken in"—eaten—in an act of "love." Indeed, this was the ultimate act of love, for it seems that what Süskind described in such concrete terms was the baby's experience of being introjected by the maternal object, an experience that the baby must have in order for him to be able to incorporate a sense of a containing object.[10] The infant's identification with such an object is absolutely necessary to the development of the all-important functions of introjection and projection.

Adhesive Pseudo-Object-Relations

Although it might be said that Grenouille lacked the capacity for object relations in the ordinary sense of the term, his behavior and experience seemed to fit the description of adhesive pseudo-object relations proposed in Chapter 8. Grenouille appeared to use his objects in much the same way that the autistic child uses objects: for the sensations they engender upon the surfaces of his body, sensations that provide a sense of impermeability, grandiosity, security, or tranquillity. Whether Grenouille manipulated or avoided his objects depended largely upon his sense of these as either protectively comforting or threateningly impinging. His repeated experience of the unreliability of his objects led him to rely

---

10. In a personal communication, Grotstein (1992), paraphrasing Fairbairn, clarified that the baby's experience of being introjected by the mother and its introjection of the mother as an object are processes that occur simultaneously and in parallel rather than in sequence; "the infant introjects the introjecting mother in the act of introjecting and thus has the object inside in whom he is inside."

upon those olfactory-sensation/objects (perfumes) he could create by himself.

At first Grenouille's idyllic existence inside the cave seemed to re-create an illusion of those earliest experiences of at-one-ment within the body of the mother. Only after many years, hidden away in his claustrum of stone, did the awareness of the black hole experience intrude into and dissolve Grenouille's illusion, an "experience of the awesome force of powerlessness, of defect, of nothingness, of 'zero-ness'—expressed not just as a static emptiness but as an implosive, centripetal pull into the void" (Grotstein 1990). I believe it was this momentary *awareness* of the aridity and bottomlessness of that black hole within, as it appeared to him in the dream, that Grenouille fled from in terror. He had moved from a state of mindless oblivion in the cave to a state of near-total collapse and, in a reflexophysiological way, he moved toward human contact, a move from avoidance of affective contact toward further sensation-dominated manipulation of humankind. Grenouille's self-generated olfactory reproductions provided him with a sensual delusion of safety. Throughout the story we can see how the failure of Grenouille's omnipotence was invariably followed by near-physiological collapse and the subsequent reconstitution of an even more impenetrable second skin.

The development of Grenouille's second skin can be traced from his earliest tick-like (muscular) encapsulation through utilization of odoriferous sensations as a protective sheath to a survival-oriented hyperactivity with the skins of animals that he learned to manipulate with great skill. The scars he acquired in his battle with anthrax served to toughen him even further against those cruel contacts with human beings, just as his ever-increasing ugliness served to ward off the threat of painful human closeness. This tough exterior secured for Grenouille an internal chamber in which he could hide away and seal off from threat of loss those precious stolen scents of the "Madonna-esque" as well as the vital essence of his own authentic self, that never-loved and therefore unborn-he.

Grenouille's experience of suffocation seemed to be a side effect of this protective sealing-off of all that was good and alive in himself and his panic, a result of the fleeting awareness that he could not access—could not smell—this aspect of his own nascent "self." Neither could he avail himself of the good objects he had sealed off inside. The fortress he had erected in avoidance of the black hole experience that threatened him became a penitentiary from which he could not escape into life.

The theme of collapse permeates Süskind's story, always coinciding with extremes of privation, disillusionment, separation, and loss. It would appear that in art, as in life, those experiences that remain untransformed and unmitigated in the mind are sometimes dealt with by assignment to and expression in the actions of others. Many of Grenouille's caretakers perished in the wake of his departure. If one can imagine that each had been experienced by Grenouille not as a separate individual but as a bodily part, then the death of each one takes on additional significance as a concrete expression of Grenouille's own recurrent experience of mutilation and psychic death. For example, just as his mother's head was severed from her body, Grenouille's own psyche was terminally dissociated from his physical being; just as Gaillard was deceived and neglected-to-death, Grenouille was left disillusioned by extremes of hypocrisy and disregard; just as Grimal was drowned in a state of self-induced stupor, Grenouille was submerged in the blocking out of his own awareness; just as Baldini's whole world suddenly and inexplicably collapsed, Grenouille had felt the collapse of the maternal environment and of the protective shell he had created as a substitute for it; and finally, just as the marquis was assumed to have disappeared atop a frozen mountain, Grenouille seemed lost in retreat from human relationships, in his frozen emotional life.

Last but not least are the deaths of all those beautiful inno-
cents. Just as they had been rendered unconscious, their hair shorn,
stripped of their clothing, and robbed of the very essence of their
being, Grenouille had been robbed of his own essence, his innocence, long ago sacrificed for the sake of survival. All these deaths,
I believe, might be seen to represent those "felt" and deflected
sensory experiences of an abandoned and dying baby-Grenouille.

CONCLUDING THOUGHTS

Hamilton (1989) reserves the word trauma "for responses to events
which arouse in most of us intense feelings of horror, a sense of
outrage and very often a feeling of revulsion and turning away. We
would rather not know and hear" (p. 74). As therapists we might
often rather turn away in order to insulate ourselves from such
trauma, as have our patients who suffered the insult of catastrophic
events at those moments in time—in earliest infancy or even before
birth—when they were ill-prepared to do otherwise.

The story of Grenouille conveys the quintessence of trauma;
it is perhaps an extreme caricature of others we have "known" and
"heard" in our consulting rooms. As psychoanalysts we strive to be
open and receptive in our attitude toward our patients in order to
experience, understand, and interpret mutatively, perhaps even in
order to imagine our patients anew, as separate and apart from the
theories within which we may find ourselves safely swaddled. We
aspire to tolerate, to accept, and initially to affirm experiences as
they are relived in the transference, this toward a modification of
experience in the long run. However, we must always be aware of
our own as well as our patients' limitations, the threshold of our
own intolerance of the horrific, the outrageous, and the revolting,
especially our own tendency to turn away from or perhaps to
"abjectify," to hurl away, or to cut off our patients' communications

prematurely when these threaten to debride our old wounds, long ago scarred over and forgotten.

Perhaps adhesive identity or adhesive equation can be relinquished by the patient only as the analyst dares to relinquish his or her insulation against the awareness of unhealed personal wounds that may constitute a black hole, this in order to allow some momentary mingling of experiences out of which true object relatedness may evolve.

10

Toward an Understanding of Unmentalized Experience[1]

Without sensibility no object would be given to us, without understanding no object would be thought. Thoughts without content are empty, intuitions without concepts are blind.

[Immanuel Kant, *A Critique of Pure Reason*]

INTRODUCTION

In Chapter 2, I addressed some of the clinical issues involved in the psychoanalytic treatment of certain patients who, while under threat of being overwhelmed by organismic panic (Grotstein 1984) or of being engulfed in a black hole of despair (Tustin 1972), protect themselves against the terrifying awareness of those early ex-

---

1. An earlier version of this chapter was presented at a scientific meeting of the Psychoanalytic Center of California on March 25, 1993, and published in *The Psychoanalytic Quarterly* in 1995.

periences of bodily separateness and loss that have yet to be mitigated through a process of human interaction. Since earliest infancy
the awareness of these experiences in their raw primordial form
has been kept at bay through the deployment of certain encapsulating forces akin to those utilized by autistic children as described
over the past three decades by Bick (1968), Meltzer (1975), Meltzer
and colleagues (1975), and Tustin (1969, 1972, 1980, 1981, 1984a,b,
1987, 1990, 1991). There I emphasized the survival function of those
auto-sensual maneuvers that form psychobiological containers for
unmentalized experience.

After the original publication of the paper on which that
chapter was based certain readers called my attention to the fact
that the term *unmentalized experience* required some elaboration
and explication as to its source and meaning. This chapter therefore aims toward a definition of this concept in order to en-
hance its usefulness for the purpose of scientific discourse and
dialogue while at the same time attempting to facilitate its use
as a model for understanding yet another dimension of human
functioning.

First, I will give a brief working definition of the term, after
which I will trace the predecessors of the concept from Freud
through the present-day object relations theorists. I will also show
how such ideas, derived from clinical experience, may be further
enhanced by mingling them with those derived from modern fetal
and infant observational research. From time to time I will return
to the clinical arena to illustrate certain aspects of unmentalized
experience and their transformation through the analytic process.
As I intend to address several divergent theoretical schools of
thought in psychoanalysis to accomplish my task (which includes a
cross-fertilization between these divergent vertices), I will attempt
to transcend the language barrier that exists between, and even
within, theoretical orientations by providing numerous footnotes
to be used by the reader as necessary.

A WORKING DEFINITION
OF UNMENTALIZED EXPERIENCE

In this chapter the term *unmentalized experience* denotes elemental sense data, internal and external, that have failed to be transformed into symbols (mental representations, organized and integrated) or signal affects (anxiety that serves as a signal of impending danger, requiring thoughtful action), but are instead perceived as concrete objects in the psyche or as bodily states that are reacted to in corporeal fashion (e.g., somatic symptoms or actions). Such experiences are merely "accretions of stimuli" that can neither be used as food for thought nor stored in the form of memories. These experiences, which have not been kept in mind, cannot be repressed. Instead they are isolated as if in quarantine, where they remain highly immutable. These unmentalized experiences therefore represent one of the most challenging aspects of our work.

I believe Freud's notion of the "anxiety equivalent" (1895b, p. 94) in actual neurosis was the first attempt to characterize this phenomenon in psychoanalysis. A brief review of Freud's thinking in this area will provide the necessary background for what is to follow.

THE ANXIETY EQUIVALENT

In 1894 Freud wrote to Fliess:

There is a kind of *conversion* in anxiety neurosis just as there is in hysteria . . . but in hysteria it is *psychical* excitation that takes a wrong path exclusively into the somatic field, whereas here [in anxiety neurosis] it is a *physical* tension which cannot enter the psychical field and therefore remains on the physical path. [1892–1899, p. 195]

Here Freud seems to be suggesting that in the case of the individual suffering from anxiety neurosis, there may exist a physical tension that may somehow be present without a psychical concomitant.

In his first model of conversion hysteria, Freud (Breuer and Freud 1893–1895) proposed that his patients had maintained psychic health until a point at which an event, idea, or sensation awakened in the ego such painful feelings that the individual was compelled to "forget" for want of alternate capabilities with respect to resolving internal contradictions. In his second model Freud understood somatic symptom formation as an organic "anxiety equivalent" (1895b, p. 94). On his way toward developing this latter model he observed that disturbances of "bodily functions . . . such as respiration" (p. 94) often accompany, mask, or even substitute altogether for anxiety and, in contrast to the anxiety of the hysteric, the analysis of such anxiety fails to uncover a repressed idea. Here, *in the case of the anxiety neurosis, or "actual" neurosis, the somatic symptom results from physical sensations that have been denied access to the psychic apparatus*—sensory experiences that have failed to be mentalized—whereas in hysterical conversion psychic stimulation induced by conflict is repressed, i.e., banished to expression in the physical organic symptom.

In either case Freud cited *"a psychical insufficiency, as a consequence of which abnormal somatic processes arise."* He suggested that in both, "instead of a psychical working-over of the excitation, a deflection of it occurs into the somatic field" (1895b, p. 115). The distinction Freud makes here is of paramount importance in that hysterical conversion is seen by him as a subtype of repression in which the organic symptom is a physical representation of a psychic transformation, while the *organic symptom of anxiety neurosis is understood as a direct expression of unmentalized somato-sensory excitation.*

In further distinguishing between hysterical conversion and the actual neuroses or anxiety equivalent, Freud described the bodily symptoms of the former as representations of psychic or mental experience that might be interpreted as stemming from an unconscious conflict between the instinctual needs and the ego's defenses. In other words, the conversion symptom constituted a compromise, with the characteristics of a symbol standing for an idea. However, the symptom of actual neuroses was thought to be the equivalent of a psychic state of an undifferentiated or primitive anxiety—not the representative or physical expression of a psychical activity gone awry but an indication that a psychic activity has failed to occur.

It might be said that the conversion symptom is a substitution of a bodily symptom for a conscious action that represents an unconscious desire to act upon an idea, while the organic symptom of the anxiety neurosis indicates a lack of mentation of a sensory experience, the idea of the action never having been formed. From this, one might conclude that there is a relationship between conversion and repression, while relating anxiety equivalents to the more primitive varieties of projection or more precisely, to the use of *projective identification for the purpose of communication* (Bion 1959, 1967a). I wish to emphasize that the distinction between these two models of somatization lies in the observation that in hysteria the excess of excitation is psychical in its origin, that is, the excitation is provoked by conflicting ideas. In anxiety neurosis, however, the excitation is purely somato-sensual, physical in its origin and as yet untransformed in the mental sphere.

In light of these findings Freud (1916–1917) concluded: "the problems of the 'actual' neuroses . . . offer psychoanalysis no points of attack. It can do little towards throwing light on them and must leave the task to biologico-medical research" (p. 389). It seems Freud relegated those neuroses of a somatic nature, neuroses devoid of psychical content, to the background of psychoanalysis. In short, such patients were assumed at one time to be unanalyzable. Fortunately, the pioneer work of Melanie Klein—and the extensions of her work by the Kleinian and Independent schools in Great Britain to the present day—has amplified our understanding of such primitive states. This understanding has led to a refinement in technique that has facilitated access to patients previously thought to be unanalyzable. Such access becomes possible through a process of analysis in which countertransference can be understood as (at least in part) an indication that a communication of a sensory experience has taken place, requiring transformation in the mentality of the analyst. Throughout this chapter I will examine some of the pivotal ideas of these British schools as they apply to the concept of unmentalized experience.

EXPERIENCES THAT REMAIN UNMENTALIZED

To begin to render the concept of unmentalized experience meaningful, it may be important to delineate those experiences most likely to remain unmentalized and how this might occur. I will therefore attempt to describe some of the elemental happenings in the life of the fetus and neonate that are sometimes foreclosed from the mental sphere due to a coincidence of vulnerability in both infant and mother, with unfortunate consequences for the development of mental structure. Here I once again return to the work of Freud on the anxiety equivalent in actual neurosis.

Freud (1926) noted that anxiety, as well as other affective states, is a precipitate of "primeval traumatic experiences, and when a similar situation occurs" (p. 93) anxiety is revived, expressing itself in a form determined by the experience that provoked it originally. He suggested that "in man, birth provides the prototypic experience" and he viewed "anxiety-states as a reproduction of the trauma of birth" (p. 133), drawing attention to "those physical sensations which clearly and frequently accompany such affective states" (p. 132).

Freud (1926) then proposed that those

innervations involved in the original state of anxiety probably had a meaning and purpose . . . at birth it is probable that the innervation, in being directed to the respiratory organs, is preparing the way for the activity of the lungs, and, in accelerating the heartbeat, is helping to keep the blood free of toxic substances. [p. 134]

He also asserted that "the baby will repeat its affect of anxiety in every situation which recalls the event of birth" (p. 135) and concluded that what is recalled and what it represents is "separation from the mother" (p. 137), which is regarded as catastrophic. Here Freud seems to imply that the purpose of the sensations that accompany the original and subsequent states of anxiety is to rid the self of the primal experience of separation, which is felt to be deadly toxic.

It has been brought to my attention (Osterweil 1990) that the presence of toxins in the prenatal environment might threaten the fetus with actual physical destruction, that the mother's emotional states affect her physical chemistry and may sometimes be at the root of spontaneous abortions in early pregnancy, and that biochemical intrauterine alterations may cause fetal distress and even premature labor in the last stage of pregnancy. Although such perils experienced *in utero* may be overcome on a physiological level with the aid of modern medical procedures, such early trauma may leave behind emotional scars, perhaps in the form of a felt threat of "discontinuity of being" (Winnicott 1960a).

Recent prenatal and perinatal research (Mancia 1981, Osterweil 1990, Piontelli 1985, 1987, 1988, 1992) seems to confirm what Freud (1926) intuited years before when he stated,

There is much more continuity between intra-uterine life and earliest infancy than the impressive caesura of the act of birth would have us believe. What happens is that the child's biological situation as a foetus is replaced for it by a psychical object-relation to its mother. [p. 138]

What Freud implied then, and what we can be more certain of now, is that the infant's immediate postnatal relationship with the breast-mother is not only the "prototype of the expression of sexual satisfaction in later life"[2] (Freud 1905, p. 182), but also a continuation and transformation of the sensory *feeling* of being inside the mother's body.

For some babies this is a tangible feeling of being held safely and securely within the mother's womb, which is, after birth, transformed into and sustained within the feeling of being held in the postnatal womb of the mother's mind as well as in her arms. However, for some less fortunate neonates, there may be instead a sensory experience of a prenatal disturbance that is tantamount to a catastrophic psychological birth (Tustin 1983), one that may remain untransformed by the mind of the mother. This sensory experience is therefore likely to elicit the most primitive forms of anxiety, which are indistinguishable from the physiological sensations of unbearably painful irritation, mutilation, burning, or tearing of the body. These experiences, if they should continue unabated, may produce an endless bodily agony of spilling, falling, dissolving, and evaporating into nothingness. This felt experience constitutes a "nameless dread" (Bion 1967a) that provokes "unthinkable anxieties" (Winnicott 1960a) and truly threatens the infant's sense of "going-on-being" (ibid.) and the "rhythm of safety" (Tustin 1986) necessary for the establishment of normal object relations. Since such catastrophes are experienced by a "body-ego" (Freud 1923) or a "felt-self" (Tischler 1979), which as yet cannot tolerate the awareness of such physical discontinuity, that awareness (or even the

---

2. Gooch (1985) has written an extensive thesis on the subject of the mother–infant nursing relationship as a prototype for sexual satisfaction in adult couples. She suggested that failures and frustrations experienced in this early nipple-mouth connection replicate themselves in a variety of sexual dysfunctions in adulthood.

capacity for awareness itself) is felt as a toxin that is expelled or perhaps withdrawn from (Grotstein 1991).

For example, Robert (who had come to analysis after numerous hospitalizations and suicide attempts) told me of a visual handicap from which he had suffered all his life. "I have this one eye which needs correction. I have no depth perception in that eye. Through it I see the world in only two dimensions. Many doctors have tried to correct it, but it can't be fixed. Although, I think I like it that way. I see the world the way I like it best. They call it a lazy eye. One time in the emergency room a doctor told me that I must have had a traumatic birth. He said that this eye problem is typical of this."

Over time we came to understand the lazy "I" as a somatic *presentation* of an unborn-he who could not bear changes in light, temperatures, or textures and so could not be *fixed by* the analysis but could only be *fixed onto* it. He could not bear the end of the hour, as it felt to him that I was peeling him off the placental walls next to the couch, which he often stroked during episodes of mute anguish. His "adhesive" way of using me in the sessions (and between times on the telephone) and his experience of being torn away from me over and over again with each separation was "felt" by my patient and "suffered" by me for many months. During holidays and sometimes even over weekends Robert would engage in behavior that would result in his being put "on hold" in the hospital. He would often describe in great detail and with much emotion previous episodes in the hospital, when he was actually placed in four-point restraints in a padded room. On one occasion when he overdosed on a mixture of substances, not only was he hospitalized but he also required renal dialysis. Thus, in a very dramatic way, Robert brought home to me his felt need, not just for the womb, but for the umbilical cord and its vital functions as well.

It seemed to me, although I had no evidence for this at the time, that he experienced all endings as re-enactments of his birth, the sense of which I gradually attempted to communicate to him as we struggled along painfully together. We finally came to discover that his actual birth had been premature (by one month), brutal (his father delivered him under primitive conditions in a place where no medical assistance was available), and dangerously complicated by *placenta previa*. The patient's recollections of this event seemed indeed to be "body memories" that were both encapsulated and expressed in behavior, character, and physiological anomaly.

With the above in mind, I will now backtrack to discuss the specific factors identified by Freud (Breuer and Freud 1893–1895) as those that prevent physical excitation from being worked over in the psychical field and precipitate the formation of the anxiety equivalent, which is a sign of unmentalized experience. Freud listed these etiological factors as (1) sexual abstinence, (2) coitus interruptus, and (3) deflection of psychical interest from sexuality. If in light of our present-day understanding we were to substitute for these three (1) the subjective experience of privation, externally or internally imposed; (2) premature disillusionment with and (3) schizoid withdrawal from the primary object (the holding and containing breast-mother of earliest infancy), it might be possible to flesh out Freud's original model of anxiety neurosis.

An updated version might read: *somatosensual excitation*, arising from a *premature awareness of bodily separateness* from the *primary caretaker* (who is at first experienced as a part of the self)[3] may result in a *felt experience of primordial terror* that must be *deflected from the psychic or mental apparatus* in the event of *psychical insufficiency* (the lack of an external or internal containing object). Subsequently, this experience that remains *unmentalized* finds aberrant means of both containment and expression in its "equivalent" (e.g., auto-sensual

---

3. This concept is addressed by a number of authors: e.g., the "subjective mother" of Winnicott (1962); the "background object of primary identification" and the "sensory floor," terms coined by Grotstein (1980); and the "archaic self object" of Kohut (1971).

encapsulation, somatic symptoms, hyperactivity), which serves to keep the felt-self free of toxic substances (e.g., awareness of the absence of the good-object, which is *felt* as a toxic substance or as a treacherous void).

Because it may seem that at this point we have entered into the internal world of objects and phantasy, I will continue my discussion with these familiar concepts, perhaps adding some new variations on several old themes. It is my intention to make clear discriminations between mental states and what Bion (1962) referred to as the "proto-mental."

THE CONCEPT OF PHANTASY

Derived from the work of Melanie Klein (1932) and others of the Kleinian group in London (Heimann 1952, Isaacs 1952), the concept of unconscious fantasy (spelled *phantasy* to discriminate this unconscious product of mentation from a *fantasy*, which is conscious) has amplified Freud's earlier notion of the term. For some time it has been a widely held belief that phantasies are processes active in the infant long before they can be represented in a symbolic or verbal manner. The earliest phantasies are presented in a somato-sensual mode (Isaacs 1952, p. 74) as bodily sensations and then as motor action.

The infant (in a position of maximal vulnerability and minimal motoric and verbal capability) employs phantasy as a means of defense, for inhibition and control of instinctual urges and for expression of wishes and desires and their fulfillment. The omnipotent character of these phantasies is directly proportionate to the degree to which vulnerability is experienced by the infant. As primitive anxieties increase, so the phantasies that constitute the pre-historic self-survival tactics of infancy proliferate, employing the senses, the viscera, and the bodily organs in the service of expression.

The form taken by these primitive phantasies in infancy is in part determined by the mother, whose own unconscious fantasies, projected into the infant at or even before birth, intermingle with innate infantile "preconceptions" to provide the primordial basis of the infant's own phantasies. In a sense the mother's phantasies provide the alphabet from which the infant begins to spell out the meaning of its own life experiences, its earliest sensory and affective states. The form or shape of the mother's phantasies about her own and her baby's emotional states are, in a sense, passed on through the placenta and in her milk (Brazelton and Cramer 1990, Mancia 1981, J. Mitrani 1987, Piontelli 1985).

Although Isaacs (1952) considered the *expression* of infantile phantasies to take place initially on a bodily level, "since the infant has so few resources at its command for expressing love or hate— his profound and overwhelming wishes and emotions" (p. 95), she maintained that the first phantasies are represented in the mental sphere. She proposed that the infant's earliest affective encounters are not merely bodily happenings but are also experienced in mental processes, namely as phantasies represented nonverbally and nonsymbolically, ostensibly in the form of images or pictographs. She also stated: "Perhaps the most convincing evidence of the activity of phantasy without words is that of hysterical conversion symptoms" (p. 90).

Here she drew our attention to the possibility that in conversion the individual returns to the use of a

primitive, pre-verbal language, and makes use of sensations . . . and visceral processes to express . . . phantasies. . . . Each detail of the symptom turns out to have a specific meaning, i.e., to express a specific phantasy; and the various shifts of form and intensity and the bodily part affected reflect changes in phantasy, occurring in response to outer events or to inner pressures. [p. 90]

This view of phantasy, which Isaacs exemplified with hysterical conversion, does not really seem to explain Freud's second area of somatic disturbance—the anxiety equivalent of anxiety neurosis—which I believe to be associated with a protomental area of experience and its concomitant realm of protophantasies.[4] The notion that an individual's earliest experiences, both pre- and postnatal, contribute to the emergence of somato-sensual protophantasies (first recorded as body-memories) and the idea that these protophantasies are both *presented* and expressed primarily on a protomental level may fill this gap, left by Isaacs, in our understanding of such primitive states of being.

A model for the establishment of body memories (which may be thought of as the prototype of later memories recorded in the mind, just as protophantasies recorded somatically may be thought of as the forerunners of their later mental counterparts) might be extrapolated from the work of Stern (1985) stemming from current infant observational research. I will attempt to formulate one such model later on in this chapter. However, I would first like to briefly clarify my substitution above of the term *presentation* for the term *representation*, which Isaacs uses in her discussion of phantasy.

I believe that the earliest phantasies are initially *unrepresented* in the mental realm. That is, primary phantasies, or what Bion called *protophantasies*, arise from central and peripheral neural perceptions of emotional experiences with objects that are *presented* (e.g., sensual experiences at the breast or even before that, *in utero*). These phantasies are concretely *recorded* (presented, rather than represented) as body-memories, later to be *presented* for expression through the visceral organs and the muscular system of the neonate.

Such experiences, although *presented* in a somatic mode as body memories, may not have attained mental representation. This

---

4. What I am referring to here is an area of experience and phantasy involving the prenatal, perinatal, and immediate postnatal existence of the fetus/infant, that area that Winnicott (1949) designates as *the realm of the "psyche-soma," in which experiences are recorded somatically*, an area later elaborated upon in an "imaginative conjecture" by Bion (1970).

area of protophantasy, associated with such early experiences, precedes those phantasies that Isaacs referred to as mental events, i.e., phantasy associated with an experience that is re-presented from the somatic to the psychic or mental realm with the aid of a containing object. The distinctions made here between *phantasy* proper and *protophantasy* and between *presentation* and *representation* are analogous to the distinctions Freud made between *hysterical conversion* and *anxiety equivalent*.

INNATE FORMS

Tustin (1987) suggested that any attempt to differentiate between the earliest *protophantasies* and later *phantasies* in the mind is somewhat complicated by the use of the term phantasy to describe both; the term phantasy can easily be misinterpreted as synonymous with sophisticated mentational processes. Tustin prefers using the term innate forms,[5] which she defines as innate biological reactions or physiological reflexes with psychic overtones.[6]

Perhaps this distinction between the protophantasy and the unconscious fantasy will become increasingly relevant to the reader if we consider how the distinction affects our approach to the treatment of our patients. Until recently, traditional psychoanalytic

---

5. The "innate form," which Tustin conceptualizes as a *biological predisposition with psychic overtones*, seems to be closer in meaning to Bion's "pre-conception."

6. I have elsewhere suggested (J. Mitrani 1993b) that, in psychosomatic patients, these have remained untransformed by reciprocal interactions with an attentive, thinking mother and have found expression in psychosomatic symptoms that block further development and transformation into symbols. In such cases the patient is transfixed on this pathological psychosomatic level and mentation is obviated.

approaches to treatment have been aimed toward seeking out conflicts and phantasies *within the mind* that seem to exert their pathological effects upon our analysands as manifested in their intra- and
interpersonal relationships, in their capacity to work and play, and
in their state of physical health. The introduction of the notion of
unmentalized experience implies an approach in which the analyst
attempts to shift somato-sensory or body-memories and protophantasies from the body into the mind, from the realm of action and
bodily events to that of logical verbal expression, where they may
be represented symbolically for the first time, finally to be introduced into the orbit of self-reflection. The aim of psychoanalysts
here is to build psychic structure, to further develop a mind-ego
from an original body-ego (Freud 1923). I believe that the key to
accomplishing this aim lies in Bion's theory of functions and his
concept of *container–contained*.

BION'S THEORY OF FUNCTIONS

Bion (1957, 1967a) traced the origins of the "psychotic part of the
personality," this corresponding with the baby's experience of the
mother's inability to provide an adequate container for its fears of
impending doom. Bion delineated a model in which the capacity
of the mother to receive the baby's anxiety, unwanted parts of the
self, of the senses, and of the mental apparatus, which are felt to
pose a threat to his existence; her ability to transform raw sensory
data (beta-elements) through her alpha-function,[7] into the stuff of

---

7. The receptive capacity of the mother which Bion called
reverie is that quality of the primary object which performs "alpha
function" (the transformational operation of the mind). The
mother's "alpha function" operates as a semi-permeable membrane
which processes the infant's "beta elements" (its raw sensory perceptions of emotional experiences), detoxifying them, imbuing them

which dreams, thoughts, and memories are made (alpha-elements); and her knack for returning them to the baby (sufficiently detoxified for his underdeveloped system to be able to tolerate) in an unimposing manner, all coalesce to make up an adequate "container" or containing object. The mother as container operates in a state of "reverie" (or receptive attentiveness) that must be adequate relative to the constitutional vulnerability of the individual infant.

Bion (1963) reminded us that at first "the infant depends on mother to act as its alpha-function" (p. 27).

> The infant, filled with painful lumps of faeces, guilt, fears of impending death, chunks of greed, meanness, and urine, evacuates these bad objects into the breast that is not there. As it does so, the good object turns the no-breast (mouth) into a breast, and the faeces and urine into milk, and the fear of impending death and anxiety into vitality and confidence, the greed and meanness into feelings of love and generosity and the infant sucks its bad property, now translated into goodness, back again. [p. 31]

Bion proposed that the development of an apparatus for thinking depended upon the "successful introjection of the good breast that is originally responsible for the performance of alpha-function" (p. 32).

It would seem that the baby must first have an experience of being introjected by the mother before it can introject the mother

---

with meaning, and returning to the baby the purified and digestible "alpha elements" which cohere to make up a "contact barrier" (Bion 1962, Freud 1895a) or "alpha membrane" (Meltzer 1978, p. 79) essential to the development of a mind for thinking thoughts; a mind with the capacity to separate conscious from unconscious, internal from external, phantasy from reality, wakefulness from sleep and dreams, with fluid communication between these dualities.

as an object with the capacity for alpha-function. It might be that this is especially crucial after the experience of being projected out of the interior of the mother in the process of birth, an experience with the potential to provoke the most terrifying anxieties. This notion would surely be in keeping with Bion's—that the infant's experience of the container precedes its own development of alpha-function.

Owing to Bion's work, we now understand that in order for the normal processes of projective and introjective identification to proceed in a healthful manner, without mutating into pathological autistic maneuvers or hyperbolic disintegration of the self, the holding mother of infancy (Winnicott 1941) must also exhibit containing[8] properties. The metabolic processing of the baby's raw sensory experience (which is initially devoid of meaning) through the mother's mental function leads to increasing development of symbol formation and a decrease in mindless action and somatization in reaction to intense affective states. Normal projective iden-

---

8. The properties necessary to adequate containment are the capacities to receive and take in projected parts and feelings of the infant; to experience the full effect of these on the psyche-soma and to bear those effects; and to think about and understand these projections, gradually returning them to the infant in due time and in decontaminated form. This assumes a mother who has her own boundaries, internal space, a capacity to bear pain, to contemplate, to think, and to reflect back. A mother who is herself separate, intact, receptive, capable of "reverie," and appropriately giving is suitable for introjection as a good containing object. Identification with and assimilation of such an object leads to the development of a capacity to make meaning (alpha-function), increased mental space, and the development of a mind that can think for itself. Bion coined the term *reverie* for the attentive, receptive, introjective, and experiencing aspect of the container and I believe that this function of the maternal environment is analogous to the mental/emotional aspect of what Winnicott (1941) referred to as holding.

tification and subsequent introjective identification with a containing object leads to a decrease in the tendency to concretize emotional experience and an increase in the development of abstract and creative thinking, replacing action symptoms related to painfully unbearable emotional states with increasing tolerance of psychic pain and mental transformations.

The overanxious mother may be impaired in her capacity for reverie. If she cannot receive her baby's communications, she may be internalized[9] as an obstructive object unwilling or unable to contain. If she cannot digest what she receives, but is instead felt to add her own anxieties to those already overwhelming the infant (using the infant as a container for her own unthinkable dreads), then what she hurriedly gives back to the baby will be suitable only for some hyperbolic form of discharge. Consequently, the baby will develop a precocious mind as an instrument for evacuating or encapsulating experience rather than as an instrument for thinking thoughts.

Federn's work (1952) preceded Bion's thinking when he suggested that, whether physical or mental, the experience of pain is relegated to the domain of the ego and he distinguished between *suffering pain* and *feeling pain*. He suggested that *suffering* is the expression of an *active function on the part of the ego*, during the course of which the pain-inducing event (frustration with or loss of the object) is taken within the boundaries of the ego and the full intensity of the event is appreciated, consumed, and digested, thus under-

---

9. In such situations incorporation rather than introjective identification and assimilation occurs and the object is not integrated into the personality, there to be mitigated or modified by other experiences/objects. As a foreign body or "undigested fact" (Bion 1962, p. 7), it is often projected either onto external objects in the present in an attempt at containment and modification, or it may be encapsulated internally, later to become the core of a pathological organization.

going transformation by the ego and, in turn, transforming the ego. *Feeling* pain is, on the other hand, a process in which the pain-inducing event cannot be endured and worked through within the bounds of the ego. Thus, the pain is not contained within the ego but merely touches upon its borders, affecting it painfully and with every recurrence meeting the ego boundary with the same intensity and traumatic effect. Therefore, such pain poses a threat to the ego's integrity and as such must be warded off. Such painful experiences are not taken within the bounds of the ego, there to be subjected to a process of mentation, but instead remain unmentalized in the form of body-memories.

Federn attributed this inability of the ego to suffer pain to a primary failure of the ego resulting from a lack of narcissistic cathexis of the ego boundary.[10] The capacity for suffering pain seems to be related to thinking. This distinction between *suffering* and *feeling* pain was later made by Bion (1965) without reference to this work of Federn, who seemed to be articulating what Bick (1968) would later term the *psychic skin* and what Meltzer (1978) would later come to call the *alpha-membrane*.

In the case of a weak ego-boundary, it would seem that the baby's painful experience has touched the mother, but has not been introjected by the mother, who, it seems cannot bear to suffer her baby and who is therefore unable to mitigate its experience. The possibility that this environmental factor not only applies to postnatal life but also prenatal embryonic development is addressed in perinatal research (Mancia 1981).

---

10. Martin James (1986), utilizing the work of Winnicott in his paper on premature ego development, clarified that the baby's ego boundary is originally cathected by the "ordinary devoted mother" in a state of near-total preoccupation with her infant. Lacking the auxiliary ego function of the mother, the baby develops his own ego prematurely and defensively.

The "body ego" (Freud 1923), which I am here equating with the "proto-mental apparatus" (Bion 1962), does not create mental representations of experiences, but instead perceives these experiences as bodily states to which it reacts with bodily states and actions on a visceral or motoric level. These reactions are manifestations of protophantasies presented in a somato-sensual mode, as bodily sensations (sense impressions) or sensory experiences devoid of meaning in the symbolic sense of the word.

It will be recalled that Freud (Breuer and Freud 1893–1895) referred to these sense impressions as somatosexual excitations felt to be physical in origin and untransformed in the mental sphere. Bion called these sense impressions of emotional experiences (which are not transformed in the mental sphere) beta-elements, noting that they are not appropriate for thinking, dreaming, remembering, or exercising intellectual functions usually related to the mental apparatus. He posited, after Kant, that they are experienced instead as "things-in-themselves," which are generally evacuated (Bion 1962).

Bion's theory of functions describes *alpha* as that function of the personality that works over these beta-elements, transforming them into alpha-elements that have been given meaning and so are able to reside within the mental sphere. These are utilized in the formation of dream thoughts, unconscious waking thought processes, and dreams themselves, and are stored as memories in the mind. Alpha-function may be said to be that function of the maternal object that provides the infant, and perhaps even the fetus (Mancia 1981), with the experience of a psychic skin (Bick 1968).

THE FUNCTION OF THE SKIN

The contribution of Esther Bick (1968) seems to articulate the first element essential to the elaboration of a model for the development of mental structure and the subsequent mentalization of experience. In her work with autistic children and normal infants, Bick noticed certain behaviors that led her to believe that these individuals experienced the absence of suitable boundaries capable of holding together mental contents not yet distinguishable or differentiated from bodily contents.

Bick proposed the notion of a psychic skin (perhaps similar to the concept of ego boundary in the primitive body-ego) that ideally serves in its function to passively bind together the parts of the nascent self. She described this psychic skin as a projection of or as corresponding to the bodily skin and posited that it is "dependent initially on the introjection of an external object, experienced as capable of fulfilling this function" (p. 484). I believe that the external object here is a complex, undifferentiated object composed of experiences of continuous interaction between a physically and emotionally "holding" and "containing" mother and the surface of the infant's body as a sensory or sensual organ. This complex notion appears to be one Freud himself struggled with, as evidenced by his statement that "the ego is first and foremost a bodily ego; it is not merely a surface entity, but is itself the projection of a surface" (1923, p. 26).

Bick (1968) hypothesized: "Later, identification with this function of the object supersedes the unintegrated state and gives rise to the fantasy of internal and external space" (p. 484). She posited this as an essential basis for normal adaptive splitting, which allows for the idealization of the self and object described by Klein. Bick warned:

> Until the containing functions have been introjected, the concept of a space within the self cannot arise . . . construction of an [internal] object . . . is therefore impaired. In its absence, the function of projective identification will necessarily continue unabated. [p. 484]

Bick was the first Kleinian to make the crucial distinction between *unintegration* as a helpless, passive state of maximal dependency and the active, defensive maneuvers of splitting or *disintegration* in the name of growth (although Winnicott addressed these issues at length some ten years earlier). She associated the former with annihilation anxiety and, I believe, particularly the fear of not-going-on-being (Winnicott 1958a), while she related the latter to persecutory and depressive anxieties.

> The need for a containing object would seem in the infantile unintegrated state, to produce a frantic search for an object—a light, a voice, a smell, or other sensual object—which can hold the attention and thereby be experienced, momentarily at least, as holding the parts of the personality together. The optimal object is the nipple in the mouth, together with the holding and talking and familiar smelling mother . . . experienced concretely as a skin. . . . Disturbance in the primal skin function can lead to development of a "second skin" formation through which dependence on the object is replaced by a pseudo-independence. [Bick 1968, p. 484]

In a paper elaborating on Bick's concept of the second skin, Symington (1985) discussed the survival function of omnipotent phantasies. She described one such phantasy as a tightening or constricting of the smooth muscles of certain internal organs. Such internal constriction, possibly resulting in spasm, provides a continuous skin, without gaps through which the self risks "spilling out into space . . . never being found and held again" (p. 481). Symington's many examples from infant observations, as well as her observations of adult patients in the analytic setting, give credibility to her conclusion that the fear of unintegration—"that very early unheld precariousness" (p. 486)—is at the root of our fears of dependency and is the prime mover of second-skin development, which is the prototype for later, more sophisticated omnipotent character defenses. Hyperactivity in children and compulsive physical action and speech used as a vehicle for action (seen in adults as well) have also been cited in the literature as other types of second-skin formation.

Anzieu (1989, 1990) and other workers in France have delineated an entire category of second-skin phenomena. They have used the term *psychic envelopes* to talk about such protections, which are constructed out of sensations of sound, touch, smell, sight, and so on, while Paul (1990) has described the phenomenon of mental pressure that also seems to provide a womblike protection against unmentalized experiences that are throwbacks to the experience of birth.

The most exhaustive study of what I call unmentalized experiences, and the sensation-dominated protections erected in avoidance of the repetition of the unbearable feeling of them, is to be found in the work of Frances Tustin (1987, 1990) on autistic states in both children and adults. In one paper (1983) Tustin extends Klein's (1930) ideas on symbol formation and ego development, drawing our attention to the severity of the consequences of a failure in the expansion of symbolic functioning beyond that of symbolic equation (Segal 1957).

THE FORMATION OF SYMBOLS

The development of the capacity for symbol formation is a necessary prerequisite for progression from evacuation to mentation—from the physical or somatic reaction to the psychic action. The development of the psychic structures, which are essential for effective handling of painful experiences inherent in living, is partially dependent upon this capacity for symbolic functioning. The earliest symbols (or more accurately protosymbols), based on sensual and perceptual input, are at best "symbolic equations" (Segal 1957), and as these are undifferentiated from the object symbolized they can hardly be called either symbols or representations. The transformation of concrete protosymbols into psychic representations of the original object depends upon the introjection of a container that can deal with anxiety arising in relation to objects in order for substitutions to be effected (Bion 1962).

Deficiencies in the earliest maternal environment abandon the infant to experience the most severe varieties of anxiety—those of unintegration (Bick 1968, Winnicott 1958), of liquefaction and evaporation, of nonbeing and total loss. One of the many reactions provoked by prolonged exposure to such anxieties is a precocious "over activity of mental functioning" (Winnicott 1949, p. 246) or "premature ego-development" (Klein 1930, p. 244).

In her paper "On the Importance of Symbol Formation in the Development of the Ego," Klein (1930) seems to expand Winnicott's notion of overactivity of mental functioning with her concept of precocious ego development, although it would seem that this is somewhat of a misnomer. What Klein described might be better termed *precocious pseudo-ego-development*. Klein further characterizes this precocious development as premature empathy for or premature identification with the object. This consists in early genitality or the premature onset of the depressive position with its incumbent anxieties related to true guilt, remorse, and the need or the desire to make reparation, all felt toward an ambivalently loved object. Since the newborn is in all likelihood inadequately prepared to deal with such complex anxieties, which require the aid and support of previously established internal containing objects, further moves toward development become inhibited and the infant may, of necessity, retreat in varying degrees within an autosensual world.

For example, one patient who had been raised by a severely disturbed mother (who, as the patient was told, closed the door to her newborn infant's room when she heard her cries because she did not know what to do for her) re-experienced in the analysis a time in early infancy when, while lying in her crib, she attempted to make meaning of her mother's failure to attend to her. Had she cried too loud or not loud enough? Was the pitch too high or too low? Should she continue to cry out or should she stop, and if so for how long? Is mother ill or asleep, or had she left forever? Was mother dead or was she? This patient was not able to be a baby-at-one-with-her-mother and so was pushed to develop her mind in service of avoiding experiences of loss; she developed as well a rather precocious concern for her caretaking object. She often became terrified when, in this avoidant state, she could not "feel her self."

This patient's ruminations were not thoughts connected to experiences, but rather an agglomeration of words that seemed to provide a cocoon of sensation within which she could wrap her fragile self for protection. Indeed, when I was able to communicate this to the patient, she recalled that she had once been told that on the day she was brought home from the hospital she was left alone, wrapped up in a blanket in the middle of mother's bed, where no one was permitted to enter to offer comfort when she cried. Mother believed that this treatment would "toughen her up" and diminish her dependency upon her caretakers. With such patients, if we attend to the content of their communications, we run the risk of colluding with their attempts to "toughen up" and to protect themselves against (while failing to help them to contain) these early experiences of loss. Such toughening leaves little room for a self, which gradually becomes compressed and out of reach of feeling.

Often at the end of the week this patient would launch a barrage of words at me, allowing me seemingly little space for interpretation should I be able to gather my thoughts together long enough to formulate one. I found that when I could interpret the content of these utterances, my interventions had little or no effect upon this patient. However, when I was finally able to understand and to point out to her the function of her speech (as a means by which she protects herself from knowing and experiencing the terror and the bodily pain of being left by me over the weekend break, which felt like a door closing, leaving her "hard and all-sandpaper"), and the way in which my interpretations and her lack of response to them kept us in a static place so that it felt to her that I could not leave her, she was quite moved. Thus, the subject of the weekend separation was opened up, along with all of the painful experiences of past abandonments. Only when I began to *suffer* these painful states, did she become more able to think about them.

Klein (1946) points out that the introjection of the good object, necessary for tolerance of anxiety, may be impeded not only when there is an excess of envy toward it, but also when "the ego is compulsively subordinated to [its] preservation" (p. 9n). Thus, in the case of premature concern for the welfare of the object or what Klein called premature empathy toward the breast, phantasy life may be truncated and restricted to expression in the visceral and muscular spheres and the process of symbol formation may be brought to a halt. In order for substitutions, displacements, and equations to be effected, anxiety must be tolerated. Intolerance results in a retreat to prenatal existence and absolute identification with the object, which perpetuates a vicious cycle; the confusion between self and object extends to a confusion of ego with the object, and consequently to a confusion of the symbol with the object symbolized.

Anxiety-provoking experiences that cannot be worked over through contact with the mother (and, through extension and symbolization, in the outside world) will remain at a concrete level, unmentalized, and perhaps finding expression in the realm of mindless action or somatization. In extreme forms this dilemma can be observed in the so-called alexithymic individual who lacks words for feelings or affective states and expresses these states somatically. The question may here arise in relation to the notion of unmentalized experience: if such experiences are foreclosed from the mental sphere, how and where are they stored and what is the process by which they are recalled? An attempt to answer this question may be taken as the focus of the following sections.

MEMORIES IN FEELINGS

Matte-Blanco (1988), in a discussion of the impact of traumatic early experiences upon the analytic process, highlights the difficulty, if not the impossibility, inherent in the process of recovering clear memories of these events. He has unearthed a 1957 quote from Klein in which she offered a solution to the problem:

> All this is felt by the infant in much more primitive ways than language can express. When these pre-verbal emotions and phantasies are revived in the transference situation, they appear as "memories in feelings," as I would call them, and are reconstructed and put into words with the help of the analyst. In the same way, words have to be used when we are reconstructing and describing other phenomena belonging to the early stages of development. In fact we cannot translate the language of the unconscious into consciousness without lending it words from our conscious realm. [p. 5n].

Perhaps, when we encounter such memories in feelings with our patients, we may not merely be encountering unconscious experience but unmentalized experience, not repressed memories but body memories entrapped in the realm of the unthought.

It is interesting to note that in that same work Matte-Blanco (1988) reported that, in his experience

> the expression of these "memories in feelings" is fundamental in the treatment of some cases. Without them, these patients could not be cured . . . [in some cases] no increase in memories *of the happenings* was obtained. The feelings, instead, were abundantly and repeatedly discharged over a long time. I feel that this repeated expression of most varied feelings connected with episodes and persons concerned, now made towards a basically respectful and tolerant analyst who tries

to understand the meaning of the emotional expression and its connections with the details of early experiences and actual relationships, is the real healing factor. [p. 163]

Matte-Blanco's conceptualization of technique in working with such memories in feelings bears a striking resemblance to those expressed by Balint (1952) and more recently by Stewart (1989) and others of the Independent group in London with regard to the "technique at the basic fault." These workers have noted that there are times in the analysis of certain patients when words do not carry the ordinary meaning for the patient that they would during other phases of the analytic dialogue. These interludes in analysis, which may be quite brief or may last for a prolonged period of time, must be borne by the analyst, who must be able to experience, in the countertransference, the full impact of what the patient cannot bear to experience *prior to the formulation and delivery of an interpretation.*

This period of interpretive inactivity could be likened to a period of mental incubation or gestation in the mind of the analyst which is an essential feature of his or her reverie. It is related to the notion of *negative capability* often referred to by Bion (a term used by the poet Keats in a letter to his brother-in-law), which may be considered analogous to the "primary maternal preoccupation" that Winnicott (1956) thought essential to normal development of the baby. Indeed, these factors are now noted by some to be essential to healthy development even before birth (Mancia 1981).

PERINATAL RESEARCH

In Mancia's paper on the mental life of the fetus (1981), empirical data from embryological and perinatal research regarding the motor functions, the sensory abilities, and the appearance of rapid eye movement (REM) or active sleep in the fetus (which can be observed between 28 and 30 weeks of gestation) are integrated with the work of Bick (1968) and Bion (1962). In formulating his hypothesis Mancia drew an analogy between this "prenatal psychic nucleus," which is based upon unconscious fantasy elements transmitted by the extrauterine objects through the intrauterine container (the original holding environment), and Bion's (1962) pre-conceptions. Mancia (1981) also discussed the role of REM sleep in the prenatal development of "the psychological function of the [psychic] 'skin' which . . . may be able to contain the self of the child and to protect it from disintegrating under the pressure of impulses which come into play at the moment of birth" (p. 355). Mancia suggested that this prenatal foundation of the psychic skin favors the inception of the container-contained relationship, which is indispensable for the development of an apparatus for thinking (Bion 1962). His interesting conjectures, which are based upon nonpsychoanalytic data, broaden this perspective just as they deepen our understanding of the impact of the earliest experiences upon mental development of the individual. Most significant are his findings in observation of both fetuses and prematurely born infants that the disruption of the maternal environment (whether physical or emotional) results in a reduction of active (REM) sleep and an increase in motor activity that Mancia noted as an indication of the evacuation of beta-elements rather than their transformation into alpha-elements that would theoretically coincide with REM sleep.

As I stated earlier, a developmental model, which might be constructed to further clarify the reader's understanding of the formation of beta-elements, can be derived from the work of Stern (1985). I will attempt to construct such a model, suggesting the process through which such undigested facts (Bion 1962) or unmentalized experiences might be stored and recalled.

THE EMERGENT SELF AND THE CORE SELF

According to recent infant observational studies, the basis for mental development seems to be determined during the first months of life by the earliest organizations of subjective experience of self-and-other. Stern's (1985) model of development for the first year of life identifies four "senses of self," which contribute to the formation of an integrated pattern of object relatedness that is sustained throughout the life cycle. Each sense of self provides a precursor to what subsequently develops. He suggested that the first to develop is the "emergent sense of self." This sense of self is both composed of the experience of the process of "emergent organization" and is also the product of that organization of experience. The experience central to the development of this first sense of self is that of the body "coming into being" and the process of organization of sensory experiences through "amodal perception,"[11] "vitality affects,"[12] and the processes of assimilation and accommodation. Thus an experience can form an "activation contour."[13] Unlike

---

11. According to present-day research in infant development, newborns are thought to have an innate capacity to take information received through one sensory modality and translate it into any other sensory modality. The resultant perception exists in some "supra-modal" form (wherein the breast that is seen, the breast that is smelled, the breast that is tasted, and the breast that is touched are linked together) and is encoded in what Stern refers to as an amodal representation that can be recognized in any of its sensory modalities.

12. According to Stern, vitality affects are formations of feelings or somatosensory experiences, that is, waves or rushes of feeling, perhaps laid down as a pattern of neural firing in a particular area of the nervous system. Vitality affects, unlike categorical affects (e.g., sadness, happiness, anger), have no symbolic content. Abstract dance and music are examples par excellence of the expressiveness of vitality affects, which do not resort to plot or categorical affect signals.

13. An activation contour is an engramatic pattern registered at the somatic or physiological level—at the level of brain, not at the level of mind.

"categorical affects"[14] there are an infinite number of possible activation contours. A single activation contour might be made up of many vitality affects that derive from a particular amodally perceived experience. Perhaps a primitive aspect of each adult individual's psyche-soma, as in the case of the newborn infant, remains endowed with a pattern detector that maintains the capacity for identifying such contours throughout life. If this were so, then extremely diverse events could thus be yoked or linked together should they happen to share the same pattern of vitality affects or activation contour.

Stern (1985, p. 58) quotes Defoe, speaking through his literary heroine Moll Flanders, who said, while incarcerated for her crimes: "I had . . . no thought of heaven or hell, at least that went any farther than a bare flying touch." It seems that the activation contour of her present situation (imprisonment) resonated with an activation contour of a particular sensation (a fleeting touch) she had previously had no thought of (no ideational content), and these evoked the same vitality affect experience. Indeed, Stern reminds us of neonatal studies that demonstrate that "not all affective life is the handmaiden of cognition" (1985, p. 66).

> To illustrate this notion, I present a clinical example. The patient Rebecca, in her third year of analysis, returned from the spring break to tell me she had missed coming more than she had imagined possible. She had attended a concert of classical music one evening during the first week of my absence and was overcome with longing for me as she listened

---

14. Categorical affects are those having a distinct quality of feeling. They have evolved as social signals commonly understood by all humans through facial expression, intensity, urgency, and hedonic tone (the quality of pleasure–unpleasure). They are discrete affects, such as sadness, happiness, fear, anger, disgust, surprise, interest, shame, or any combination of these.

to the first work on the program. After the concert, unable
to get the music out of her mind, she purchased it on audio-
tape and played it over and over again in her car during my
absence. Each time she heard the music, it invoked intense
feelings and she found herself longing for my return so she
could tell me about it. However, she was now dismayed to find
that she could not put into words her many-faceted experience, which had seemed so clearly presented in the music.

Rebecca felt certain that embedded in the music were
important aspects of her experience with me in her analysis. "I
wish I could just bring the tape here for you to listen to it with
me—so that we could think about it together," she said. "But I
have the feeling that its meaning is idiosyncratic to me. It's not
that I think you would not appreciate the beauty of the music,
but I sense that it is *my* experience of this *and* of you—not just
a single feeling, like love or hate or excitement, but a whole
rainbow of feelings that seem to span my very being."[15]

Of course, this material brought forth with it a torrent
of emotion and further material regarding the impossibility
of representing and therefore of communicating such an
experience verbally. The analysis of this, in consort with my
own emotional experience in the countertransference and
Rebecca's subsequent dreams and associations over the next
few weeks and even months, were helpful in teasing out and
articulating some aspects of her emotional experience of
her relationship with me. I believe that taken as a whole the

---

15. Rayner (1992), in a paper discussing the concepts of
amodal perception and preverbal attunement in the dialogue between patient and analyst, noted that "Music, being presentational
and an efficient vehicle of affect, might also be an appropriate form
of communication about the indistinct, largely pre-verbal analytic
times ['unformulated sequences'] for there is then perhaps a dance
or tune of the two protagonists' interpenetrating moods" (p. 40).

musical interlude must have also approximated for Rebecca a very early experience of her relationship with her mother, which had been somehow recorded in the far distant past as an activation contour in unmentalized and encapsulated form, only to be played out in the transference relationship with the analyst, where it might be presented for the purpose of under-standing.[16] It appeared that, in the presence of the analyst, Rebecca was finally able to develop thoughts to represent her experience, which, it would seem, had been relegated to the domain of the unthought prior to the analysis.

This notion seemed to fit the patient's history, since her mother had been severely depressed both before and for the first year after the birth of Rebecca. In such a depressed state Rebecca's mother may not have been able to share or appre-ciate her baby's intense states of ecstasy or tantrum and all the waves and rushes of affect in between. Unable to be suffi-ciently mindful of her experience, Rebecca's mother may have unwittingly failed her as a containing object, leaving her unable to metabolize and digest (in her mentality) these very early amodal experiences of herself in relation to her primary caretaker. Unable to create a mental record of her early rela-tionship with her mother, Rebecca had little in the way of experience-in-memory to fall back on during times of separa-tion, relying instead on external objects and sensory experi-ences to fill the black hole (Tustin 1981) created by that early disillusionment, as well as each new experience of loss.

---

16. Boyer (1992) reported the case of "a severely regressed man whose unconscious early pre-oedipal ties to his mother were expressed through the concretization of music in a fantasized umbilical cord. The clinical data clearly support the findings of the previous observers that music per se serves more primitive func-tions than do its themes and lyrics, which symbolize, express and defend against more specific unconscious conflicts" (p. 65).

It might be hypothesized that early experiences (e.g., prenatal experiences or very early experiences at the breast), recorded as body memories in the shape of activation contours of vitality affects, could conceivably remain unmentalized, only later to be linked with situations in the present that share that same pattern or contour.[17] The nature of the link is not necessarily cognitive-affective (Stern 1985) or logical-verbal (T. Mitrani 1992), but may be the specific neural pattern or contour of the sensorial or sensual arousal.

I would here put forth the notion (to use the language of infant observation) that until such time as "Representations of Interactions [with self regulating others] that have been Generalized (RIGs)" (Stern 1985, p. 97) have been internally established (what Bion might term introjective identification with mother's alpha-function or of the container-contained relationship), these activation contours of vitality affects must remain excluded from the symbolic chain. The primordial processes, which are in operation prior to the development of primary and secondary process thinking and which continue to function in the primitive areas of the psyche-soma, perpetuate the production of action symptoms that guarantee survival on one level while at the same time interfering with the development of "Generalized Event Structures (GERs), the basic building blocks of cognitive development" (Stern 1985, p. 97) as well as a verbal memory.

Following the development of what Stern called RIGs (1985, p. 97), the "sense of a Core Self" (p. 69) begins to form between

---

17. Greenacre (1952), in a discussion of the influence of the birth experience upon the earliest pre- and postnatal narcissistic organization and the predisposition to anxiety, suggests that these nascent experiences are laid down as "unique somatic memory traces" that may coalesce with later experiences to create a situation of psychobiological tension.

two and seven months, along with a concomitant sense of "core others." This core consists of (1) self-agency (e.g., the sense that your leg moves when you want it to); (2) self-coherence (e.g., the body as a whole, moving or stationary); (3) self-activity; and (4) self-history (e.g., Winnicott's going-on-being). "These senses are distinct from concepts, knowledge or awareness in that they are meant to connote palpable experiential realities of substance, action, sensation, affect, and time" (Stern 1985, p. 71). Stern pointed out that the absence of any one of these four subsenses, which constitute the core sense of self, have dire consequences for psychological health.[18]

Of these subsenses, it appears that the most crucial, or what the other three pivot upon, is the sense of continuity or historicality, which I believe is very much like Winnicott's (1949) sense of going-on-being. This inner sense of "writing" one's own history depends upon the infant's capacity to *remember*, which is non–language-based, i.e., it is based on memory that resides "in voluntary muscle patterns and their coordinations" (Stern 1985, p. 91) and in "activation contours of vitality affects" (p. 54) that are perhaps analogous to body memories—what Klein referred to as "memories in feelings" (1957, p. 5n), or what Winnicott (1949) described as a "catalogue" of experience. These protomemories must be able to be transformed into internal objects in the mind for the structure of the mental apparatus to develop to its fullest capacity.

---

18. For example, absence of agency can be manifest in catatonia, hysterical paralysis, derealization, and some paranoid states; absence of coherence can be manifest in depersonalization, fragmentation, and psychotic experiences of merger or fusion; absence of affectivity can be seen in anhedonia of some schizophrenias and absence of continuity can be seen in fugue or other dissociative states (Stern 1985, p. 71).

DETECTING UNMENTALIZED EXPERIENCE

Often, when attempting to use the concept of unmentalized experience in clinical/scientific discussion, the following question arises:
how can we differentiate between unmentalized experience and
experience that has undergone a destructive process of "dismantling"[19] (Meltzer et al. 1975), "reversal of alpha-function"[20] (Meltzer
1978), or disintegration, fragmentation, and splintering (Klein 1946,
H. A. Rosenfeld 1950), those passive and active attempts at evad-
ing or avoiding the persecutory feelings associated with the paranoid-schizoid position, or the guilt and remorse of the depressive
position (Klein 1946)? Toward making such a discrimination com-
prehensible, it may be helpful to conceptualize unmentalized experiences as constituting a lacuna in the mind, a hole in the ego
(Ammon 1979), a tear in the psychic skin (Bick 1968), or an area of
the personality that lacks a supporting structure.

As Federn proposed (1952), experiences felt but not suffered
do not affect the ego, i.e., they do not result in learning, nor do
they contribute to the development of mental structure. It might
be said that unmentalized experiences leave circumscribed areas
of the personality frozen at an extremely primitive level of development. It is as if in infancy the baby has looked into the mother's
eyes, only to be met with the "black hole" of her depression, which

---

19. Dismantling of the sensual apparatus into its component
parts is defined as a mindless passive falling to pieces in defense of
depressive feelings and conflictual states (Meltzer et al. 1975). By
this definition, dismantling can be seen to be compatible with evasive or evacuative modes of dealing with sense data and affective
experiences in the absence of a mind for thinking (Bion 1962).

20. Reversal of alpha-function is described as the cannibal-
ization of previously bound alpha-elements, resulting in the creation
of bizarre objects, albeit under omnipotent control, i.e., defensively
(Meltzer 1978).

has rendered her unable to think or to imagine her baby (Winnicott 1960). Consequently, the baby acquires no meaning for what it experiences. There is only the "presence of the absence" (Bion 1962).

By way of extending Bick's (1968) model of second-skin formation, I propose that at times the more sophisticated areas of mind and personality, which have developed parallel (Grotstein 1986) to those areas left barren by unmentalized experience, function as camouflage for those less developed aspects of the personality. This occurrence may result in frequent misdiagnoses. Klein (1961), in her narrative of Richard's treatment, talks about memories that provide a "cover" for "concrete memories" (p. 136) she observed arising as a consequence of the revival of early infantile emotional experiences in the transference. As I have previously mentioned, Klein (1961) also refers to these concrete memories as "memories in feelings" (pp. 136, 217, 235, 315, 318, 338). Her description of cover memories gives additional significance to (what Strachey translated as) Freud's screen memories, and she stressed the point that these cover-memories lose their importance in analysis unless what is *covered over* is *dis-covered*.

While working with psychosomatic patients, I have found that sophisticated and elaborate defenses often substitute for somato-sensual protections, from time to time filling the lacuna, gap, or hole in the ego (Ammon 1979) created in the wake of "privation" (Winnicott 1965, p. 226). This finding is consistent with observations of many workers, among them Alexander (1950), Atkins (1968), Balint (1968), H. A. Rosenfeld (1985), and Sperling (1955), who have each written about the alternation between the action symptom and other diverse symptoms, such as hallucinations and delusions. These substitute protections may be thought of as emanating from the more developed areas of the psyche, bringing along with them the anxieties against which they defend. These seem to compensate for or cover over the faulty part of the personality; accordingly, they seem to block out the gap or hole left in the path of privation. Kohut (1977) addressed this phenomenon in his discussion of "defensive and compensatory structures" that function to cover over or compensate for a "primary defect in the self" (p. 3).

It may help the reader to imagine a whirlpool or a pothole in a fast-moving river. Such holes are barely visible as one traverses the river, appearing only as slight indentations of whirling water because the surrounding waters camouflage the depth and breadth of the void. Consequently, when an object, for example a man in a kayak, nears a pothole, it is forcefully and suddenly sucked down in a spiral motion, sometimes dozens of feet to the bottom of the riverbed. Similarly, the analyst may be deceived by what *appear* to be clearly observable and quite well-structured defenses, anxieties, conflicts, and symptoms in the mind. Entering into the analysis of their content, without having had the experience of what lies beneath, may result in the analyst's being sucked into an endless void of impasse (H. A. Rosenfeld 1987), enclave (O'Shaughnessy 1992), and collusion in which the psychoanalytic dialogue functions as an "autistic shape" (Tustin 1984b) or an "autistic object" (Tustin 1980) that further blocks out awareness of catastrophic separation for both analyst and analysand (Gomberoff et al. 1990).

In my experience working with adult analysands with a pocket of autosensuality (Mitrani 1992)—within which are sequestered those very early unmentalized experiences—I have sometimes been compelled to "act-in" in a very specialized way. For example, in one case I found myself interpreting within the you-me form, called for by the transference material presented. I tied this to the patient's external situation and the dynamics of her internal object relations, only to find later that I had helped the patient create a quite cozy state of at-one-ment within the transference–countertransference relationship. Only after some time did I come to realize how stuck and stale the work was feeling to me, as nothing appeared to come as a surprise, either to the patient or to myself.

Eventually, when I was able to experience, detect, and understand this mutual enactment, I found that it was once more within my power to effect a resumption of the analytic interpretive work, which then could emanate from my experience within this protective niche. What had appeared to me to be material representing the patient's experience as it was being played out in the transference was revealed as an expertly constructed camouflage, all too neatly laid over an experience of emptiness and void, that the patient did not dare enter into and that I had been all too willing to help her to cover up with so-called "good" analytic interpretive work, firmly rooted in my theories. However, this missed the point of the patient's earliest experiences: the loss of boundary and feeling. The generic experience I have observed arising in the countertransference, while entrapped within such mindless capsules, is that of deadness, time-lessness, flatness, stillness, changelessness, and numbness, all devoid of anxiety, although permeated by a feeling of despair.[21]

I believe that when we can convey to the patient, with genuine passion and conviction, the experience of this void, we will have truly given him a piece of our minds, adding to his own perspective a new vertex from which to operate without robbing him of his own hard-won solutions to the problems he presented (Joseph 1992). In a sense, the patient's solution to his experience of the absolute-zero or noth-ingness of privation, which is felt as intolerable, is to transform this zero into a "minus-one" experience (Bion 1965) of continued mis-

---

21. Perhaps if we do not allow our patients to sufficiently touch us or to adequately infuse us with these meaningless experi-ences—if we move too quickly to apply our theories so as to render the unknown known through interpretations, attempting to avoid or evade too assiduously the enactment of the patient's experi-ences—we may run the risk of leaving our patients without suffi-cient containment for such experiences, causing them to fall back upon the use of an already established internal, autosensual enclave or even to convert (or pervert) a physiological function or an organ system into a somatic container.

understanding. Perhaps the difficulty in describing this phenomenon is a reflection of the unthinkability of the notion of the lacuna left in the wake of mental and emotional privation.

Bion (1965) attempts to confront this mathematically, but perhaps artists and writers do so more eloquently and accessibly for us (e.g., Stephen King's [1981] *Dead Zone* of the mind, filled with premonitions of violence about to happen to others, all the while obscuring the incident of one's own demise). Filling up the mental void created in the disaster of privation with the memories, symptoms, and defenses associated with parallel experiences of deprivation, resentment, and destructive envy is one way of ensuring a precarious sense of survival.

I would like to put forth here the idea that there may be a specific area of our work in which the concept of innate or primary envy has little applicability. When the notion of privation is at issue— that is, when there has been, on a given level, no experience of a good-breast-present against which to define absence (which is experienced as the bad-breast-present)—it makes little sense to talk about an envious part of the infant "which doth mock the meat it feeds on . . ." (Klein 1957, p. 182).

In privation there can be no experience of a "mean and grudging breast" (Klein 1957, p. 183) or a bountiful good-breast upon which one must rely for supplies. Therefore, there can be no sense of "losing and regaining the good object," nor can there be operations attributable to "the innate conflict of love and hate" (p. 180). What I am talking about differs from the instance of envy provoked by absence and frustration, as in the case of "deprivation which increases greed and persecutory anxiety" (p. 183) and consequently envy. Instead there is a black hole (Tustin 1981) or an intolerable gap in meaningful experience, which results in hyperbolic and distorted efforts to fill the hole or gap—a specialized or defensive use of the reparative drive (Khan 1979, Winnicott 1948).

On this level there are no "flickering states of awareness" (Tustin 1981) in which to experience loss against a background of satisfaction or security (in terms of specific or circumscribed areas of experience), only a sensation of nothingness or an absolute zero. Of course, if this were not confined to a circumscribed area or cluster of areas, the infant would not survive at all or, at best, extensive physiological and psychological pathology would inevitably result (e.g., schizophrenia or failure-to-thrive infants, or the "hospitalism" babies described by Spitz [1950], many of whom died. These might be examples of the outcome of absolute-zero registering in a preponderance of interactional experiences across the board). While the envy involved in the deprivation experience can be observed in those individuals "who can think of nothing but what they have not got" (Riviere 1937, p. 29), the individual who has experienced privation simply has not got what to think of or with.

Finally, I would like to add that since the unmentalized part of the personality derives from early somatosensual experiences that have failed to attain mental representation, that is, that have never progressed to the level of symbol (e.g., anxiety experienced as the thing-in-itself, not as a signal), this part of the personality cannot be said to regress. Regression implies previous progression, just as disintegration implies or takes for granted previous integration, without which we must use the term unintegration.[22] To the extent that regression can be considered a rather elaborate phantasy, I propose that there are more primitive mechanisms at work with

---

22. The primitive state, which Winnicott (1960) defined as a stage of "absolute dependence," consists in a two-dimensional world of "adhesive identification" (Bick 1968, Meltzer et al. 1975, Tustin 1981) in which there is little or no tolerance for separateness, space, or absence and little capacity to differentiate self from object or "me" from "not-me." While this latter position, in health, is a primarily normative phase of total dependency of the infant upon the maternal environment, the subsequent failure of that environment results in the individual's entrapment in this position that constitutes Tustin's (1981) world of the "encapsulated" child.

respect to the production of some of the symptoms manifested in our patients. As I have elsewhere suggested (Mitrani 1993b), the anxiety equivalent/action/somatic symptom may be a primary protective maneuver, a protophantasy executed on a somatosensual level in reflexive reaction to a primal "prey-predator anxiety" (Grotstein 1984) experienced on the somatosensual level. This would be consistent with Freud's idea that in anxiety neurosis a somatic excitation is denied access to the psychical apparatus due to a psychical insufficiency and is consequently expressed in the somatic realm. In sum, I would suggest here that the psychical insufficiency is related to a circumscribed privation experienced in the earliest postnatal environment (rather than to a deprivation) and that such privation consists in the lack of some functionally specific alpha-element in the maternal aspect of the nursing couple.

The above notions differ from those of the original Kleinian perspective, from which we might view action symptoms as a means of omnipotent control over the object, which is both loved and envied; or as a means of evacuating persecutory anxiety; or perhaps in the case of obsessional behavior, as a means of manic reparation by which a pseudo-restoration of the good object is effected in phantasy. While these are all plausible interpretations, I believe they would be more applicable in the realm of some sophisticated mentalized or dementalized state. Such states might coincide with operations of disintegration and its concomitant anxieties, or with "resomatization" and anxiety that has previously attained mental representation. These aforementioned states would be provoked by the deprivation of something once possessed, or might develop as a result of envious feelings toward the good-object-present.

It is not my intention to diminish the validity or the importance of Klein's theory of primary envy, nor do I mean to imply that envy does not operate significantly and require interpretive attention in the treatment of most of our patients. I wish, however, to propose that in some patients, at times, the destructiveness of envy and its paranoid-schizoid and depressive consequence cannot be effectively addressed before the underlying "unthinkable anxieties" (Winnicott 1962, p. 61), created in the wake of privation, have gained access to and been given meaning through the interaction with the analyst that facilitates mentation. Such anxieties may not be immediately analyzable or interpretable (Mitrani 1993a). They must first be experienced *for* the patient (Meltzer 1986). Only when *we can bear to remain in contact with and to think about our experience of the totality of the patient's experience*, including those endlessly terrifying perceptions of utter helplessness, perpetual meaninglessness, and infinite void (Grotstein 1990), can we expect our patients to be able to remain in contact with themselves as well as with the new perspective we offer to them in the analytic encounter.

CONCLUSION

I have attempted in this chapter to begin to clarify the concept of unmentalized experience that has been addressed in the literature in several ways, using many different terms. Since Freud first delineated the area of the unanalyzable anxiety equivalent, notions such as body memories (Federn 1952), memories in feelings (Klein 1946), beta-elements (Bion 1962), and activation contours of vitality affects (Stern 1985) all seem to have been the products of various efforts to describe clinical encounters with those emotional experiences of our patients yet to be worked over in the mental sphere. This is a difficult task, since such experiences, which have been ineffable, undergo transformation even as we attempt to speak about them. Such experiences seem to have remained unthought until, in the process of analysis, they have chanced to arrive *in* the analyst, who has been capable of keeping them in mind for a sufficient period of time to be able to suffer and think them and give them logical, verbal meaning, to be conveyed to the patient, all in good time.

11

Deficiency and Envy: Some Factors Impacting the Analytic Mind from Listening to Interpretation[1]

Si nous n'avions point de defaults, nous ne prendrions pas tant de plaisir a en remarquer dans les autres.[2]

[La Rochefoucauld, *Maximes*]

INTRODUCTION

Almost invariably at psychoanalytic meetings, what has become a familiar discussion makes its way to the foreground. It might sound something like this: is the patient under discussion suffering from a deficiency in his earliest experience, perhaps the lack of a containing object? Was he therefore attempting to reinstate an experi-

---

1. The paper on which this chapter is based was published in *The International Journal of Psycho-Analysis* in 1993.
2. "If we had no faults, we would not take so much pleasure in noticing those of others."

ence of at-one-ment through the use of projective identification in order that he might fill the gap in his experience, felt as a danger-ous void through which he may slip away, to be lost forever? Is he overcome by his envy of the good analyst-present, whom he is now attempting to control through intrusive projective identification? Is he perhaps launching devaluating attacks on the analyst, destroy-ing what is good, either as a manifestation of or as a defense against such unbearable feelings of envy? Could it be that he is communi-cating something about the failure of the "self-object" function of the analyst, and is the attack therefore to be understood as a signal of this breach in the empathic connection between the analyst and the patient? Is the assault on the analyst and his interpretations an expression of an infantile libidinal and/or aggressive drive-discharge in action?

Exchanges with colleagues and evidence obtained from the literature examined have led me to conclude that these controver-sies are not idiosyncratic to any particular psychoanalytic society nor are they restricted to the above-stated theoretical perspectives. However, in this chapter I do not offer to examine the problem of the various theoretical/political disagreements within or even between psychoanalytic societies, nor do I propose to focus my dis-cussion on the pros and cons of any orientation or model. This chapter emanates from a wish to share a question, or perhaps a series of musings, that came to mind as I listened to a discussion much like the one I have approximated above, a discussion that seemed to be centered on the *analysand's* mental and emotional machinations. Mine is *not* an inquiry into the patient's dynamic psychology, but instead is one aimed toward a better understand-ing of what unconscious, dynamic processes might be taking place at times in the analyst, that is, toward a better understanding of what may be deeply hidden beneath this incessant argument between those who consistently identify the problem of impasse (either in the patient's development or in the analytic process) as attributable mainly to *deficiencies* in the patient's early environment and those who emphasize the role of certain innate predispositions in the patient, among them, what Klein (1957) referred to as *primary envy*.

INQUIRY

The question that occurred to me is as follows: Are *we* as analysts at times suffering from a deficiency with respect to our patients, one for which we need the patient to compensate us? It might be said that we suffer from *a deficiency of experience*; more specifically, a deficiency of the *patient's experience, which is unique to him.* Could it be that it is we who need the patient to supply us with such an experience, which we may then use as food for thought about the patient? Are not those experiences the patient grants us in the transference-countertransference interaction the *sine qua non* of our creative interpretive interventions? It seems to me that without the patient's experiences we cannot survive professionally. We are dependent upon the patient not only in order that we may be able to practice our chosen occupation, but also in order that we may be able to expand upon our theories and grow as a discipline.

But how are we to obtain such experiences? One might say that, if we are not too consumed with envious feelings toward the patient as the sole bearer of those experiences we need to do our work, then perhaps we will be able to introject (or perhaps we will introjectively identify with) the patient. However, if envy is so great that we find ourselves putting our own ignorance into the patient in order that we may rid ourselves of an unbearable state of "unknowing" as well the painful awareness of our own interdependency, we may find *ourselves* unwittingly using projective identification for purposes of control. In this way we may be effectively rendering the patient deficient of experience, while re-establishing ourselves as the ones who have it all, the ones who have it all to give, and therefore as the primary source of knowledge and supplies.

In order to sustain such tacit omnipotent phantasies of superiority over our analysands, we are likely to grow overly dependent upon our theories, applying them to or superimposing them on the patient, rather then allowing him to help us to "re-find" our theories (Parsons 1992) or, better still, to discover a *truth* about him and ourselves within that unique interactional experience we call psychoanalysis.

Perhaps the following vignette, from my own clinical experience, may serve as a fitting preamble to some of the issues I will attempt to address in this chapter. Later I will review two additional cases, both previously published in another context, to aid in continuing the discussion.[3]

---

3. Bion, referring to his Grid, suggested that analysts might do well to play what he called *psychoanalytic games* as a part of our work. One such game or "mental exercise" proposed consisted in supposing "what the interpretations would have been and what course the analyst might have taken if, instead of the actual conjectures and interpretations, the material had been categorized quite differently" (Bion 1965, p. 128). Bion also suggested that what is reported of a given session is but a "theory" or a "transformation of a realization" (p. 6) of what took place between patient and analyst, which may be assessed differently according to the facets that each individual sees. However, he warned that such "assumptions about assumptions" are merely models and must not be mistaken for the actual event. Bion encouraged analysts to "make as many models as [we] choose out of any material available to [us]" (1962, p. 80). In keeping with the spirit in which he intended the Grid and the principles underlying its structure to be used, I here suggest that the reader may gain something of value from the models presented in this chapter, to be considered "not as [substitutes] for observation or psychoanalysis, but as a prelude to it" (Bion 1977b, p. 39).

Clinical Case #1

A 27-year-old man entered treatment complaining of severe difficulties in his relationships as well as problems in his work. As an aspiring screenwriter, Brad felt stuck and doomed to repeat a pattern he felt helpless to alter. He would begin a piece of work and just as the ideas seemed to develop on the page he would crumple up the paper and toss it into the trash, erasing all traces of the piece from the memory banks of his word processor, ending all possibility of returning to his ideas at a later time. This pattern had its equivalent in his relationships with women friends, as he could never seem to consummate a relationship or to commit to anyone, breaking off contact in such a violent way that there was little chance for reconciliation.

Feelings of dependency either in himself or in others were intolerable, and complete isolation seemed to him to be the only (if unsatisfactory) solution. Cut off from his feelings, he found that he was increasingly unable to create lively characters who could interact, just as he was unable to bear lively interactions between objects in his internal world. His frustration with and intolerance of any nascent attempt at creating a story that could come alive on the printed page added to the vicious cycle that seemed both to begin and end with crumpling and discarding.

In spite of his extreme ambivalence, lively interactions between Brad and me did develop early in the analysis; these were experienced as both exciting and frightening to him. For example, in the beginning of the third week of the analysis, I described to him some of the very painful states of mind that he had gradually been relating to me in the sessions, helping him to see how they were linked in the transference to his hopes and fears with respect to our relationship. He was both startled and relieved to find that he was not "all alone at his computer, writing stories which no one would ever read," but that he was, in fact, being "read" by a thinking and feeling presence "looking over his shoulder all the time."

Although seemingly minor failures in understanding on my part often precipitated a ripping and crumpling of the "story" we had begun to write together, and threats of termination were frequent, early discovery of each failure and the subsequent analysis and interpretation of these events set the treatment once again in train. Although little was brought in the way of detail about Brad's early history, he told me that his mother, a manic depressive, was ill throughout his childhood and that she had finally taken her own life when he was 21 years old and away at the university. His father, a physician, had remarried and Brad's relationship with him was "polite but distant."

Each day at the end of the analytic hour Brad would linger at the door of my consulting room (where he invariably stored his numerous belongings), offering additional comments and associations, and I often gave in to his provocations, giving off-the-couch interpretations. As my next patient was nearly always waiting, I frequently (and quite automatically) gathered up the tissues and paper head towel from the couch, throwing them in the trash basket while Brad collected his gear at the door, stealing a final and prolonged look at myself and the room before leaving. I often felt he had stolen an extra bit from me in the end and I was aware of my feelings of irritation toward him each time he dawdled at the door. I thought at first that perhaps I was being made the recipient of an aspect of the patient that felt irritation with an infantile and dependent part of himself. I also came to feel over time that just as we had begun to develop some tender and meaningful contact in a given hour he would arrive the next day seemingly untouched by the previous day's work, "trashing" me for my inability to give him any help or understanding, and accusing me of "ripping him off" when it came time to pay me my fee.

In one session he began by deriding me in a particularly cruel way, and I felt at the same time irritated and hurt as he seemed to twist my words around, claiming that the insight he had gained on the previous day was owing to his own self-examination after the session had ended. I thought about the last interpretation from the previous day, one I had given him as he stood (as usual) lingering at the door, one he was now repeating to me as if he had given it to himself. I was absolutely crushed, feeling he had stolen my "good" understanding and was now threatening me with abandonment. In summary, I told him I thought that there was an aspect of himself that was quite angry and irritated with a very-little-him who had grown to rely upon the mommy-me for support and care, that this angry-he was feeling threatened by and in competition with a mommy-analyst who might be able to give the baby-him something he could not, and that he had, during the night, robbed me of my caring and thoughtful understanding, which he then gave to the baby-him, representing it as his own. I also said that, having emptied me of my goodness, he was now crumpling me up and throwing me away like a piece of trash.

The patient seemed to be affected by my interpretation, letting me know that he had often been angry with himself for feeling so attached to me during the week as this made him feel lost without me over the weekend. However, the next day he came in complaining about a painful rash he had developed on his hands during the night. Indeed, his hands looked red and irritated and Brad seemed more depressed than usual. I felt as the hour continued that perhaps I had misunderstood something about the source of the "irritated" feelings I had identified with a narcissistic object that might be feeling usurped by the connection between the patient's infantile self and the analyst. My dis-ease with the session lasted on and off throughout the day and continued as Brad began the following day's hour with a pregnant silence. When he spoke it was to tell me that he had gone to his father's office the night before and had noticed that his father used the same kind of paper towels in his examining room that I use to protect the pillow of my couch. He also gave me the impression that his father had been quite emotionally distant with him and seemed unable to hear about his difficulties and the fact that he had begun analysis in order to deal with them.

I told him that I thought he was also telling me that he was experiencing me as a distant father who could not bear the pain of the little-him who came for understanding to my office and of how it felt that I had left him raw and oozing out of his skin, feeling misunderstood and alone, in order to protect myself from these unbearable hurts. After a short silence he recalled how he had felt the previous day when he was leaving and that now the thought was dawning on him, in his silence, that he had felt the same way on numerous other occasions at the end of the session. He proceeded by telling me that on such days he would remain in the stairwell of my building for 30 minutes to an hour, crying his eyes out and unable to go into the street. He said he often wanted to tell me about it, but could not find the words to describe either the feelings he had or the events connected with them. Today however, upon entering the consulting room, he had caught sight of the towel on the pillow and had flashed on the image of my crumpling the towel and throwing it in the trash on the previous day; at that instant the sadness of the stairwell had returned, rendering him mute. Then he sighed and exclaimed, "I'm wasted!"

I was now painfully aware of the error I had made in my interpretation of a competitive and envious-him who either twisted and trashed my interpretations or ripped them off, presenting them as his own. My feelings of irritation at the end of almost every hour and of feeling crushed, emptied, and cast off seemed now, at least in part, to belong to the baby-him who felt torn from me—crumpled, trashed, abandoned, and wasted at the end of the hour as he watched me clean up after him in preparation for my next patient. When I told him this, adding that he felt like a "paper boy" being disposed of by a cold and uncaring daddy at the end of the hour, acknowledging how he longed to feel held softly and securely, folded gently and "saved" by me, he responded by telling me that when his mother was too ill to care for him, his father would send him away to live with some "distant relation." Each time he was "dropped" in a different place, never feeling at home, always feeling "cut off" from the source and never feeling there was a place where he could "open the fridge and take food when he was hungry."

It seems in retrospect that I had at first been unable to tolerate the full extent of the state of uncertainty and suspension Brad had been subjected to as a small and helpless child. I was deficient in my knowledge of his personal history and could not wait for him to bring this "home" to me. Relying on theory was perhaps my way of compensating for and dealing with those unbearable feelings of helplessness Brad evoked in me. Although I may have been correct in my sense of the nature of the caretaker within him, which he had created in order to survive his childhood disillusionment, I had failed to provide him with adequate containment for that little-him who had been so abandoned once the atmosphere of that abandonment was unwittingly re-created in the analytic setting. Not until I began to rethink my own experience was I able to provide sufficient "holding" for the baby-him, so that Brad could relax his attachment to that self-made caretaker that had isolated him from human bondedness.

SOME RECENT DEVELOPMENTS

In a refreshing discussion of "Varieties of Envious Experience," Spillius (1993) expresses some of her considerations regarding Klein's (1957) concept of primary envy. In this paper Spillius examines a few of the factors that contribute to or actively provoke envy in our patients, those elements "in the perceived giver/receiver relation [that] make envy more bearable or less bearable" (p. 10). Her comprehensive model highlights many of the feelings, perceptions, and misperceptions (both conscious and unconscious) that may persist in both "giver" and "receiver" and that contribute to the overall experience of envy and its interpretive handling in the analytic process.

Spillius's model is bipolar. On the positive end the giver derives gratification from giving and is aware that the receiver may resent being on the receiving end of the relationship. The receiver accurately perceives the giver as sensitive to and understanding of these resentful feelings, and in this way is also able to acknowledge his envy, which he may then be free to balance out with his positive feelings. The giver, acknowledging the coexistence of such positive feelings, willingly becomes the receiver. Thus a benign process of giving and receiving is put in play in the analysis as the receiver introjectively identifies with an object who gives and receives with pleasure.

Although Spillius does not explicitly mention it, I think it is implied that in this benign cycle both analyst and analysand partake in and are enriched by this process of introjective identification, as each in turn has the opportunity to take up the role of the receiver as well as of the giver.

On the negative end Spillius proposes that the giver experiences little pleasure in giving. Instead he feels imposed upon and drained by the demands of the receiver and is motivated to give primarily by his need to feel superior, a need derived from and perhaps covering over a fear that what he has to give is bad. Should this attitude on the part of the giver be accurately perceived by the receiver, envy will be exacerbated, resentment will be increased, and gratitude will be diminished if not altogether absent. The giver, deprived of gratitude, "gives less or more aggressively, and the deprivation/envy cycle continues" (p. 10) with both giver and receiver taking in and identifying with a joyless object in an endless battle for superiority and omnipotent power as compensation for a pervasive sense of discontent.

To this aspect of Spillius's model I would add that perhaps it is not only that we are fearful that what we have to give to the patient is bad, but that we are even more fearful of having "no-thing" to give to the patient. The awareness of this fear may resonate with a very primitive experience of "nothingness and emptiness" (Grotstein 1991, 1992, Winnicott 1974) and the concomitant terror of being a "no-body," which Tustin (1986) describes so poignantly from her experience with autistic children. Such elemental terrors, associated with unmentalized experiences belonging to earliest infancy (Mitrani 1992), have been noted to exist in encapsulated form in many neurotic adults (S. Klein 1980, Mitrani 1992, Ogden 1989a, Tustin 1986, 1990) and may be reactivated in the countertransference with our most difficult-to-reach patients (Joseph 1975).

In providing us with the aforementioned model, Spillius gives cause for re-evaluation of our attitudes and theories. I would like to call the reader's attention to the way the analyst's unconscious perception of his own deficiencies may compel him to rely upon his theories with more regularity than he cares to recognize. This situation may result in the formulation of interpretations that might constitute a misunderstanding rather than an understanding of the patients' most vulnerable experience.

Bion (1967b), in his pithy and provocative paper "Notes on Memory and Desire," admonishes us as he suggests a technique of analysis in which we might step aside from all we "know" about a patient (or in the case of a new patient, from all we know about patients-who-come-to-analysis in general) as this knowledge is primarily derived from our theories. He asks us to allow ourselves to see the patient with eyes unclouded by yesterday's visions, to listen to the patient with innocent ears, to let go of our theories that secure us firmly in our own identities so that, while in a state of "negative capability," a fresh idea may germinate within us as a result of a marriage between the emotional experience of both analyst and analysand. Bion admits this is no easy task as it requires us to tolerate the vast void of the unknown that, in my experience, harkens back to our earliest infantile insecurities (Mitrani 1992).

O'Shaughnessy (1992), in her paper "Enclaves and Excursions," describes a patient who attempts to make the analysis into a safe refuge, where a homosexual at-one-ment dominates the analytic relationship. O'Shaughnessy seems in that paper to be suggesting that our patients have a knack for getting us to "act in" or to collude with them to this end by creating an atmosphere of overcloseness that aims to shut out the external world as well as the internal world of objects that represents the patient's experiences. She appears to imply that this is a part of the natural process of the analytic experience for some patients at some times and for other patients nearly all of the time.

O'Shaughnessy recounts her experience with a patient with whom she is compelled to act in, thus creating such an "enclave" of at-one-ment; her subsequent realization of this mutual "enactment"; and finally the resumption of the analytic interpretive work, which clearly emanates from and is made possible by her experience from within this enclave of over-close mutuality that is created in part through the patient's misuse of transference interpretations.

Reporting on a second case in contrast to the first, O'Shaughnessy illustrates how another type of patient will attempt to avoid close contact with the analyst by using what she terms the *excursion*. As a quite concrete example of this "philobatic tendency" (Balint 1959) in some of our analysands, she puts forward one patient's suggestion that the analyst accompany her, hand in hand, on a stroll overlooking the railroad tracks, ostensibly to get a breath of fresh air. Although O'Shaughnessy interprets this as the patient's attempt to get her analyst off track—inviting her to abandon the analysis and the patient's internal reality in favor of a manic flight into the external world—one wonders whether the patient may not also be asking if the analyst can abandon her theories long enough for the two of them to be in touch with one another from a new and perhaps fresh vertex of understanding, that is, inviting the analyst to get back on track.

O'Shaughnessy's paper inspires a series of questions. What happens if we do not allow our patients to "touch" us sufficiently or to adequately infuse us with their infantile experiences and/or archaic internalized objects (through the processes of projective identification on the part of the patient and introjective identification on the part of the analyst)? In attempting to avoid or evade too assiduously, in the name of "good analysis," some re-enactment of the patient's internal experiences, do we run the risk of leaving our patients without sufficient containment for such objects and experiences? Might we thus be provoking them to fall back on the use of an already established internal, autosensual "enclave" (S. Klein 1980, Tustin 1986) or even to create one anew? Might such an enclave be established by converting (or perverting) a physiological function or an organ system into a somatic container (e.g., asthma)? Could the patient's use of this mode of managing "unthinkable anxieties" be analogous to the analyst's retreat into an enclave of theory that soothes and protects him, substituting for the more painful experiencing of and thinking about the patient's unbearable inner realities? Could our refusal to be led off our theoretical "track" (or perhaps onto another track) mirror precisely that aspect of the patient's one-track mindedness and the universal human tendency toward repetition?

In an attempt to further investigate some of these questions, I present two additional vignettes that may suggest, among other things, our tendency to use theories to block out the painful awareness of the unbearable experiences our patients attempt to communicate to us through "projective identification" (Bion 1962).[4] I preface these two vignettes by stating that in the original contexts they were presented to substantiate theory concerning the etiology of pathological processes, but the same clinical material may be of use to illustrate the ways in which we as analysts think and work and also provide a vivid background for discussion of the dynamics of the analytic process in general.

Clinical Case #2

The following concerns the case of a male patient who suffered from asthma and claustrophobia, a patient in whom

> anxieties [of suffocation] seemed to date back as far as feeding during infancy for according to his mother he would choke when he fed from her breast until her doctor advised the use of a nipple shield through which her nipple protruded during feeding. When I recall how this patient would thrust his way into my office, sometimes bumping into me on the way, and how his voice bored into my head and his eyes penetrated me with a steely blue glance, I had little doubt that the nipple shield prevented him from asphyxiation because of *his invasive thrusting into the breast*. I often longed for the psychic equivalent of a nipple shield during sessions when he bored into my mind. From the patient's point of view the thrust was experienced the other way round, and he complained about my

---

4. Bion is credited with making the distinction between "pathological" forms of projective identification used primarily as a means of omnipotent control and evacuation, as first described by Melanie Klein in 1930, and "normal" projective identification used as a primitive method of communication between the infant and its primary objects.

thrusting interpretations down his throat, and recalls how his mother "cornered" him in the morning with a bowl of corn flakes, and how suffocated he felt by her "pushing the food at him." [Mason 1981, p. 148, *my italics*]

The analyst seems to be inferring, both from the patient's behavior and his own countertransferential experience of being thrust into, that what is being split off and projectively identified in him by the patient is the maternal object who was greedily intruded upon by the infant in his omnipotent attempts to control the breast.

One alternative inference to be made from the maternal given is that what is being projected into the analyst is the infant part of the patient, which had *in fact* (as reported) been suffocated by the over-full breast in its thrust to feed—perhaps in its attempt to rid itself of painful "accretions of stimuli" (the milk)—possibly related to the mother's own anxieties about her baby's welfare as well as a lack of confidence about her capacity to satiate him. The patient would then be introjectively identified with the intrusive nipple/mother (the suffocating internal object incorporated in the actual feeding situation), a primitive identification with the aggressor (A. Freud 1936). The latter would account for the analyst's experience of being thrust, bored, bumped, and penetrated into, although this alternative does not appear to have been explored by the analyst.

When the analyst identifies the activity of penetration with the "greedy baby" who thrusts his way intrusively into the breast, the patient then has the experience of the analyst's "thrusting interpretations down his throat." Here the patient may be complaining of his experience of the analyst, who perhaps, while in a state of "projective counteridentification" (Grinberg 1962)[5] with the intru-

---

5. Grinberg (1962) coined this term to represent a specific response on the part of the analyst to the patient's projective identification which is not consciously perceived by the analyst, who is

sive and suffocating breast/mother, pushes back too soon (and in unmodified form) the patient's projected infantile part-self that has felt suffocated.

If this were the case, it would appear that what has been re-created in the transference-countertransference interaction is the "minus container-contained" experience of infancy (Bion 1963) that the patient is attempting to communicate to the analyst. The patient may have been attempting to give his analyst a first-hand experience approximating the nature and origins of his difficulties, hoping to find containment for it in the mind of the analyst. If this experience is received but misinterpreted, "the patient feels surrounded not so much by real objects, things-in-themselves, but by bizarre objects . . . stripped of their meaning and ejected" (Bion 1962, p. 11).

If a benign and receptive environment necessary for the development of thoughts and thinking is deficient (in the mind of the mother and later in the mind of the analyst), the infant or infantile part-self of the patient might create a malignant container for itself, a second skin (Bick 1968) established through a process of mind constriction, projective identification with an internal (archaic persecutory superego) object, or the bronchoconstriction of asthma (Mitrani 1993b).

Subsequent projection of the "parental" object (the "suffocating superego") into the analyst might then be understood as a secondary elaboration, the result of the analyst's collusion with the patient in a repetition of the relationship with the primary object. I suggest that this might occur in the following manner: the patient first attempts to find containment for his suffocated infant-self in the

---

consequently "led" passively to carry out the role that, actively though unconsciously, the analysand has forced upon him. When this happens—although it may be only for a short space of time, but sometimes dangerously prolonged—the analyst will resort to every kind of rationalization to justify his attitude or his disturbance.

mind of the mother/analyst (normal projective identification for purposes of communication and/or as a survival tactic aimed at obtaining relief from overwhelming and unbearable anxieties); if he is rejected, such rejection may constitute an experience of abrupt disconnection (e.g., of being dropped or of dissolution); projection then becomes hyperbolic, that is, the maternal object is thrust violently into the mind of the analyst, who is subsequently experienced by the patient as suffocating. In this manner the patient's greatest (primary) fear, of being left unheld and uncontained, is replaced by the lesser fear of being suffocated; just as the fear of being eaten (being back inside the mother's body) is preferable to the terror of nothingness (dissolving, diffusing, evaporating).

Without the nipple shield, which here might represent the alpha-membrane (Bion 1963) or contact barrier (Freud 1895a) created by the mother's mental holding (Winnicott 1958a) and containing (Bion 1963)—the original nursing experience of at-one-ment may be left overflowing (Tustin 1980) and might result in an experience of suffocation. The patient subsequently may feel drowned in the overflow of the dangerous "not-me" elements (Winnicott 1958a) that overwhelm or suffocate his infantile-part-self.

Clinical Case #3

This is the case of a 7-year-old girl who was referred for the treatment of asthma and depression (Karasic 1991), a treatment that lasted a brief 42 hours. The family history is permeated by situations of violent action and painful separations beginning with the patient's maternal grandmother, who was interned in a Japanese POW camp in the Philippines at the age of 9, where she was exposed to much terror and deprivation. After the war, she was released along with a man who had been paid by her father to protect her. She eventually married this man and bore him three daughters. The patient's mother was the youngest of these daughters.

When the grandfather died, the grandmother married a man she fought with violently. The patient's mother reportedly intervened as they often threatened one another with knives. When the grandmother acted on one of her threats, she was imprisoned for six months, presumably for assault against her husband with a deadly weapon. The patient's mother was 14 at the time.

The mother supported her unemployed Vietnam vet husband throughout their marriage, which ended when the patient was 2 years old. The father abandoned the patient at the time of the divorce. That same year, the patient was nearly drowned when she was thrown into a swimming pool by an adolescent uncle, but was rescued by an aunt.

The mother remarried and had a son by her second husband when the patient was 4 years old. Incidents of sibling rivalry provoked the mother to punish her in a severe and impulsive manner. The mother reported that she often chased the patient to her room, trapping her there and hitting her. On one of these occasions the patient slammed the door of her room and threw a dresser down in front of the door. "Her mother was blocked from coming in, but [the patient] was trapped inside. Her stepfather had to climb through a window to rescue her." The stepfather reportedly loved the patient so much that he later adopted her after her own father (who had come back into her life when she was 6) once again abandoned her at some point midway in the analysis.

When the patient was 7 she had her first asthma attack on the eve of her first swimming lesson. The analyst reported that "Mother suspected that the patient's asthma was psychogenic" in origin and that she "knew the patient was depressed, because she had been drawing pictures of a little girl, probably herself, with a cartoon bubble over her head." Inside the bubble she wrote, "I'm very sad—I want to die." Alarmed, the mother began to search for a therapist for her daughter.

In the first week of the analysis, the patient answered her analyst's questions, made "Lego" houses, and talked about her father; she seemed to develop a strong positive transference. In the Friday hour she appeared quite manic and the analyst "commented to her that she did not seem sad anymore" (Karasic 1991, p. 8) although she had been quite depressed in the first hours of the week. She now seemed remarkably cheerful as she played "one game after another" (p. 8). The analyst then reminded the patient of the drawings, which the mother had told him about; the patient acknowledged them while insisting that he should "not talk about them because they were silly" (p. 8).

The patient then proceeded to make a "trap" out of blocks and a paper bag. She described how she would trap the mother inside the bag by dropping a toy knife on her hand as she reached inside for some playdough that the patient planned to place there. The patient became more and more excited as she described this game and soon began to cough a "characteristic asthmatic cough." She then had to go to bathroom to urinate.

When she returned she began to cut a hole in the paper bag while the analyst asked her "about some spanking which the mother had told [him] about during [his] history taking" (Karasic 1991, p. 9). The patient continued to prepare her trap for a "trial run" in which *she* volunteered to play the mother while instructing the analyst on "how to hold the knife so that [he] would not miss" (p. 9). When the analyst intervened by telling the patient that "children get mad enough to hurt their parents when their parents hurt them," she associated to the occasion when she was trapped in her room while fleeing from her mother and the subsequent rescue by the stepfather. She then told him that "once my mother got so mad she punched a hole in the wall."

The analyst responded by telling the patient a story that

he "used as a distancing device to make the patient more comfortable with her anger." The story was about a little girl "who
used to come to see [him], who was very angry at her mother,
but who could not express her anger because of her fear of
her." The analyst reports that at this point the patient wrote
a note "to use with the trap." The note read, "I love you" and
she repeated the plan to entrap Mother once again, emphasizing how "she would not miss with the knife."

With little further response from her analyst, the patient
brought her mother into the room and executed her plan. The
session ended on a note of tension, with the patient cough-
ing and wheezing and laughing to the very end. The analyst
explained that in the Monday hour he learned that the patient
had one asthma attack after another over the weekend. He
reported that the "trap-play" was repeated twice more in the
treatment, with the subsequent asthma attacks decreasing in
duration until they stopped just prior to the mother's abrupt
interruption of the treatment due to the patient's increasing
aggression toward her at home.

The analyst admitted candidly that he did not know what
to make of the session at the time, but later came to conceptualize it in the following way:

[The patient] turns passive into active . . . using the defense
of identification with the aggressor . . . then was obviously
aggressive toward Mother . . . the patient also had accompa-
nying anxiety as evidenced by her trip to the bathroom . . .
the onset of the asthma represents a shift from conscious
aggression in play and its discharge in laughter to a regressive expression of that aggression in her autonomic nervous
system. [p. 11]

After several years of follow-up, the analyst noted that the
patient's asthma had remained in remission and that she had

become an outstanding member of the school swim team. In concluding, the analyst denied that this was a "transference cure" and stated:

Though I think transference played an important role, the trap-play appeared early in the analysis in direct connection with the patient's anger toward her mother, *not toward her analyst*. [p. 15, *my italics*]

This last remark may indeed be significant since the analyst reports that the treatment was abruptly terminated upon the recommendation of the mother's church advisors, who blamed the analysis for exacerbating the child's aggressive acting out toward the mother. I suggest the possibility that such acting out might be attributable, at least in part, to the lack of transference interpretation, which is striking in the session and throughout the analyst's discussion of the material. Instead of gathering the transference, it appears as though the analyst has recoiled from becoming an active recipient of and a participant in the sort of "acting-in-the-therapy" that constitutes a re-enactment of the patient's emotional experience, essential when mental representatives for such an experience are lacking.

If such acting in is not allowed, experienced, and understood, the analyst might remain restricted to the role of an observer to the patient's relationship with the external mothering-object while the internal object is left unmodified in a kind of behavioral or somatic exile. In this case the child seems to have been left alone, the sole recipient of multiple generations of violence unmodified by understanding. We may assume from the patient's history that both Grandmother's and Mother's inability to contain these violent experiences resulted in their merely being passed on (projected?) throughout at least three generations. In order to halt the "regeneration" of such violence, the patient's experiences must be contained in the mind of the analyst.

Provided that the analyst is willing and able to take up the transference roles assigned him by the patient, he will come into direct contact with the patient's anger felt toward the entrapping mother as well as with the loving feelings and gratitude felt toward the rescuing father. When viewed from the vertex of the various transference relationships, the trap-play that first appeared in the last session of the first week of the analysis might be seen in a new light.

Perhaps the patient's cheerfulness on Friday might alternatively be understood as an expression of her need to maniacally deny the unbearable upcoming loss of the good-daddy-analyst, whom she had experienced all week as rescuing her feelings and thoughts from within a "trap" of depression inside her mind, where she had to hide them for protection from an intrusive and hostile mother. This the analyst appears to sense, as he notes the positive transference that developed in these first days of the treatment. However, this connection is not made for his little patient, a connection that might have offered the patient an alternative for her use of denial of the separation (e.g., one might have said to the patient: "It appears that today you must abandon the sad little-girl-part of you who wishes to die, just as you feel I abandon her over the weekend").

Instead, by "trapping" her and "hitting" her with the "fact" of her depression without also "containing" and address-ing the underlying separation anxiety and feelings of despair, the denial (a mental mechanism) fails, and seems to be re-placed by an action (construction of a trap) that serves not only as an action-defense but also as yet another attempt at communication with the analyst. One might conjecture that the patient sets up the trap in hopes of capturing the good-daddy-analyst so that he cannot leave her, and perhaps also to take revenge on the bad-mommy-analyst he became when he confronted her with her unmodified and frightening suicidal feelings and her painful feelings of missing him over the weekend.

Subsequently the patient, in her manic triumph, appears still to be filled up with anxiety, which she attempts to rid herself of through urination. Upon returning from the bathroom she cuts a hole in the paper sack, which seems to speak of the breach she experiences in her capacity to contain her own hurt and angry feelings about her analyst, and may also represent a new attempt to give him some access to the phantasies inside her mind. However, a reminder from the analyst about the painful and frightening punishment meted out by a mother who cannot tolerate or understand the hurt and angry little girl (who may have felt left out after the birth of her baby half-brother) seemed to be misinterpreted by the patient as a warning that there may also be a misunderstanding-mommy-analyst who might likewise hurt and frighten her.

The patient then appears to attempt to save herself and the experience of a good-daddy-or-mommy-analyst while continuing her communication in play. Identifying herself with the analyst-mommy, she volunteers to play the role of the mother in the trial run of the trap-game. She then seems to be attempting to clarify, by writing the note, that the knife is not to be used to kill the mommy/analyst, but only to trap him so that he cannot leave her over the weekend and so that she "will not miss" him so painfully.

Perhaps the analyst gets trapped here in what might easily be taken as an aggressive act by the patient toward the mother, as he appears to interpret retaliation as the patient's motivation for the trap-play. The patient's association to this felt-misunderstanding is to tell her analyst about how she is now feeling persecuted by him, just as she had felt persecuted and trapped by the mother. She now seems to feel the analyst to be both frightening and angry. His "distancing device" seems to prompt the patient to clarify once more that she only wishes to trap him out of feelings of love and longing and her inability to bear her feelings of missing him.

It seems that this failure of the patient's *psychic* defenses against anxiety and the pain of loss throw her back upon a more primitive means of containing her experience—the somatic defense—as she seems to lock up a terrified-baby-her inside her bronchial tubes, constricting it there for the weekend, while keeping out the violent threat of the experience of the mother-analyst's misunderstanding.

Perhaps the experience of rescue by the good-father-analyst finally freed the patient from her somatic prison/entrapment when the analytic work resumed in the following week. It might be said that the gradual development of the patient's faith in the certitude of a rescuing object—the experience of the good daddy/analyst who returned to her each week with steadfast devotion, continuing to check in on her in the years after termination, and perhaps the experience with the stepfather who loved and adopted her—may account for her dramatic "recovery" and the remission of the asthmatic symptoms. It may also be that the stepfather's willingness and ability to understand and protect the child (perhaps serving the function of a "contact barrier" or "alpha-membrane" for the little girl) eventually enabled her to develop some capacity to mentalize her experiences well enough so that she could institute more adaptive and efficient defenses against pain (e.g., the apparent "reaction formation" implied in her later becoming an active member of the swim team).

CONSIDERATIONS

Against the background provided by the various clinical examples presented in this chapter, certain issues appear to be highlighted, issues that merit serious consideration. To begin with, I suggest

there is the tendency in or perhaps the temptation for us as analysts to distance ourselves—unconsciously or intentionally—from our
patients' most primitive and painful experiences as they are evoked
or provoked in the analytic process, experiences that may threaten
to overwhelm, crush, entrap, and suffocate. Such distancing may
severely limit our receptive capacity, rendering us unable to adequately contain our patients' infantile projections, containment that
is essential for mental transformations to be effected. When the
emotional distance between analyst and analysand is too great (relative to the patient's needs), the experience may be "felt" but not
"suffered" (Bion 1962, Federn 1952) or may merely be considered
on an intellectual level, far removed from first-hand experience.

For example, at times we may feel ripped off, crushed, led
astray, trapped, intruded into, penetrated, or smothered, and may
not be able to bear or to "suffer" these painful experiences under
conditions of identification with the helpless baby in a state of total
dependency—a state that is part and parcel of earliest infancy. Relief
from such an unbearable state may be obtained by a subtle shift in
the cognitive focus, so that this experience of intrusion might be
felt as the experience of the maternal object rather than that of the
baby-self. It may at times be less painful and terrifying for the analyst to identify himself with the maternal object who, when intruded
into by the baby, *can* provide protective shielding for herself. However, if this occurs, those awful experiences of the baby-within-the-
patient may be pushed back too soon and in unmodified form. What
I am describing might be indicative of a certain kind of splitting in
the analyst, who may be able to accept the feelings of pain (e.g.,
the sensations of suffocation) but not the premise for these experiences and feelings (e.g., that what is being received is the experience of the baby at the breast). Perhaps this might be considered a
type of "reversible perspective" taking place in the mind of the
analyst. Bion (1962) first thought this phenomenon was related to
the unbearable pain of envy. I believe it may also be associated with
feelings of unbearable pain and the terror concomitant with a state

of "not-knowing" whether or not such feelings will result in death, a state of "not-knowing," which is characteristic of earliest infancy, when an experience of the "goodness" of the environment is limited and uncertain.[6]

Just as problematic may be a situation in which the patient's distress is not *experienced* by the analyst but merely *witnessed* from a distance. In this instance the patient's infantile experiences may not be allowed to penetrate the analyst, but may be intentionally deflected out of awareness by the analyst who then remains a distant observer rather than becoming a responsive participant in the projective-introjective process of communication and modification. Perhaps in such instances the analyst, in unconscious collusion with the patient's defense, is compelled to barricade his mind, thus preventing the patient's anxieties from touching him painfully.

Some years ago I became interested in certain notions in the field of ethology (Miller 1972) that link the psychology of animal behavior to the Darwinian concept of survival of the fittest. These notions apply to those behaviors established to ensure survival of the individual as well as the species. The tendency to distance may be related to some primitive instinctual response. To better comprehend this response one might borrow from ethological wisdom. For example, ethologists tell us that horses shy and bolt when frightened, running away without looking first to see just what is doing the frightening; they do not stop to ascertain whether what is perceived, just barely within their peripheral vision, is a leaf flying in the wind or a mountain lion running and about to attack. The curious but unfortunate animal who stops *before* running to deter-

---

6. Such feelings were addressed by Bion in his discussion of "catastrophic change" (1965), although he did not seem to apply this notion directly to the understanding of the phenomenon of "reversible perspective."

mine what "it" is rarely survives to reproduce his kind. The animal who runs first, however, who gets out of range of being eaten and *then* turns to have a look (or perhaps never does, but is just grateful to be alive), goes on "being" to produce offspring who behave in like manner.

I suppose that, not unlike our patients, *we* may at times be taken over by prey–predator anxieties (Grotstein 1984) that dwell in the far reaches of the psyche-soma. Perhaps even the most well-analyzed mind is subject to takeover, if only at times, by the primitive experiences and reflexive actions of early infancy. On such occasions we may find ourselves fleeing from some undetermined threat that enters into our peripheral awareness. We may act first to preserve ourselves, only stopping to "see" the source and to "think" a solution (interpretation) after the hour (or the patient) is gone. Perhaps there are even times when we avoid looking back altogether, and so are unable to learn from our experiences. Instead we may remain safely entrenched in our theories, *surviving but not evolving as analysts.*

I believe there is always the danger that we may take refuge in our theories as an alternative to receiving and/or suffering the terrifying and painful experiences of the baby-within-the-patient that consequently remain walled off and encapsulated in the somatic symptom or its equivalent. Without the opportunity for refuge and rehabilitation in the mind of the analyst, these experiences remain "out of mind" (Britton 1992) in the analysand.

Malcolm (1990), expanding on the work of Bion (1963) on the phenomenon of reversible perspective, clarifies the concept, locating it at the root of the failure to bring about psychic change in analysis. Malcolm states that in the case of reversible perspective the patient *appears* to accept the analyst's interpretations; however, through a subtle shift of focus, he manages to replace the *premise* for the interpretation with one of his own authorship, one that will serve to maintain his psychic equilibrium. To this I would add that it may also be that by extracting out and disposing of the (new?) meaning contained in the analyst's interpretation the patient increases his armamentarium of "meaninglessness" that, as Grotstein points out (1991), is preferable to the nothingness he might otherwise experience. Perhaps the resultant sense of meaninglessness is used by the patient as a comforter and shield against the painful awareness of nothingness that is an ever-lingering threat (Tustin 1986, 1990).

To add another dimension to this concept, it might also be helpful to entertain the notion that if the *patient* can be thought to engage in reversible perspective to avoid the turmoil of emotional learning, then perhaps there might be times when the same may be said of the *psychoanalyst*. We may appear to ourselves (in keeping with our analytic ego-ideal) to be receiving, accepting, and transforming the communications of our patients. However, through a subtle shift of focus (motivated by self-preservation and facilitated by our own particular theoretical lens), we may be blurring the patient's meaning (one that may be new and therefore threatening to us) and—by substituting our own meaning—effectively replenishing our theoretical armory against the awareness of the experience of catastrophic change (Bion 1965).[7]

---

7. Bion (1965) suggested that one function of analysis is to enable the analysand to "become" whatever he or she is within the realm of his or her own personal psychic reality—what he designated as "O"—as well as enabling the patient to evolve in O. He emphasized the importance of the capacity to tolerate and to "suffer" the frustration and pain that accompany "not knowing" and "not understanding"—a capacity that favors and sustains a state of "being." Because the process of psychic change (i.e., evolution in O) demands a destructuring of the mind and the capacity to tolerate and withstand anxieties about disintegration, annihilation, and death, Bion suggested that all psychic change is potentially catastrophic in nature.

CONCLUDING THOUGHTS

Freud (1937) anticipated that not all psychoanalysts attain the level of psychic health they desire for their analysands, and he admonished us that training analysis does not carry with it a lifetime warranty. He emphasized the dangers in analysis that threaten to reactivate infantile experiences in the analyst as well as in the patient. In line with Freud's thinking, Grinberg (1963) points out that the analyst not only has to endure and sustain "his own conflicts reactivated by the impact of transference vicissitudes, but also the various conflictual situations his patients project into him . . ." (p. 363).

Today we might also consider not only the dangers inherent in intrapsychic conflict and the anxieties provoked by such conflicts, but the dangers of re-experiencing certain elemental states of terror that have failed to attain mental representation and are "felt" on a bodily level. The caesura between the experience of such states of being and the act of mentalizing such an experience can at times be unbearable for the patient or the analyst or both. That temporal space between receiving the patient's experience and the development of understanding may itself be felt as the catastrophe of falling forever, of spilling out uncontrollably, of evaporating into nothingness, or of floating endlessly in a void of aloneness—those catastrophes that characterize our most primitive anxieties. This may very well be a state in which the necessary basic "illusion of omnipotence" (Winnicott 1965, p. 146) is absent (e.g., the experience of the presence of the "holding" mother). When the analyst reaches the point where he must abandon his "reverie" in favor of his theory, he cannot be very far removed from the infant-in-the-patient who clutches at (or is in the clutches of) his own infantile omnipotent phantasies in order to survive.

When we take the above into consideration, it is a wonder that we can *ever* be even reasonably certain, especially in the heat of the analytic hour, that our interventions are not bound and determined by those very "faults" (i.e., anxieties and the defenses against them) that we find remarkable in our analysands. However, if we are able to sustain the uncertainties inherent in those elemental states of being, if we can sufficiently endure the reflection of our own humanness, mortality, envy, and deficiency, we may be freer to hear the patient as he endeavors to aid us in our attempt to understand his own unique dilemma.

References

Alexander, F. (1950). *Psychosomatic Medicine: Its Principles and Applications.* New York: Norton.

Alexander, F., and French, T. (1948). *Studies in Psychosomatic Medicine.* New York: Ronald Press.

Ammon, G. (1979). *Psychoanalysis and Psychosomatics.* New York: Springer.

Anzieu, D. (1989). *The Skin Ego.* New Haven: Yale University Press, 1985.

—— (1990). *Psychic Envelopes.* London: Karnac.

Atkins, N. (1968). Acting out and psychosomatic illness as related regressive trends. *International Journal of Psycho-Analysis* 49:221–223.

Balint, M. (1952). *Primary Love and Psycho-Analytic Technique.* London: Hogarth.

—— (1959). *Thrills and Regressions*. New York: International Universities Press.

—— (1968). *The Basic Fault*. London: Tavistock.

Barendregt, J. T. (1961). *Research in Psychodiagnostics*. The Hague: Mouton.

Bianchedi, E. (1991). Psychic change: the "becoming" of an inquiry. *International Journal of Psycho-Analysis* 72(1):6–15.

Bick, E. (1964). Notes on infant observation in psychoanalytic training. *International Journal of Psycho-Analysis* 45:448–466.

—— (1968). The experience of the skin in early object-relations. *International Journal of Psycho-Analysis* 49:484–486.

—— (1986). Further considerations on the function of the skin in early object relations. *British Journal of Psychotherapy* 2(4):292–301.

Bion, W. R. (1957). Differentiation of the psychotic from the nonpsychotic part of the personality. *International Journal of Psycho-Analysis* 38:266–275.

—— (1959). Attacks on linking. *International Journal of Psycho-Analysis* 40:308–315.

—— (1962). Learning from experience. In *Seven Servants*. New York: Jason Aronson, 1977.

—— (1963). Elements of psychoanalysis. In *Seven Servants*. New York: Jason Aronson, 1977.

—— (1965). Transformations. In *Seven Servants*. New York: Jason Aronson, 1977.

—— (1966). Catastrophic change. *Bulletin of the British Psycho-Analytic Society* 5:18–27.

—— (1967a). *Second Thoughts*. London: Heinemann.

—— (1967b). Notes on memory and desire. *Psychoanalytic Forum* 2(3):272–273.

—— (1970). Attention and interpretation. In *Seven Servants*. New York: Jason Aronson, 1977.

—— (1976). On a quotation from Freud. In *Clinical Seminars and Four Papers*, ed. F. Bion. Abingdon: Fleetwood Press, 1987.

—— (1977a). *Seven Servants*. New York: Jason Aronson.

—— (1977b). *Two Papers: The Grid and Caesura*. Rio de Janeiro: Imago Editoria, Ltd.

—— (1979). *The Dawn of Oblivion*. Perthshire: Clunie.

Boyer, B. (1990). Countertransference and technique. In *Master Clinicians on Treating the Regressed Patient*, ed. L. B. Boyer and P. L. Giovacchini. Northvale, NJ: Jason Aronson.

—— (1992). Roles played by music as revealed during counter-transference facilitated transference regression. *International Journal of Psycho-Analysis* 73(1):55–70.

Brazelton, T. B., and Cramer, B. G. (1990). *The Earliest Relationship: Parents, Infants, and the Drama of Early Attachment*. Reading, MA: Addison-Wesley.

Breuer, J., and Freud, S. (1893–1895). Studies on hysteria. *Standard Edition* 2:1–310.

Britton, R. (1992). Keeping things in mind. In *Clinical Lectures on Klein and Bion*, ed. R. Anderson, pp. 102–113. London: Routledge.

Cannon, W. B. (1932). *The Wisdom of the Body*. New York: Norton.

Coolridge, J. (1956). Asthma in mother and child as a special type of intercommunication. *American Journal of Orthopsychiatry* 26:165–178.

Deutsch, F. (1939). The choice of organ in organ neurosis. *International Journal of Psycho-Analysis* 20:252.

—— (1949). Thus speaks the body I, an analysis of postural behavior. In *Transactions*. New York: Academy of Science Series 2(19):2.

—— (1959). *On the Mysterious Leap from the Mind to the Body*. New York: International Universities Press.

Deutsch, H. (1942). Some forms of emotional disturbance and their relationship to schizophrenia. *Psychoanalytic Quarterly* 40:301–321.

Dunbar, H. (1943). *Psychosomatic Diagnosis*. New York: Hoeber.

Elkan, J. (1977). Stages toward the containment of mental experience as illustrated in the treatment of a young girl with asthma. *Journal of Child Psychotherapy* 4:90–97.

Engel, G. L. (1954). Selection of clinical material in psychosomatic medicine: the need for a new physiology. *Psychosomatic Medicine* 16:368–377.

—— (1962). Anxiety and depression-withdrawal: the primary affects of unpleasure. *International Journal of Psycho-Analysis* 43:89–97.

Etchegoyen, H. (1991). *Fundamentals of Psychoanalytic Technique.* London: Karnac.

Fairbairn, W. R. D. (1952). *Psychoanalytic Studies of the Personality.* London: Tavistock.

Federn, P. (1952). *Ego Psychology and the Psychoses.* New York: Basic Books.

Fenichel, O. (1931). On respiratory introjection. In *Collected Papers of Otto Fenichel: First Series.* New York: Norton.

Freud, A. (1936). *The Ego and the Mechanisms of Defense.* New York: International Universities Press.

Freud, S. (1892–1899). Extracts from the Fliess papers. *Standard Edition* 1:173–280.

—— (1894). The neuro-psychoses of defense. *Standard Edition* 3:41–61.

—— (1895a). Project for a scientific psychology. *Standard Edition* 1:281–397.

—— (1895b). On the grounds for detaching a particular syndrome from neurasthenia under the description "anxiety neurosis." *Standard Edition* 3:85–120.

—— (1895c). Studies on hysteria. *Standard Edition* 2:1–310.

—— (1905). Fragment of an analysis of a case of hysteria. *Standard Edition* 7:3–122.

—— (1906). Delusions and dreams in Jensen's *Gradiva. Standard Edition* 9:7–94.

—— (1910). The psycho-analytic view of psychogenic disturbance of vision. *Standard Edition* 11:209–218.

—— (1914). On narcissism. *Standard Edition* 14:67–102.

—— (1916-1917). Introductory lectures on psychoanalysis. *Standard Edition* 16:241-463.

—— (1922). Two encyclopedia articles. *Standard Edition* 18:235-259.

—— (1923). The ego and the id. *Standard Edition* 19:3-63.

—— (1926). Inhibitions, symptoms and anxiety. *Standard Edition* 20:75-175.

—— (1933). New introductory lectures on psychoanalysis. *Standard Edition* 22:7-158.

—— (1937). Analysis terminable and interminable. *Standard Edition* 23:211-253.

Gaddini, E. (1959). Rumination in infancy. In *Dynamic Psychology in Childhood*, ed. L. Jessner and E. Pavensteat, pp. 166-185. London: Grune and Stratton.

—— (1969). On imitation. *International Journal of Psycho-Analysis* 50(4):475-484.

Giovacchini, P. L. (1984). *Character Disorders and Adaptive Mechanisms*. New York: Jason Aronson.

Gomberoff, M. J., Noemi, C. C., and Pualuan de Gomberoff, L. (1990). The autistic object: its relationship with narcissism in the transference and countertransference of neurotic and borderline patients. *International Journal of Psycho-Analysis* 71:249-259.

Gooch, S. (1985). *Primitive psychosomatic states and adult sexual dysfunction*. Unpublished doctoral dissertation.

Greenacre, P. (1952). *Trauma, Growth and Personality*. London: Hogarth.

—— (1971). *Emotional Growth*. New York: International Universities Press.

Greene, W. A. (1958). Early object relations, somatic, affective and personal: an inquiry into the physiology of the mother–child unit. *Journal of Nervous and Mental Disorders* 126:225-234.

Grinberg, L. (1962). On a specific aspect of countertransference due to the patient's projective identification. In *Classics in Psy-*

choanalytic Technique, ed. R. Langs, pp. 201–206. New York: Jason Aronson, 1981.

—— (1963). Relations between analysts. *International Journal of Psycho-Analysis* 44(4):362–367.

Grinker, R. (1953). *Psychosomatic Concepts.* New York: Norton.

Groddeck, G. (1928). *The Book of the It.* New York: Vintage.

Groen, J. J. (1964). *Psychosomatic Research: A Collection of Papers.* Oxford: Pergamon.

Grotstein, J. S. (1980). A proposed revision of the psychoanalytic concept of primitive mental states: part I. *Contemporary Psychoanalysis* 16:479–546.

—— (1983). A proposed revision of the psychoanalytic concept of primitive mental states: part II. The borderline syndrome. Section I: The disorders of autistic safety and symbiotic relatedness. *Contemporary Psychoanalysis* 19:571–609.

—— (1984). A proposed revision of the psychoanalytic concept of the death instinct. In *The Yearbook for Psychoanalytic Psychotherapy*, ed. R. J. Langs, pp. 299–326. Hillsdale, NJ: Analytic Press.

—— (1986). The dual track theorem. Unpublished manuscript.

—— (1989). Of human bondage and of human bonding: the role of friendship in intimacy. *Contemporary Psychotherapy Review* 5(1):5–32.

—— (1990). Nothingness, meaninglessness, chaos, and the "black hole." I. *Contemporary Psychoanalysis* 26(3):257–290.

—— (1991). Personal communication. Los Angeles.

—— (1992). Personal communication. Los Angeles.

—— (1993). Discussion of "The idealization of safety and the terror of change" by M. Shatz. Paper presented for the Psychoanalytic Center of California, Los Angeles, CA.

Hamilton, V. (1989). The mantle of safety. *Winnicott Studies* 4:70–495.

Hansen, Y. (1994). The importance of the birth experience in early integrations. Unpublished paper presented at the Psychoanalytic Center of California Extension Division Conference: The

Detection and Understanding of Primitive Mental States, Santa Monica, CA.

Heimann, P. (1952). Certain functions of introjection and projection in early infancy. In *Developments in Psychoanalysis*, ed. J. Riviere, pp. 122–168. London: Hogarth.

Innes-Smith, J. (1987). Pre-oedipal identification and the cathexis of autistic objects in the aetiology of adult psychopathology. *International Journal of Psycho-Analysis* 68:405–414.

Isaacs, S. (1952). The nature and function of phantasy. In *Developments in Psychoanalysis*, ed. J. Riviere, pp. 67–121. London: Hogarth.

James, M. (1986). Premature ego development: some observations on disturbances in the first three months of life. In *The British School of Psychoanalysis: The Independent Tradition*, ed. G. Kohon, pp. 101–116. London: Free Association Books.

Jessner, L. (1955). Emotional impact of nearness and separation for the asthmatic child and his mother. *Psychoanalytic Study of the Child* 10:353–375. New York: International Universities Press.

Joseph, B. (1975). The patient who is difficult to reach. In *Tactics and Techniques in Psychoanalytic Therapy*, vol. 2, ed. P. Giovacchini, pp. 205–216. New York: Jason Aronson.

—— (1982). Addiction to near death. *International Journal of Psycho-Analysis* 63:449–456.

—— (1992). Psychic change: some perspectives. *International Journal of Psycho-Analysis* 73:237–243.

Karasic, J. (1991). A fragment of an analysis of a latency child with asthma: infantile discharge as a link between asthma and affect. Paper presented to The Los Angeles Psychoanalytic Society.

Karol, C. (1980). The role of primal scene and masochism in asthma. *International Journal of Psychoanalytic Psychotherapy* 8:577–592.

Khan, M. (1964). Ego distortion, cumulative trauma and the role of reconstruction in the analytic situation. *International Journal of Psycho-Analysis* 45:272–279.

——— (1979). *Alienation in Perversions*. New York: International Universities Press.

King, S. (1981). *The Dead Zone* [Film]. Los Angeles. United Artists Motion Pictures.

Klein, M. (1928). Early stages of the Oedipus complex. In *Contributions to Psycho-Analysis*, pp. 202–214. London: Hogarth.

——— (1930). The importance of symbol-formation in the development of the ego. In *Contributions to Psycho-Analysis*, pp. 236–250. London: Hogarth.

——— (1932). *The Psychoanalysis of Children*. New York: Dell.

——— (1935). Contribution to the psychogenesis of manic depressive states. *International Journal of Psycho-Analysis* 16:145–174.

——— (1945). The Oedipus complex in the light of early anxieties. In *Contributions to Psychoanalysis*. London: Hogarth.

——— (1946). Notes on some schizoid mechanisms. In *Envy and Gratitude and Other Works*, pp. 1–24. New York: Dell.

——— (1948). *Contributions to Psycho-Analysis, 1921–1945*. London: Hogarth.

——— (1952). Some theoretical conclusions regarding the emotional life of the infant. In *Developments in Psychoanalysis*, pp. 198–236. London: Hogarth.

——— (1955). On identification. In *Envy and Gratitude and Other Works*, pp. 141–175. New York: Dell.

——— (1957). Envy and gratitude. In *Envy and Gratitude and Other Works*, pp. 176–235. New York: Dell.

——— (1961). *Narrative of a Child Analysis*. London: Hogarth.

——— (1975a). *Envy and Gratitude and Other Works, 1946–1963*. New York: Dell.

——— (1975b). *Love, Guilt and Reparation and Other Works*. New York: Dell.

Klein, S. (1980). Autistic phenomena in neurotic patients. *International Journal of Psycho-Analysis* 61(3):395–401.

Knapp, P. (1971). Revolution, relevance and psychosomatic medicine: where the light is not. *Psychosomatic Medicine* 33:363.

Knapp, P., Mushatt, C., Nemetz, S. J., et al. (1970). The context of reported asthma during psychoanalysis. *Psychosomatic Medicine* 32(2):167.

Kohut, H. (1971). *The Analysis of the Self. A Systematic Approach to the Psychoanalytic Treatment of Narcissistic Personality Disorders.* New York: International Universities Press.

—— (1977). *The Restoration of the Self.* New York: International Universities Press.

Kristeva, J. (1982). *The Powers of Horror: An Essay on Abjection.* New York: Columbia University Press.

Mahler, M. (1958). Autism and psychosis: two extreme disturbances of identity. *International Journal of Psycho-Analysis* 39:77–83.

Malcolm, R. R. (1990). The as if: phenomenon of not learning. *International Journal of Psycho-Analysis* 71(4):385–392.

Mancia, M. (1981). On the beginning of mental life in the foetus. *International Journal of Psycho-Analysis* 62(3):351–357.

Marty, P. (1968). A major process of somatization: the progressive disorganization. *International Journal of Psycho-Analysis* 49:246–249.

Mason, A. A. (1959). The place of suggestion and hypnosis in the treatment of asthma. In *Bronchial Asthma: A Symposium.* London: The Chest and Heart Association.

—— (1960). Hypnosis and suggestion in the treatment of allergic phenomena. *Allergologica* 7:332–338.

—— (1965). Psychotherapeutic and hypnotic treatment of asthma. In *Transactions of the World Asthma Conference.* London: The Chest and Heart Association.

—— (1981). The suffocating super-ego: psychotic break and claustrophobia. In *Do I Dare Disturb the Universe,* ed. J. Grotstein, pp. 139–166. London: Karnac.

Matte-Blanco, I. (1988). *Thinking, Feeling, and Being: Critical Reflections on the Fundamental Antimony of Human Beings and World.* London/New York: Routledge.

Meltzer, D. (1968). Terror, persecution and dread: a dissection of paranoid anxieties. *International Journal of Psycho-Analysis* 49:396–400.

—— (1975). Adhesive identification. *Contemporary Psychoanalysis* 11(3):289–310.

—— (1978). *The Kleinian Development, Part III: The Clinical Significance of the Work of Bion*. Perthshire: Clunie.

—— (1986). *Studies in Extended Metapsychology*. Perthshire: Clunie.

Meltzer, D., Bremner, J., Hoxter, S., et al. (1975). *Explorations in Autism*. Perthshire: Clunie.

Miller, R. M. (1972). Personal communication.

Mitrani, J. (1987). The role of unmentalized experience in the emotional etiology of psychosomatic asthma. Unpublished doctoral dissertation.

—— (1992). On the survival function of autistic maneuvers in adult patients. *International Journal of Psycho-Analysis* 73(2):549–560.

—— (1993a). Deficiency and envy: some factors impacting the analytic mind from listening to interpretation. *International Journal of Psycho-Analysis* 74(4):689–704.

—— (1993b). "Unmentalized" experience in the etiology and treatment of psychosomatic asthma. *Contemporary Psychoanalysis* 29(2):314–342.

—— (1994a). On adhesive-pseudo-object relations: part I—theory. *Contemporary Psychoanalysis* 30(2):348–366.

—— (1994b). Unintegration, adhesive identification, and the psychic skin: variations on some themes by Esther Bick. *Journal of Melanie Klein and Object Relations* 11(2):65–88.

—— (1995a). On adhesive-pseudo-object relations: part II—illustration. *Contemporary Psychoanalysis* 31(1):140–165.

—— (1995b). Toward an understanding of unmentalized experience. *Psychoanalytic Quarterly* 64:68–112.

Mitrani, T. (1987). The use of archaic selfobject interpretations in object relations psychotherapy. Unpublished doctoral dissertation.

—— (1992). Personal communication.

Mohr, G. J. (1963). Studies of eczema and asthma in the preschool child. *Journal of Child Psychiatry* 2:271–291.

Money-Kyrle, R. E. (1969). On the fear of insanity. *The Collected Papers of Roger Money-Kyrle*, pp. 434–441. Perthshire: Clunie.

Mushatt, C. (1975). Mind, body, environment. *Psychoanalytic Quarterly* 44:81–105.

Ogden, T. (1989a). *The Primitive Edge of Experience*. Northvale, NJ: Jason Aronson.

—— (1989b). The autistic-contiguous position. *International Journal of Psycho-Analysis* 70(1):127–146.

O'Shaughnessy, E. (1964). The absent object. *Journal of Child Psychotherapy* 1:134–143.

—— (1981). A clinical study of a defensive organization. *International Journal of Psycho-Analysis* 62:359–369.

—— (1992). Enclaves and excursions. *International Journal of Psycho-Analysis* 73:603–611.

Osterweil, E. (1990). *A psychoanalytic exploration of fetal mental development and its role in the origin of object relations*. Unpublished doctoral dissertation.

Parsons, M. (1992). The refinding of theory in clinical practice. *International Journal of Psycho-Analysis* 73(1):103–116.

Paul, M. I. (1983). A mental atlas of the process of psychological birth. In *Do I Dare Disturb the Universe*, ed. J. Grotstein, pp. 551–570. London: Karnac.

—— (1989). Notes on the primordial development of a penitential transference. *Journal of Melanie Klein and Object Relations* 5(2):43–69.

—— (1990). Studies on the phenomenology of mental pressure. *Journal of Melanie Klein and Object Relations* 8(2):7–29.

Piontelli, A. (1985). *Backwards in Time*. Perthshire: Clunie

—— (1987). Infant observation from before birth. *International Journal of Psycho-Analysis* 68:453–463.

—— (1988). Pre-natal life and birth as reflected in the analysis of a 2-year-old psychotic girl. *International Review of Psycho-Analysis* 15(1):73–81.

—— (1992). On the continuity between pre-natal and post-natal life: a case illustration. Paper presented to the Psychoanalytic Center of California, Los Angeles.

Rank, O. (1924). *The Trauma of Birth*. London: Routledge & Kegan Paul.

Rayner, E. (1992). Matching, attunement and the psychoanalytic dialogue. *International Journal of Psycho-Analysis* 73(1):39–54.

Reiser, M. (1975). Changing theoretical concepts in psychosomatic medicine. In *American Handbook of Psychiatry, vol. 4*. New York: Basic Books.

Riviere, J. (1936). A contribution to the analysis of a negative therapeutic reaction. *International Journal of Psycho-Analysis* 17:304–320.

—— (1937). Hate, greed, and aggression. In *Love, Hate and Reparation*, ed. M. Klein and J. Riviere, pp. 3–56. New York: Norton, 1964.

Rosenfeld, D. (1984). Hypochondriasis, somatic delusions, and body scheme in psychoanalytic practice. *International Journal of Psycho-Analysis* 65:377–388.

Rosenfeld, H. A. (1950). Notes on the psychopathology of confusional states in chronic schizophrenias. In *Psychotic States: A Psycho-Analytical Approach*, pp. 52–62. New York: International Universities Press.

—— (1964). On the psychopathology of narcissism. *International Journal of Psycho-Analysis* 45:332–337.

—— (1971). A clinical approach to the psychoanalytic theory of the life and death instincts: an investigation into the aggressive aspects of narcissism. *International Journal of Psycho-Analysis* 52:169–178.

—— (1985). Psychosomatic symptoms and latent psychotic states. *Yearbook of Psychoanalysis and Psychotherapy* 1:381–398.

—— (1987). *Impasse and Interpretation: Therapeutic and Anti-Therapeutic Factors in Psychoanalytic Treatment of Psychotic, Borderline, and Neurotic Patients.* London: Tavistock.

Sarlin, C. N. (1970). The current status of the concept of genital primacy. *Journal of the American Psychoanalytic Association* 18(3):285–299.

Segal, H. (1957). Notes on symbol function. *International Journal of Psycho-Analysis* 38:391–397.

Share, L. (1994). *When I Hear a Voice, It Gets Lighter.* New York: Analytic Press.

Sperling, M. (1955). Psychosis and psychosomatic illness. *International Journal of Psycho-Analysis* 36:320–327.

—— (1967). Transference neurosis in patients with psychosomatic disorders. *Psychoanalytic Quarterly* 36:342–355.

—— (1968). Acting-out behavior and psychosomatic symptoms: clinical and theoretical aspects. *International Journal of Psycho-Analysis* 49:250–259.

—— (1978). *Psychosomatic Disorders in Childhood.* New York: Jason Aronson.

Spillius, E. (1993). Varieties of envious experience. *International Journal of Psycho-Analysis* 74:1199–1212.

Spitz, R. (1950). Anxiety in infancy: a study of its manifestations in the first year of life. *International Journal of Psycho-Analysis* 31:138–143.

Steiner, J. (1982). Perverse relationships between parts of the self. *International Journal of Psycho-Analysis* 63:241–251.

—— (1987). The interplay between pathological organizations and the paranoid-schizoid and depressive positions. *International Journal of Psycho-Analysis* 68:69–80.

—— (1990). Pathological organizations as obstacles to mourning. *International Journal of Psychoanalysis* 71:87–94.

Stern, D. L. (1985). *The Interpersonal World of the Infant. A View from Psychoanalysis and Developmental Psychology.* New York: Basic Books.

Stewart, H. (1989). Technique at the basic fault: regression. *International Journal of Psycho-Analysis* 70:221–230.

Süskind, P. (1986). *Perfume: The Story of a Murderer.* New York: Knopf and Pocket Books.

Symington, J. (1985). The survival function of primitive omnipotence. *International Journal of Psycho-Analysis* 66:481–488.

Tischler, S. (1979). Being with a psychotic child: a psychoanalytic approach to the problem of parents of psychotic children. *International Journal of Psycho-Analysis* 60:29–38.

Tustin, F. (1969). Autistic processes. *Journal of Child Psychotherapy* 2(3):23–38.

—— (1972). *Autism and Childhood Psychosis.* London: Hogarth.

—— (1980). Autistic objects. *International Journal of Psycho-Analysis* 7:27–38.

—— (1981). *Autistic States in Children.* London/Boston: Routledge & Kegan Paul.

—— (1983). Thoughts on autism with special reference to a paper by Melanie Klein. *Journal of Child Psychotherapy* 9:119–132.

—— (1984a). The growth of understanding. *Journal of Child Psychotherapy* 10(2):137–149.

—— (1984b). Autistic shapes. *International Journal of Psycho-Analysis* 11(3):279–290.

—— (1986). *Autistic Barriers in Neurotic Patients.* London: Karnac.

—— (1987). Personal communication. London.

—— (1990). *The Protective Shell in Children and Adults.* London: Karnac.

—— (1991). Revised understanding of psychogenic autism. *International Journal of Psycho-Analysis* 72(4):585–592.

—— (1992). Personal communication. London.

Tyler, A. (1974). *Celestial Navigations.* New York: Berkeley.

Weiner, H. (1977). *Psychology and Human Disease.* New York: Elsevier North-Holland.

Williams, D. (1992). *Nobody Nowhere: The Extraordinary Autobiography of an Autistic.* New York: Times Books.

Wilson, C. P. (1980). Parental overstimulation in asthma. *International Journal of Psycho-Analysis* 8:601–621.

Winnicott, D. W. (1941). The observation of infants in a set situation. In *Collected Papers: Through Paediatrics to Psycho-Analysis*, pp. 52–69. New York: Basic Books.

—— (1945). Primitive emotional development. In *Collected Papers: Through Paediatrics to Psycho-Analysis*, pp. 145–156. New York: Basic Books, 1958.

—— (1948). Reparation in respect to mother's organized defense against depression. In *Collected Papers: Through Paediatrics to Psycho-Analysis*, pp. 91–96. New York: Basic Books.

—— (1949). Mind and its relation to the psyche-soma. In *Collected Papers: Through Paediatrics to Psycho-Analysis*, pp. 243–254. New York: Basic Books, 1958.

—— (1951). Transitional objects and transitional phenomena. In *Collected Papers: Through Paediatrics to Psycho-Analysis*, pp. 229–242. New York: Basic Books, 1958.

—— (1956). Primary maternal preoccupation. In *Collected Papers: Through Paediatrics to Psycho-Analysis*, pp. 300–305. New York: Basic Books, 1958.

—— (1958a). *Collected Papers: Through Paediatrics to Psycho-Analysis*. New York: Basic Books.

—— (1958b). The capacity to be alone. In *The Maturational Processes and the Facilitating Environment*, pp. 29–36. New York: International Universities Press, 1965.

—— (1960). The theory of the infant-parent relationship. *International Journal of Psycho-Analysis* 41:585–595.

—— (1962). Ego integration in child development. In *The Maturational Processes and the Facilitating Environment*, pp. 56–63. New York: International Universities Press, 1965.

—— (1965). *The Maturational Processes and the Facilitating Environment*. New York: International Universities Press.

—— (1974). Fear of breakdown. *International Journal of Psycho-Analysis* 1:103–106.

Credits

The author gratefully acknowledges permission to reprint material from the following sources:

"Unintegration, Adhesive Identification, and the Psychic Skin: Variations on Some Themes of Esther Bick," by Judith L. Mitrani, in *Melanie Klein and Object Relations* vol. 12:(2) 65–88, December 1994. Copyright © 1994 by *Melanie Klein and Object Relations*, and the Ontario Institute for Studies in Education.

"Unmentalized Experience in the Etiology and Treatment of Psychosomatic Asthma," by Judith L. Mitrani, in *Contemporary Psychoanalysis*, vol. 29(3) 314–342. Copyright © 1993 by *Contemporary Psychoanalysis*.

"On Adhesive Pseudo-Object Relations: Part I: Theory," by Judith L. Mitrani, in *Contemporary Psychoanalysis*, vol. 30(3) 348–366. Copyright © 1994 by *Contemporary Psychoanalysis*.

Author Index

Subject Index